The Religious Condition

The Religious Condition

Answering And Explaining Christian Reasoning

iUniverse, Inc.
New York Bloomington

The Religious Condition
Answering And Explaining Christian Reasoning

iUniverse books may be ordered through booksellers or by contacting:

iUniverse
1663 Liberty Drive
Bloomington, IN 47403
www.iuniverse.com
1-800-Authors (1-800-288-4677)

ISBN: 978-1-4401-0648-4 (pbk)
ISBN: 978-1-4401-0649-1 (ebk)

Printed in the United States of America

iUniverse rev. date: 12/08/2008

To the billions who have died believing in myths

"I prayed for twenty years but received no answer until I prayed with my legs."

Frederick Douglass, on escaping slavery

Contents

An Introduction

It is a curious thing that most of us ardently believe that we solved the ultimate question of the universe before we even learned how to tie our shoelaces. If philosophers, theologians, and scientists have struggled with the concept of existence for millennia without arriving at a definite solution, our naïve childhood assessment that a divine entity simply wished it were so certainly requires a reevaluation. This painfully obvious appraisal would seem readily acceptable if I were talking about something other than our sacred religious beliefs, but the growing dangers from religious fanaticism do not permit me the freewheeling luxury of discussing anything else. I find it nothing short of an incomprehensible tragedy that anyone in this age of reason would have to write a book debunking a collection of ridiculous fantasies from an era of rampant superstition. I find myself consistently preoccupied with how it is possible that humans have been able to cure disease, travel to the moon, and create nanotechnology in an era where we still worship a creator who allegedly inspired one of the foulest books ever produced.[1] This manuscript is my attempt at an explanation of how we arrived in our present state.

To support my behavioral observations of those I believe to be mired in false superstition, I will frequently reference the two most widely consulted books ever written on persuasive psychology: *Influence: The Psychology of Persuasion* by Robert B. Cialdini and *Attitudes and Persuasion: Classic and Contemporary Approaches* by Richard E. Petty and John T. Cacioppo. Social psychologists have long considered these two books to be the cornerstones for explaining the oft-irrational methods through which people acquire and maintain their beliefs. Whenever I find that I can never hope to express certain religious ideas with equal justice as those who preceded me, I will cite additional texts on religious thought, relying heavily on the following works: *The Demon Haunted World: Science as a Candle in the Dark* by Carl Sagan, *Why People Believe Weird Things* by Michael Shermer, *Atheist Universe: The Thinking Person's Answer to Christian Fundamentalism* by David Mills, *Atheism: The Case Against God* by George H. Smith, *The God Delusion* by Richard Dawkins, and *The End of Faith: Religion, Terror, and the Future of Reason* by Sam Harris.[2]

I hope that my latest endeavor will take the best of these efforts and incorporate them with my own responses to those who have disparaged progressive-thinking disbelievers for not accepting fairy tales like Noah's Ark, Balaam's talking donkey,[3] and the resurrection of Jesus as historical events. As a great deal of these correspondence originate from individuals who, due to their isolated Christian environments,[4] could never develop reasonable unbiased arguments, I'll allocate a large portion of the text for explaining what I suspect are the psychological processes that form their arguments and block them from accepting more rational perspectives. In other words, we will see why certain people continue to believe the silly things that they believe despite facts to the contrary.

Human psychology plays such an enormous and indispensable role in forming and maintaining religious beliefs that I have dedicated more material to this matter than any other topic in this book. I cannot emphasize enough how people are victim to the persuasions of society and the natural gullibility of human rationale. Conditioning, bias, dissonance, and intelligence are all factors that play enormous roles in our decision-making. We will eventually consider each of these aspects and discover to what extent people shun rational thought in favor of observing their indoctrinated religious beliefs throughout life.

The standalone-italicized portions you will see throughout the text are authentic past reader statements that have been presented to me in defense of God, Christianity, the Bible, or all of the above. These reader opinions are often condensed or summarized–without destroying the original connotation or stripping it of supporting ideas–and brushed up grammatically; I would otherwise be accused of doctoring a number of them with terrible grammar in order to make the arguments look even shoddier than they sometimes reveal themselves to be. I fully appreciate that many of these responses are not indicative of the preeminent apologetic works available, but I believe they are an accurate portrayal of the objections that embolden the minds of *mainstream* Christians.

In addition to the upcoming excerpts from letters of criticism that range anywhere from pleasantly constructive to feloniously malicious, there have been a number of subsequent supportive letters thanking me for my work, a few that credit me with starting or assisting in the deconversion process, and plenty from those who wanted me to know that their faith is now stronger than ever. I am not at all surprised with the results from the latter since it has long been said that more faith is required in the presence of growing counterevidence. Many Christian readers have also taken the time to inform me that they have prayed for my soul so that I might somehow understand how I have been misguided into not understanding their particular interpretations of the Bible. Although on some level I appreciate their good intentions, I highly doubt that God is going to appear and defend the seemingly innumerable logistical and ethical problems of the Bible. Instead, the infallible God apparently relies on fallible apologetic messengers who utilize bankrupt logic and disagree even among themselves on how to set everything straight for the nonbelievers. I will leave it to the readers to consider the fundamental ramifications of such a curious decision from the almighty.

Religious Thought, Or The Lack Thereof

When writing on the topic of why people hold religious beliefs, my mind always drifts back to the story of *The Crucible*. The tale was based upon the seventeenth-century religious community of Salem, Massachusetts who zealously executed an incredible number of people accused of practicing witchcraft and conspiring with the devil. As I recall details of the town's gullibility, I can think of nothing else but how absurdly hypocritical it is for any modern Christian to believe that the people of Salem were in any way more foolish than the people living there now. I am completely unsurprised that a small town of ignorant people was fooled into believing that the devil was among them because the difference in the absurdity between the people of the colonial period and the citizens of modern-day America is relatively minor.

I can show you, at this very moment, a civilized nation (the world's only remaining superpower, no less) in which the majority of its people believe in things even more preposterous than this. I can show you a country with a majority of citizens who believes in the ability to predict specific details in the distant future, the existence of winged-messengers living in the sky, the worldwide flood as told in Genesis, and the resurrection of a man who had been dead for many hours.[5] While these individuals believe they are enlightened enough to explicitly claim the veracity of such outlandish beliefs, is there any doubt that they are mentally ill-equipped to provide the name of one famous psychic, the name of one angel in any piece of literature, the name of the mountains in which the ark landed, or the names of the four canonical gospels that tell of the resurrection?[6] They believe simply because they want to believe, they have always believed, and others around them have the same beliefs.

If you can place a young boy within a society that widely believes in the Tooth Fairy, and teach him the sacred importance of believing in the Tooth Fairy, he will most likely believe in the Tooth Fairy until the day he dies. If you can place him within a society that widely believes the earth is flat, and teach him the sacred importance of believing the earth is flat, he will most likely believe that the earth is flat until the day he dies. In either scenario, he will almost certainly teach his children to believe the same and to pass those beliefs on to his grandchildren, great-grandchildren, etc. People believe what they are taught it is important to believe, and the vast majority will stick to those beliefs throughout life despite overwhelming evidence and observations to the contrary.

Individuals in the Islamic states were not taught about Tooth Fairies or flat earths, but rather about the final prophet riding a winged horse into heaven and suicide bombers who receive a reward of seventy-two virgins in paradise. Individuals in American Mormon communities were not taught about tooth fairies or flat earths, but rather about an enormous Jewish kingdom in North America many centuries ago and golden tablets translated by studying rocks placed in a hat. While these ideas might seem ridiculous to contemporary Americans, most in this society believe in an omnipotent deity that is petty enough to torture his underlings forever if we do not satisfy his ego by worshipping him.

While God *could* choose any absurd method of interaction he wanted, we never stop to consider if God *would* manifest in this way. God *could* choose to continue his declaration to the world by having a man read it out of a hat, but *would* he? God *could* choose to retrieve his final prophet by sending him a winged horse, but *would* he? God *could* choose to communicate with a man through a talking donkey, but *would* he? God *could* choose to give salvation to the world by sacrificing and resurrecting himself in bodily form, but *would* he? Since any of these scenarios is physically possible if we assume the existence of an all-powerful deity–and since rational evidence for these claims is practically nonexistent–belief boils down to whichever book you were raised to think is reliable. It is not a matter of accepting that one *must* be true and deciding that our hastily chosen belief sounds the least superstitious (or perhaps just as good as the next), but rather determining if any suggestion can stand on its own as a sensible avenue for God to take. The reasons given for each belief are driven not by rational thought and reasoned arguments, but in response to indoctrination, bias, and cognitive dissonance, which too often yield rationalizations and other superficial answers. So you must excuse me for not joining the crowd who laughs at specks in the Puritans' eyes when there are planks in just about everyone else's.[7] Harris puts the matter in perspective quite bluntly:

> It is merely an accident of history that it is considered normal in our society to believe that the Creator of the universe can hear your thoughts, while it is demonstrative of mental illness to believe that he is communicating with you by having the rain tap in Morse code on your bedroom window. And so, while religious people are not generally mad, their core beliefs absolutely are. This is not surprising, since most religions have merely canonized a few products of ancient ignorance and derangement and passed them down to us as though they were primordial truths. This leaves billions of us believing what no sane person could believe on his own. In fact, it is difficult to imagine a set of beliefs more suggestive of mental illness than those that lie at the heart of many of our religious traditions.[8]

Indeed. The Puritans taught themselves that it was normal to believe that the devil was lurking in the shadows, and they were constantly able to find him. The Muslims taught themselves that it was normal to believe that Allah would provide a paradise for suicide bombers, and they are constantly able to recruit them. The Mormons taught themselves that it was normal to believe in a pre-historic Western Jewish kingdom, and they are constantly able to find scholars who will attest to its existence. The Christians taught themselves that it was normal to pray to an earthly savior who miraculously rose from the dead, and they are constantly finding miraculous evidence of his benevolence. Christians believe this notion because, like the others, they are lifelong members of a society that has continually reinforced the "special" nature of their beliefs. It should go without saying that every religion is "special" in its own isolated environment of observance. Christians believe strange things for what objective outsiders perceive to be very strange reasons. What one society perceives as normal, another perceives as collective insanity.

Explaining the various thought processes behind why people belong to a certain religion is not intended to serve as proof that the belief system in question is wrong, but rather to demonstrate that the belief system is being observed in a fashion that is completely void of rational and independent thought. In other words, the religious belief was offered, it was accepted, it was practiced, it was justified, and it was passed; but it was *not* seriously questioned. A particular religion will be a strong presence in surroundings where children are continuously taught that it cannot be seriously questioned, much less possibly proven false. Christian environments, particularly fundamentalist ones, provide such conditions. I would never deny that exceptions to this process exist (as just about everyone claims to be such an exception–the possibility of which we will investigate shortly), but I will indefinitely stand by my position that the overwhelming majority does not join a religion in this fashion. The only major religious study of the twenty-first century dealing with this question reports that 84 percent of Americans belong to the exact same religion as their parents.[9] Coincidence? Hardly.

Does it come as any surprise that the self-proclaimed exceptions who claim to have chosen Christianity through rational deduction just *happened* to pick the one religion out of hundreds that was already widely practiced and accepted in their environment? Is there any reasonable doubt that if they had been born in Morocco, Egypt, or Iraq under similar conditions, they would have arrived at the parallel conclusion that Islam was the correct religion? Is there any reasonable doubt that they would have been just as confident about the Qur'an–

through the use of equally effective self-convincing rationalizations–as they are now about the Bible?

The oversimplification of my position from one apologist, "you believe what your parents taught you," will apply an overwhelming majority of the time to religious preference and serves as the primary reason that Christianity has flourished to enormous proportions in the West. Followers of Christianity are great in number because their predecessors spread, conquered, and converted in a very efficient manner during an era in which people rarely chose to question Christianity.[10] The masses of people following Christianity today are not doing so because God wants to ensure that the correct religion has a sizable lead over the others. This would be a ridiculous *ad hoc* claim, one that any religion in the lead could utilize.

People who purportedly "choose" Christianity do not consider the religion as the first belief for consideration as a result of this large society having studied its history and declaring its veracity, but rather because this large society (the product of migration, conquest, and conversion) presented the religious belief as the most, if not the only, viable option. Even in homes where parents raise children without religion, the religious beliefs of a society are vocal enough and widespread enough to suggest constantly to a young child that there might be some sort of legitimacy to the religion. If 90 percent of people in your extended society believe in something you do not, you are likely to soon begin looking for reasons why this is so. Individuals who claim to have made a rational, uninfluenced decision to join Christianity seem oblivious to how likely it was that they would walk right into the church. If that society had been propagating an Islamic viewpoint, the odds are that it would be right into the mosque. If that society had been propagating a Jewish viewpoint, it would be right into the temple. I could continue with a seemingly endless list of buildings for worship, but I hope the point is clear.

A treatise on why a considerable portion of the world's population belongs to the Christian faith is beyond the scope of this book. To summarize two thousand years of religious history in a paragraph, Paul of Tarsus and other early Christian writers presented a much more digestible version of the old Hebrew religion to the Roman Empire, which in turn promoted its newly found religious persuasion as it extended its borders throughout the European continent. While the philosophies of Islam began to flourish several centuries after the fall of Rome, pre-existing religions in the East and a series of Crusades with the Christians in Europe led to a defeat for those wanting to advance the ideas of Islam to unconquered regions of the globe. The explorers who would eventually find a new world in the Western Hemisphere came primarily from England, Spain, France, or Portugal–areas that resided within and shared the religious philosophies of the defunct Roman Empire. We are discussing Christianity instead of some other religion primarily for these reasons. While this summary may help explain why we are destined to enter the world as Christians, it is an entirely different matter as to why we leave it as such. For this, we must turn to childhood indoctrination.

It is not a shocking discovery that parents pass on their religious beliefs through their children. Muslim parents tend to have Muslim children; Christian parents tend to have Christian children; atheist parents tend to have atheist children. As I mentioned earlier, studies have consistently shown that children will habitually accept their parents' religious beliefs as their own. This trend remains true, as far as researchers have investigated, throughout the ten thousand distinct religions still in observation.[11] I think it would be perfectly fair to say that if the most avid Christian preacher of your hometown had been born in Israel to Jewish parents, there is a great possibility that he would have been the most avid Rabbi in a comparable Israeli city. Subsequently, he would have been just as certain that he was preaching the truth about Judaism as he is now doing for Christianity. It also follows that he would view Christians as misguided and pray to God in order for them to stop acknowledging Jesus as his son. The man's parents would have raised him to practice Judaism, and he would have likely believed anything else that they instructed was sacred to believe. Petty and Cacioppo summarize what is already obvious:

> Since most of the information that children have about the world comes directly from their parents, it is not surprising that children's beliefs, and thus their attitudes, are initially very similar to their parents. For example, social psychologists have well documented that children tend to share their parents' racial prejudices, religious preferences, and political party affiliations.[12]

Such consistent traditions simply cannot be maintained by chance alone. Because religious beliefs are certainly not in our DNA, a child's environment must necessarily affect his religious affiliation to an extensive degree. In fact, all children are born without specific religious ideas and remain in a state of impressionability until influenced by the religious convictions of their parents or other similarly motivated individuals. In effect, all children are born classical atheists. Smith rightly points out that some readers will have problems with the observation that children are born atheistic, to which he offers the following reply:

> If the religionist is bothered by the moral implications of calling the uninformed child an atheist, the fault lies with these moral implications, not with the definition of atheism. Recognizing this child as an atheist is a major step in removing the moral stigma attached to atheism, because it forces the theist to either abandon his stereotypes of atheism or to extend them where they are patently absurd. If he refuses to discard his favorite myths, if he continues to condemn nonbelievers per se as immoral, consistency demands that he condemn the innocent child as well. And, unless the theist happens to be an ardent follower of Calvin, he will recognize his sweeping moral disapproval of atheism for what it is: nonsense.[13]

We can safely say that individuals become members of their respective religious groups primarily because their parents were also members. Likewise, the parents are probably members because *their* parents were also members. This developing pattern should prompt the question of how far back this visionless trend continues–and who knows why that first person decided what he did. Instead of initiating an honest and impartial analysis of the new evidence that science and enlightened thinking have provided, people simply bury their heads in the sand and continue to observe whatever beliefs they were conquered with or whatever religion their ancestors thought they needed thousands of years ago. They believed it as children, and they will continue to believe it as adults. Moreover, this type of reckless behavior goes unnoticed because religious individuals exhibit it throughout almost every culture around the globe.

Psychologists have further linked the increased tendency for children to share such beliefs, rather convincingly, to the level of indoctrination. One important study in social psychology by Frank Sulloway revealed that birth order was the strongest factor in determining intellectual receptivity to innovation in science–stronger than the date of conversion, age, sex, nationality, socio-economic class, number of siblings, degree of previous contact with leaders of the innovation, religious and political attitudes, fields of scientific specialization, previous awards and honors, three independent measures of eminence, religious denomination, conflict with parents, travel, education attainment, physical handicaps, and parents' ages at birth. In our example, the order of birth correlates to the level of indoctrination because firstborn children receive more attention from their parents than their younger siblings receive. Earlier born children also have more responsibilities to maintain the status quo while their younger counterparts are further removed from parental authority. For this reason, children further down in the birth order are less inclined to adopt the beliefs of their parents and are therefore less likely to have their parents indoctrinate them with fantastical beliefs.[14]

Shermer explains that of the components of the Five Factor model, the most popular trait theory in psychology for the moment, openness to experience is the most significant predictor of an individual's levels of religiosity and belief in God. However, the results are quite the opposite of what you might anticipate. Despite pleas from the religious crowd geared toward the skeptics for open-mindedness, a study by Shermer and Sulloway showed that people with open minds compose the one group *less* likely to be religious or have a belief in God.[15] This conclusion might seem counterintuitive, especially considering how mystical ideas are commonly purported to reveal their veracity to those with open minds, but the results should be obvious upon further reflection. Skeptics are doubtful but willing to consider; the religious are indoctrinated not to seriously question. It does not take a willfully open mind to accept the existence of God because it is essentially the default position. People accept such beliefs during childhood, a stage of development known for its readiness to accept ideas as outrageous as Santa Claus and the Tooth Fairy. It *does* take an open mind, however, to consider the possibility that one's most sacred beliefs might be false.

Let us take a closer look at this coerced process of indoctrination taking place within religious communities across the globe. When children in the United States are at a very young age, most parents unknowingly initiate the conditioning process by informing their children that we are all imperfect and need to take on the perfect Jesus Christ as a role model. By turning their lives over to Jesus, they receive forgiveness for their imperfections and inadequacies. Fundamentalist parents also make their children fear the consequences of remaining alone with their imperfections by convincing them that hell, a place where you suffer through perpetual agony, is the ultimate destination for people who don't rely on the provided support system. Since the consequences of not accepting the support system are so horrific, and the steps necessary to eliminate the consequence are so simplistic, children will learn to adopt these beliefs, if only to keep a distance from the supposed punishment. By this point, children certainly become willing to follow those who know this system best.

The influence that such fear messages holds over an audience is two-fold and certainly not to be underestimated. Petty and Cacioppo offer a study to explain how high-fear messages can be so upsetting that the audience engages in defensive avoidance and refuses to think critically about or be motivated by the issue.[16] Additionally, high-fear messages are more effective than moderate-fear or low-fear appeals when supporting arguments are reassuring and leave the audience with effective means of protecting themselves. The psychologists summarize the thought process quite nicely, and it is worth quoting at some length:

> Let's look more closely at how fear-arousing messages are constituted. These messages describe: (a) the *unfavorableness* of the consequences that will occur if the recommended actions are not adopted; (b) the *likelihood* that these consequences will occur if the recommended actions are not adopted; and (c) the likelihood that these consequences will *not* occur if the recommended actions *are* adopted. In other words, the message arouses fear in a person by questioning the adaptiveness of the current state of affairs. In addition, the message arguments motivate a person to accept the recommendations by outlining explicit undesirable consequences of doing otherwise. That is, the message arguments explain the high likelihood that a set of dire consequences will occur if the recommendations are ignored, consequences whose seriousness and unpleasantness are graphically depicted. The better understood and the more reassuring the message arguments, the more attitude change toward the recommended action that should occur…In sum, fear-arousing messages are effective in inducing attitude change particularly when the following conditions are met: (a) the message provides strong arguments for the possibility of the recipient suffering some extremely negative consequence; (b) the arguments explain that these negative consequences are very likely if the recommendations are not accepted; and (c) it provides strong assurances that adoption of the recommendations effectively eliminates these negative consequences. [17]

According to Petty and Cacioppo, as the message bearer more clearly defines the three message points, the speaker will convince a larger portion of the audience to adapt to his position. With respect to these three points regarding our discussion of hell, the unfavorableness of the consequences that will occur if the recommended actions are not adopted is *absolute* because hell is complete (and often asserted to be eternal) agony;[18] the likelihood that these consequences will occur if the recommended actions are not adopted is *absolute* because it is decreed as the rule of an all-powerful being;[19] and the likelihood that these consequences will not occur if the recommended actions are adopted is *absolute* because it is likewise decreed as the rule of an all-powerful being.[20]

Hardly any conceivable message could be more motivating than the threat of hell, and we have good reason to believe that the nature of the message can be upsetting enough to deter critical thinking, especially when the audience is too young and tender to have developed a discipline that would rationalize or challenge the validity of such assertions. Just the opposite, children habitually give benefit of the doubt to their parents and other role models. Petty and Cacioppo report that children are "increasingly persuasible until around the age of eight, after which time the child becomes less persuasible until some stable level of persuasibility is reached."[21] Naturally, religious indoctrination is firmly in place well before the age of eight, making any subsequent attempts to remove the indoctrination quite difficult to say the least. After all, since parents tend to be correct on just about every other testable matter of importance, it is unfortunately reasonable for a child to extend this pattern into the realm of non-falsification. There is obviously good reason why a large number of children do not question the veracity of hell. According to Dawkins:

> More than any other species, we survive by the accumulated experience of previous generations, and that experience needs to be passed on to children for their protection and well-being. Theoretically, children might learn from personal experience not to go too near a cliff edge, not to eat untried red berries, not to swim in crocodile-infested waters. But, to say the least, there will be a selective advantage to child brains that possess the rule of thumb: believe, without question, whatever your grown-ups tell you. Obey your parents; obey the

> tribal elders, especially when they adopt a solemn, minatory tone. Trust your elders without question. This is a generally valuable rule for a child. But, as with the moths [flying into a flame], it can go wrong.[22]

To continue the conditioning process, parents must successfully keep their children free from external contradicting influences by encompassing them within a Christian environment in a Christian country often with weekly Christian refreshment.[23] Even the more advanced instructors of a child's religion, such as Sunday School teachers, are reasonably consistent with parental beliefs. Do they tell their students that they should impartially study both sides of the religious debate in order to discover the truth, or do they tell them that Christianity is true and give them reaffirming material if they have doubts? If any such teacher fits the former category, I would be very impressed since I have yet to hear of anyone who does. Instead, they use the latter method because alternative religious and secular sources would obviously present conflicting information and weaken their bonds with Jesus Christ, the head of the religious support system. The other religions would also illustrate the contradictions and consequential uncertainties shared amongst all faith-based beliefs. A young child fortunate enough to appreciate this contrast would certainly be much more likely to question his beliefs than one who is not.

Just as Paul told his various audiences that there was a sense of urgency in accepting Jesus, many fundamentalist parents graciously tell their children that they believe people who know about Jesus and refuse to worship him might go to hell.[24] Since Jesus could possibly return today or tomorrow, time is of the utmost essence. The requirement to accept Jesus is absolute, and it would be beneficial to do so as soon as possible in order for God to save them from the chance of perpetual punishment. If they choose not to accept Jesus before death, that trip to hell may very well be in order.

While we have spent considerable time describing the punishment of refusing Jesus, we must not forget about the ultimate reward for accepting him: an eternal stay in heaven with infinite happiness. How many impressionable young children could possibly refuse this "genuine" offer? By this point, children have heard and hastily accepted the proposal. As time goes by, the vast Christian American environment gently but consistently drives the imperative system into their heads day after day, week after week, month after month, and year after year. By their teenage years, most Christians could not possibly consider the presence of a fundamental error in the Bible, much less a completely erroneous foundation, because it is already–unquestionably–the perfect word of God to them. And for what other reason than the perceived importance?

Any attempt to educate children based solely on the facts, instead of faith, is seen (ironically) by many Christians as attempted indoctrination. Consider this excerpt from an article that contains the opinion of a Christian mother of two who is speaking out against the refusal to allow Intelligent Design into public schools: "'If students only have one thing to consider, one option, that's really more brainwashing,' said Duckett, who sent her children to Christian schools because of her frustration."[25] The irony in that line is *astonishing*. Moreover, just for the sake of pointing out even further irony, Jesus himself even seems to have appreciated the notion that children are unbelievably gullible and may have had this observation in mind when he declared, "Unless you change and become like little children, you will never enter the kingdom of heaven."[26] Smith elaborates beautifully on the danger of this idea:

> To be moral, according to Jesus, man must shackle his reason. He must force himself to believe that which we cannot understand. He must suppress, in the name of morality, any doubts that surface in his mind. He must regard as a mark of excellence and unwillingness to subject religious beliefs to critical examination. Less criticism leads to more faith–and faith, Jesus declares, is the hallmark of virtue...The psychological impact of this doctrine is devastating. To divorce morality from truth is to turn man's reason against himself. Reason, as the faculty by which man comprehends reality and exercises control over his environment, is the basic requirement of self-esteem. To the extent that a man believes his mind is a potential enemy, that it

> may lead to the 'evils' of question-asking and criticism, he will feel the need for intellectual passivity–to deliberately sabotage his mind in the name of virtue. Reason becomes a vice, something to be feared, and man finds that his worst enemy is his own capacity to think and question. One can scarcely imagine a more effective way to introduce perpetual conflict into man's consciousness and thereby produce a host of neurotic symptoms.[27]

Following their childhood indoctrination, individuals exhibit their desire to be in groups by surrounding themselves with those who hold similar interests in order to reinforce the perceived appropriateness of their beliefs and opinions. When I was younger, I also underwent this near-universal conditioning process and tried to recruit/assimilate others into my group because that is what my environment told me that God wanted me to do. I discovered that this was my reality when I was sitting in church one Sunday and realized that I would believe in the veracity of whatever religion was instilled within me. I understood that I would have believed in Hinduism if I had been born in India. I understood that I would have believed in Islam if I had been born in Iraq. But somehow, I was "lucky." I was born with the "correct" religion. And how did God decide who would have the advantage of being born into the proper religion? For whatever reason, the system was inherently unfair. Dawkins describes the dilemma wonderfully:

> If you feel trapped in the religion of your upbringing, it would be worth asking yourself how this came about. The answer is usually some form of childhood indoctrination. If you are religious at all it is overwhelmingly probable that your religion is that of your parents. If you were born in Arkansas and you

> think Christianity is true and Islam false, knowing full well that you would think the opposite if you had been born in Afghanistan, you are the victim of childhood indoctrination. *Mutatis mutandis* if you were born in Afghanistan.[28]

If you believe in a book with a talking donkey[29] because you feel it is the special exception to the rules of common sense, but realize that you would believe in a different book, perhaps one with a dancing giraffe or a flying horse, if you had been born elsewhere, something has obviously gone very wrong with your way of thinking. Otherwise, our reality is an omnipotent creator of the universe carrying out some sort of game in which his test subjects must suspend common sense and choose the correct religion from thousands, of which any can be accepted with a little bit of faith.

That Sunday morning in church, I wondered why the adults did not realize this and reevaluate their own beliefs.[30] In addition to their oblivious decision to follow Christianity, I later came to realize that most adults don't even know what they really believe because they never take the time to read a considerable amount of the Bible, much less the whole text. In fact, only 40 percent can name *half* of the Ten Commandments.[31] Because of this shockingly lazy choice exercised by the vast majority of Christians, they are ill-equipped to answer challenges to their belief system. As a result, the common response to presented complications usually boils down to "The Bible says it. I believe it. That settles it." When it comes to religion, the mainstream believers exhibit no more in-depth thinking than members of any local cult. Regardless of the actions such religious people take, however, I could never deem them evil because I now understand that they are victims of an unfortunate destiny (or more accurately, an unfortunate hardwiring of the brain) misleading them down a path of ignorance and unwitting gullibility.

Many Christian readers who have taken the time to write me will admit that nothing I say will convince them that the Bible is not the word of God. It's quite pointless to speak to people who admit that they will not change their minds on an issue no matter what evidence is presented and no matter to what extent their arguments for the position are destroyed. The exercise of this book isn't an attempt to change the minds of such individuals, but rather to provide a perfect illustration for the more rational audience members on how people are conditioned to accept whatever society informs them is critical to accept. How many Hindus, Jews, Muslims, and Mormons would respond exactly like these Christians had I asked them if they were willing to admit that it is possible that their respective holy books were wrong? I can imagine nothing other than a perfect parallel.

Religion thrives with stubborn behavior implemented by years of conditioning. It is not the perceived high quality of evidence apologetically offered in favor of the Bible that makes religious people feel comfortable maintaining their beliefs. After all, they will not change their minds under *any* circumstances. One could offer perfect evidence of the Bible's moral and historical bankruptcy if it existed, yet the believers would not accept it because the conditioned indoctrination has made the belief concrete. As Harris brilliantly puts it:

> Tell a devout Christian that his wife is cheating on him, or that frozen yogurt can make a man invisible, and he is likely to require as much evidence as anyone else, and to be persuaded only to the extent that you give it. Tell him that the book he keeps by his bed was written by an invisible deity who will punish him with fire for eternity if he fails to accept its every incredible claim about the universe, and he seems to require no evidence whatsoever.[32]

To compound further this obtuse mental fallibility, researchers have shown that people become more confident about their decisions as time progresses, despite a complete lack of evidence to support the veracity of their choices. Cialdini reports that after placing a bet at a racetrack, and with no additional information to consider, individuals are much more confident of their chances of winning than they were just before laying down the bet.[33] As humans, we simply are not as comfortable considering the notion that we might be wrong. We enjoy being right. As a result, on some inexplicable level, we strive to convince ourselves that we have followed proper revenues of belief rather than consider the possibility that we might have behaved improperly. This nature is highly illogical, intellectually dishonest, and potentially dangerous. In an upcoming section, we will consider the implications of an individual confronted with the notion that his most sacred beliefs have come into question–decades after those beliefs have been set.[34]

To what great extent are people of deep religious faith conditioned to avoid questioning their core beliefs? Consider the following example. Suppose the world witnesses the descent of a great entity from the sky. This being proclaims that its name is God and the time for the world to end has finally arrived. It should go without saying that people are going to want to see proof of its claims. Whatever miracles one requests of God, he is happy to oblige. He has the power to make mountains rise and fall at will. He can set the oceans ablaze at the snap of a finger. He can even return life to those who died thousands of years ago. God can do *anything* asked of him. Then, someone from the gathered crowd makes an inquiry as to which religion holds the absolute truth. God replies, "The religion of truth is Islam. The Qur'an is my one and only holy word. All other religious texts, including the Bible, are entirely blasphemous. All those who do not acknowledge my word will undergo a lengthy punishment for not following my teachings. Now is your chance to repent."

What choice does the Christian community make in this situation? This entity has already demonstrated that it possesses the omnipotence and omniscience of a supreme being. Do Christians readily switch over to the side of observable and testable evidence, or do they declare that this being is the Devil tempting their faith in God? Stop and think about it for a minute because it's an interesting predicament. After careful consideration, I believe we all know that a good portion of Christians would denounce this new being in order to please "The One True God, Heavenly Father of Jesus." As a result of their collective decision, the supernatural entity forces them to undergo unimaginable torment for a few weeks before offering them a final chance to repent. Do the

Christians embrace the teachings of this creature after experiencing its capabilities firsthand, or do they still consider it the final test and refuse to denounce their faith in the Bible? We should not be at all surprised to find that a large portion would still maintain their present beliefs. Childhood indoctrination is *that* strong and *that* crippling to sensibility. Once the concept of faith is introduced, the test is simply not fair; yet if Christianity is true, it is the very test that we would all be expected to pass.

While many believe that they have arrived at their Christian beliefs through logical deduction and not childhood indoctrination of faith, Shermer demonstrates the existence of an *Intellectual Attribution Bias*, which will help support my earlier insinuation that people claim far too often to be an exception to the indoctrination process. One of his studies shows that an individual is nearly nine times more likely to believe that he arrived at his religious position from critical thinking than he is to believe that any other Christian chosen at random did the same. Shermer argues that "problems in attribution may arise in our haste to accept the first cause that comes to mind" and that "there is a tendency for people to take credit for their good actions…and let the situation account for their bad ones."[35] He continues:

> Our commitment to a belief is attributed to a rational decision and intellectual choice; whereas the other person's belief is attributed to need and emotion. This intellectual attribution bias applies to religion as a belief system and to God as the subject of belief. As pattern-seeking animals, the matter of the apparent good design of the universe, and the perceived action of a higher intelligence in the day-to-day contingencies of our lives, is a powerful one as an intellectual justification for belief. But we attribute other people's religious beliefs to their emotional needs and upbringing.[36]

In other words, people are able to recognize that many religious believers are only in the faith because of the influence from society, but they are more than willing to pass over such consideration for themselves and will instead seek out a rational explanation for a belief that they never freely chose. Finding the gullibility of others is an easy task; finding it within ourselves can be a difficult and discomforting one.

I will indefinitely stand by my observation and the identical observation made by countless other freethinkers who have left organized religion: almost all religious people, Christian or not, have been strongly conditioned as children to believe what society has encouraged them to believe. It is my hope that readers can appreciate that people tend to believe in whatever religion their society believes and that religious believers are typically able to rationalize their beliefs even in the presence of overwhelming contrary evidence. This rationalization process, to which we will now turn our attention, is the result of the believer's favoritism toward his preconceived notions.

If you wanted safety information on a used car, would it be wiser to trust the word of a used car salesperson or the findings of a consumer report? I hope that you would trust the consumer report over the salesperson because the salesperson has a vested interest in the quality of his products and an even larger one in getting you to accept his opinion on his products. The consumer report, on the other hand, would likely have no interest in advancing a one-sided view of any product. Similarly, if you wanted to obtain information on the historicity and veracity of Islam, would you ask an Islamic scholar who has been taught about Islamic sanctity since childhood, or would you ask a secular scholar with no emotional investment in Islam? Would you not also do the same for Hinduism, Mormonism, Buddhism, etc? If you utilize the same reasoning and choose the unbiased scholar in each instance, as you very well should, why make an exception only for Christianity? People who study a concept in which they have no emotional investment are going to offer more reliable conclusions than those who want the concept to yield a specific result. The decision in each case should be easy.

Scholars who began with no emotional investments in Christiani present the most unbiased conclusions on Christianity simply because they are more open during their studies to accept evidence that contradicts their tentative conclusions. Just as the used car salesperson will be hesitant to acknowledge and relay information that is damaging to the quality of his vehicles, the Christian scholar will be hesitant to acknowledge and relay information that is damaging to the veracity of his religion. We have no reason to think that belief in Christianity provides a special insight into the veracity of it because every religion can make a parallel claim. The opinions of individuals with ego involvement, emotional investments, or vested interests in the outcome of a debatable issue are less likely to change when confronted with new information because people have an innate inclination to seek only evidence that confirms their pre-established beliefs. We can describe this phenomenon, termed *confirmation bias,* as the tendency to seek out answers that will confirm our beliefs and ignore answers that will not. Research has long established the presence of this phenomenon in persuasive psychology. Shermer put it best:

> Most of us most of the time come to our beliefs for a variety of reasons having little to do with empirical evidence and logical reasoning…Rather, such variables as genetic predispositions, parental predilections, sibling influences, peer pressures, educational experiences, and life impressions all shape the personality preferences and emotional inclinations that, in conjunction with numerous social and cultural influences, lead us to make certain belief choices. Rarely do any of us sit down before a table of facts, weight them pro and con, and choose the most logical and rational belief, regardless of what we previously believed. Instead, the facts of the world come to us through the colored filters of the theories, hypotheses, hunches, biases, and prejudices we have accumulated through our lifetime. We then sort through the body of data and select those most confirming what we already believe, and ignore or rationalize away those that are disconfirming.[37]

According to Shermer, psychologists have discovered a process that people follow when given the task of selecting the right answer to a problem. Individuals (a) will immediately form a hypothesis and look only for examples to confirm it, (b) do not seek evidence to disprove the hypothesis, (c) are very slow to change the hypothesis even when it is obviously wrong, (d) adopt overly-simple hypotheses or strategies for solutions if the information is too complex, and (e) form hypotheses about coincidental relationships they observe if there is no true solution.[38] Moreover, by adopting these overly simple hypotheses and strategies for complex issues, we gain immediate gratification. Shermer elaborates:

> Good and bad things happen to both good and bad people, seemingly at random. Scientific explanations are often complicated and require training and effort to work through. Superstition and belief in fate and the supernatural provide a simpler path through life's complex maze.[39]

Cialdini provides a personal anecdote that exemplifies the beginning of this practice quite well:

> I had stopped at the self-service pump of a filling station advertising a price per gallon a couple of cents below the rate of other stations in the area. But with pump nozzle in hand, I noticed that the price listed on the pump was two cents higher than the display sign price. When I mentioned the difference to a passing attendant, who I later learned was the owner, he mumbled unconvincingly that the rates had changed a few days ago but there hadn't been time to correct the display. I tried to decide what to do. Some reasons for staying came to mind–'I really do need gasoline badly.' 'This pump is available, and I am in sort of a hurry.' 'I think I remember that my car runs better on this brand of gas.'

> I needed to determine whether those reasons were genuine or mere justifications for my decision to stop there. So I asked myself the crucial question, 'Knowing what I know about the real price of this gasoline, if I could go back in time, would I make the same choice again?' Concentrating on the first burst of impression I sensed, the answer was clear and unqualified. I would have driven right past. I wouldn't even have slowed down. I knew then that without the price advantage, those other reasons would not have brought me there. They hadn't created the decision; the decision had created them.[40]

People who begin with specific beliefs on an issue are highly unlikely to be persuaded by counterarguments, even when those arguments are greatly superior to the internal justifications for the previously established beliefs. Shermer reports that he has demonstrated this experimentally–with subjects ignoring, distorting, and eventually forgetting evidence for theories that they do not prefer. Moreover, as the degree to which the subjects internally justified their beliefs increased, so did the confidence of their positions.[41] With respect to religion, this phenomenon is certainly expected. Independent of the amount of influence and persuasion that Christians have absorbed, would we not expect the lukewarm followers to be far more reachable through logic and reason than the ardent ones? Petty and Cacioppo elaborate:

> Social judgment theory emphasizes the importance of one additional factor in determining the amount of persuasion that a message will produce–the person's level of ego involvement with the issue…Since involved persons have larger latitudes of rejection, they should be generally more resistant to persuasion than less involved persons, because any given message has a greater probability of falling in the rejection region for them.[42]

Our analysis of emotionally involved scholars should lead us to an important question in desperate need of an answer. What good is a researcher who will preclude viable possibilities and refuse to consider that his point of view may simply be wrong? If past research tells us that there are three hypothetical scientific disciplines capable of yielding a hypothetical cure for a hypothetical disease, would we ever trust a scientist who was indoctrinated since childhood to believe that only one of the three could produce a cure? Should we honestly believe that apologists for biblical inerrancy, who began with the notion of a perfect Bible, would readily consider the possibility of a textual error? Should we honestly believe that other biblical apologists, who began with the notion of an inspired Bible, would readily consider the possibility that their holy book is fundamentally flawed? Many of the top Christian apologists even admit that when the data conflicts with the text, we should trust the text.[43] So I ask, what's the point in listening to them?

This is the problem with all religious apologists, regardless of the specific belief. They will begin by presuming certain premises to be true (e.g. talking donkey, man coming back to life, DNA changes via peeled branches,[44] moon splitting in half[45]) and mold an explanation to patch the apparent problem, no matter how insulting the explanation and the claim itself are to common sense.[46] Are these implausible solutions not the superficially confirming answers that doubting Christians want to find? This practice is how religions thrive in the age of scrutiny and reason.

I am not foolish enough to think that defenders of the Bible cannot find a "resolution" to any problem that I or other rationalists mention. It has been done a million times before, and it will be done a million times in the future. No skeptical author can offer anything that Christian apologists think they cannot answer. The consideration we need to give with respect to those answers is the likelihood of the offered explanation and how an unbiased, dispassionate individual would rule on the explanation. Is the suggestion a likely solution to the problem, or is it a way of maintaining predetermined apologetic beliefs? Since most staunch Bible defenders have already declared that nothing is going to change their minds (and the solutions to presented biblical complications often reflect this disposition), we must be highly suspicious of the intellectual honesty put forth toward the development of the apologetic solutions. After all, as we will see, there are even apologists for specific, contradictory schools of thought within Christianity itself. How could two groups of people consistently use two contradictory avenues of thought yet consistently arrive at the same answer unless the conclusion itself consistently preceded the explanation?

In short, either religious followers ignore evidence that is contradictory to their beliefs, or they superficially rationalize it. They interpret according to their preconceived notions and biases. When a skeptic points out a likely error, the Christian begins with the premise that it is not an error and then proceeds to defend by any means necessary what he is already convinced is the truth. Misguided believers often accomplish this intellectually dishonest defense by citing a biblical authority who may have been influenced and conditioned to a degree even greater than that of the Christian who is repeating it. After all, God wrote it, so it must be true–even if it violates common sense. Shermer provides a wonderful example of how a premature conclusion influences observations from those who are not even affected by indoctrination:

> When Columbus arrived in the New World, he had a theory that he was in Asia and proceeded to perceive the New World as such. Cinnamon was a valuable Asian spice, and the first New World shrub that smelled like cinnamon was declared to *be* it. When he encountered the aromatic gumbo-limbo tree of the West Indies, Columbus concluded it was an Asian species similar to the mastic tree of the Mediterranean. A New World nut was matched with Marco Polo's description of a coconut. Columbus's [sic] surgeon even declared, based on some Caribbean roots his men uncovered, that he had found Chinese rhubarb. A theory of Asia produced observations of Asia, even though Columbus was half a world away.[47]

In the same manner that Columbus' theory of Asia produced observations of Asia, I would suggest that a Christian's theory of a divinely inspired Bible produces observations of biblical veracity. All of the observations tend to make sense to the believer once the faulty premise is accepted. It is human nature to base explanations on premature conclusions, but knowing that it is human nature to do so allows us to think outside the box and subsequently consider uncomfortable possibilities.

As a terrific religious example of confirmation bias, Sagan provides his readers with data for miraculous healings attributed to the Virgin Mary in Lourdes, France. The Catholic Church recognizes less than a hundred miraculous healings over the past 150 years, but they claim that these recoveries are proofs of supernatural intervention. The spontaneous remission rate of cancer, on the other hand, would accumulate a hundred such "miracles" in a population far smaller than those who have actively sought a cure from the Virgin Mary. "The rate of spontaneous remission at Lourdes seems to be lower than if the victims had just stayed home. Of course, if you're one of the [survivors], it's going to be very hard to convince you that your trip to Lourdes wasn't the cause of the remission of your disease."[48] If you have been indoctrinated to believe in the reasonable possibility of your hypothesis beforehand, and you get the result you are expecting, an explanation of your bad reasoning isn't going to convince you that a miracle did not occur. You believed in miracles from the start, sought a way to obtain one for yourself, and never considered the possibility of an alternative explanation. Preconceptions make all the difference.

The importance of the fact that religious apologists were often indoctrinated with outlandish beliefs from childhood simply cannot be overstated. This is why Christians must excuse me for wanting authorities, if they must constantly appeal to them, who have started with minimal religious influence in their environment. Practice of religion clouds judgment; understanding of religion does not. In the same vein, if an atheist represses evidence for God, he is committing the same mistake as the Christian who represses evidence against God. Someone who has been convinced since childhood that God does not exist is of no better use to us than a person who has been convinced since childhood that he does. The trouble for members of the religious side, however, is that the vast majority of disbelievers were not heavily influenced with hostility toward Christianity during childhood. In fact, most were once believers. Even with years of reinforcement from the environment working against them, the number of people leaving religion greatly outweighs the number joining it.[49] Uninfluenced people rarely join Christianity because they recognize the absurdity of it just as easily as a Christian recognizes the absurdity of Wicca, Hinduism, or any other religion that is not closely related to his own.

Very, very rarely do we see experts skilled in skepticism become religious. You might hear of apologists claiming that they were once atheists, but these claims are highly dubious and depend on the specific quality of atheism. If we are speaking of the classical definition of having no specific beliefs or disbeliefs, the point of claiming a conversion is moot because they lacked familiarity with the subject. Their inability to provide skeptics with remotely reasonable arguments for their conversions lends credence to this position.[50] Conversely, there are scores of well-known skeptics who are former ministers with doctorates in religious studies. Unlike a person who would have been instilled with atheism since birth, these skeptics are not experiencing any detectable psychological glitches that drive their defense of freethinking atheism/agnosticism/deism. A lack of a belief based upon a known lack of evidence is not the same as a lack of a belief based upon being told there is a lack of evidence. Freethinkers did not earn their name by starting with no influence from their parents, their peers, and their society; they typically fought their way through it.

Some of my Christian readers have provided examples that perfectly demonstrate my position that many cannot differentiate a biased conclusion from an unbiased one. The most comical of which was a hypothetical verbal exchange between two individuals that an apologist named Jim and Bob. In his example, Jim informed Bob that Bob's mother was a prostitute, to which Bob offered a vehement denial. Jim then concluded that Bob was wrong simply because Bob was biased toward loving his mother and did not want to accept the rational conclusion about her line of work.

This example was somehow supposed to parody my argument that bias prevents religious people from impartially weighing evidence. This apologist's interpretation of my position was greatly disappointing because it did not have any bearing on the process of weighing and validating known evidence to draw a conclusion–much less a conclusion on a matter with extreme emotional significance attached. As the verbal exchange between Jim and Bob does not afford the opportunity to weigh evidence, it is irrelevant to the issue of how bias can interfere with rational decision-making. Of course, with no evidence to offer, Bob's opinion, due to his presumed familiarity with his mother's activities, is going to trump Jim's opinion.

Consider, however, a situation in which Jim actually saw the evidence that Bob's mother was a prostitute. Suppose that Jim saw a police video of Bob's mother clearly propositioning men for financial gain. In this scenario, there can be several obstacles for Bob to accept Jim's story readily. Perhaps Bob's mother raised him to believe that she was an engineer or a member of some other socially acceptable profession. Perhaps his mother always told Bob elaborate stories about her engineering projects. Like many people, Bob does not approve of prostitution and believes his mother would never engage in such activities. Bob loves his mother and has great respect for her, but he has no respect for prostitutes. Considering all of these factors, the notion that she has been working as a prostitute obviously does not sit well with Bob. It is only natural that he is going to strive to vindicate his mother. It is highly unlikely that Bob is going to weigh the evidence objectively and render a dispassionate verdict.

Once Jim shows Bob the video, uneasy feelings are going to stir within Bob and drive him to create possible scenarios that would explain what he has seen. Perhaps it is a scripted movie; perhaps it is a practical joke; perhaps the woman only looks like her; perhaps his mom has a long-lost twin sister. As far as Bob is concerned, any one of these scenarios is more likely to be factually correct than what the evidence plainly indicates because the evidence directly contradicts Bob's core beliefs of his mother having a different profession. Bob must ask himself if it is truly more likely for his mother to have a long-lost twin sister than it is for her to have deceived him out of fear of ridicule. He must decide how a dispassionate person would rule on the evidence.

Bob's bias prevents him from accepting the most rational conclusion on his mother's occupation. In short, Bob has an enormous emotional investment that renders his conclusions much less reliable because he does not want his mom to be a prostitute. Jim, on the other hand, is thoroughly dispassionate and does not care about Bob's mother one way or the other. We should therefore consider Jim more reliable than Bob on the subject at hand *because Jim is able to view the evidence without bias*. The most likely conclusion, given the weight of the evidence, is that she works as a prostitute.

As this example relates to biblical study, Bob would be the religious scholar who has been told by his peers, his parents, his mentors, and his society for as long as he can remember that the Bible is a sacred book. Jim would be the secular scholar who has no emotional investment in the Bible and has recently stumbled upon overwhelming evidence and a number of solid arguments that indicate its complete lack of reliability. Just as the apologist will invent unlikely scenarios to explain the new evidence (and we will see many such examples), Bob has invented unlikely reasons why the evidence is not what it seems. It will be extremely difficult for Bob to accept Jim's story, just as it is extremely difficult for a Christian to accept evidence against the Bible's reliability. If the video were of anyone other than Bob's mom, Bob would have no problem concluding that the woman was engaged in prostitution. Correspondingly, if the evidence were against any religion other than Christianity, the Christian apologist would have no problem seeing how the evidence was detrimental to that religion.

Even with this demonstration in mind, biblical apologists will continue to protest such an inevitable conclusion because they claim that nonbelievers also have biases that prevent them from drawing rational conclusions. This is no doubt true on occasion, but apologists cannot deny the existence of a great disparity between skeptics and believers. How many religious skeptics actually have emotional investments with atheism, and how important is that lack of belief to them? How many religious believers have spent their lives observing their sacred belief systems, and how deep do those emotional bonds run? There simply can be no comparison between the levels of importance placed on the respective beliefs.

I have no emotional attachment, ego involvement, or confirmation bias toward relatively minute biblical inconsistencies, such as whether or not there is a contradiction about the permissibility of public prayer.[51] If the evidence pointed away from my current position, and it seemed as though I had made an error in judgment, I would have no problem in admitting so. My world does not come crashing down around me when I am wrong. There are several passages that I previously believed were erroneous or contradictory, and I had no problem letting them go once I found a sufficient (or at least a vaguely plausible) explanation. The passages that I continue to regard as contradictions do not have a known feasible rectification, and it will take an enormous philosophical rethinking to demonstrate otherwise. In great contrast to my outlook, an apologist of biblical inerrancy cannot allow even the smallest of problems to enter the text because each one destroys the whole foundation of infallibility. Thus, as Bob invented unlikely scenarios to protect his deepest convictions, so will the apologist.

The thought processes of liberal Christian scholars who uphold the Bible but realize its limitations from human authorship are not much different. Instead of premises based around inerrancy, their convictions are often built around an unalterable foundation. While they might accept that there is a historical inaccuracy in one passage, a difference of author opinion in another, and a scientific absurdity in a third, the idea that the Judeo-Christian God never existed is an inconsiderable position because it conflicts with the foundation that has likely been in place since childhood. While they believe that mistakes, contradictions, cruelties, and absurdities are human reflections of an infallible god, they never seriously consider the ramifications of an infallible god that would allow a great measure of mistakes, contradictions, cruelties, and absurdities to be his textual reflection. It is much more sensible to say that a perfect being had absolutely nothing to do with the Bible, but since they prematurely used their conclusion as a premise, these Christians will not seriously consider such a possibility. A dispassionate outlook is an indispensable necessity when in search of the truth. Religious scholars who began as religious believers lack that critical component.

It is an inescapable reality that the vast majority of people who have spent a great deal of time studying the Bible believe it is the word of God. While stating that 90 percent of experts agree with a given position is usually a valid point to make, it is a mere appeal to authority on its own. Should we then at least leverage some credibility to specific claims based on the position of the authorities? My answer is that it depends.

I am perfectly aware that the vast majority of experts in the history of the Ancient Near East will back positions that are beneficial to Christianity–but that is because the vast majority of experts in the history of the Ancient Near East were born in a Christian society. The majority of those who will back the Qur'an were born in an Islamic society. The majority of those who will back the Torah were born in a Jewish society. We can best predict the distribution of experts on a highly emotional issue by evaluating biases toward their respective predetermined conclusions, not by weighing the evidence.

My claim of bias refers not only to the confirmation bias practiced by the experts, but to the affiliation bias of the sample as well. People who have an interest in pursuing knowledge of the history of Christianity are most certainly those who have already been indoctrinated with the importance of it. If they believe in Christianity ardently enough to pursue a career from it, they are unquestionably more likely to interpret evidence so that it is favorable to their preconceived notions. Should it come as any surprise that the vast majority of experts in *any* religion believe in the very religion that they study, even though no religious belief is even close to holding a majority opinion in the world? Christians make up 33 percent of the world, yet 90 percent of experts in Christianity probably practice it. Muslims make up 21 percent of the world, yet 90 percent of experts in Islam probably practice it. Mormons make up far less than 1 percent of the world, yet 90 percent of experts in Mormonism probably practice it.[52] I could continue with Hinduism, Buddhism, Judaism, Jainism, Shintoism, etc., but I trust that I have made the point that the scholars long believed in their respective religions before they ever studied them in depth.

If one wishes to argue that the number of Christian scholars is disproportionately larger than that of other religions, we need only remind ourselves that most religions are not in the business of defending their claims and proselytizing potential converts through structured argumentation. Hindus and Buddhists generally do not feel the obligation to convert others or threaten them with eternal punishment for not accepting their respective positions. The distribution of religious scholars might also parallel the availability of such studies within each region. Religious believers in impoverished areas of the world are more likely to be concerned with feeding their families than building advanced universities for studying the intricacies of their beliefs using Western methods.

As for confirmation bias, it is clear that apologists of every religion begin with the conclusion that their scriptures are true and work backwards to find the supportive evidence. They are not interested in the most likely conclusion that they can draw from the evidence, but rather the most likely conclusion that does not invalidate their beliefs. We can say with unflinching near-certainty that if Christian apologist *A* were born with religion *X* instead of Christianity, Christian apologist *A* would instead be just as confident that religion *X* was the correct belief. There are countless apologists for every religion who claim to be able to prove, beyond all reasonable doubt, that each of their respective, contradictory belief systems is true. If 90 percent of scholars studying Christianity agree with a position on a hypothetical dichotomy that favors Christianity, I would make the bet every time that roughly 90 percent of the scholars came into the field as Christians. The opinion of such authorities, who began with a certain conclusion instead of analyzing the evidence to reach that conclusion, cannot be trusted simply because they are authorities. Conclusions based upon evidence are important; conclusions based upon evidence that has been interpreted to support an *a priori* assumption are what we should take with a handful of salt.

Rightfully so, I put little stock in the opinions of people who began studying Christianity years after they accepted the existence of a talking donkey. If we brought in an intelligent, rational group of people who were never indoctrinated, who were never even *exposed* to the idea of religion, and asked them to become experts in the ancient history of the Near Middle East, I would be extremely confident that it would be the *unanimous* consensus of the group that the Bible is bunk. They would not be subjected to the centuries of aura and mystique that society has placed on the Bible, and there is absolutely nothing in the book that would impress critically thinking dispassionate outsiders. To them, the Bible would be just another book in the mythology section of the library. You simply cannot trust those with huge emotional investments to be objective on critical issues.

Not only does the problem of experts with premature conclusions reach outside of Christianity, it continues outside of religion. Think of other fields of study that skeptics and rationalists regard as mythical. For example, consider UFOs. What percentage of people who are UFO experts believe that UFO sightings are evidence of flying saucer-shaped vehicles piloted by gray aliens? I have not been able to find a statistic on the question, if such a study has even been undertaken, but should we not feel confident that the vast majority of UFO experts are UFO apologists? People with such interests will naturally flock to such fields, initiating their studies with the determination to validate their unusual beliefs, continuing with the notion that seemingly inexplicable phenomena have radical solutions, and striving to convince people of their outlandish beliefs. The problem is multiplied for religion because we must appreciate the much greater impact that society has on reinforcing an expert's belief in a personal god compared to an expert's belief in UFO visits, as well as the overwhelming elevation of emotion and identity that experts have invested in religion compared to UFOs.

Just like the biblical defenders who are prone to practice confirmation, UFO apologists do not pay much attention to evidence and explanations that debunk their beliefs; they find ways of making it consistent. Since they are not interested in simple, rational explanations for sightings–just as religious believers are not interested in simple, rational explanations for miracles–they begin with the premise that the sighting is authentically alien–just as religious believers begin with the premise that the miracle is authentically divine–and mold explanations without breaking their foolish premise.[53]

Have you ever seen the pseudoscientific techniques and equipment used on television shows that delve into the world of ghost hunting? Like the Young Earth Creationists who inappropriately use carbon dating on living organisms in an attempt to discredit the method,[54] these ghost hunters will determine that unusual electromagnetic fields present in old houses, typically caused by bad wiring, are spirits of the deceased looking for someone among the living to avenge their deaths. While this ghost hunting process may seem foolish to discerning Christian readers, it is no different from Christian scholars using ridiculous apologetic and hermeneutical studies to eliminate obvious textual inconsistencies. The answers are obvious, but they aren't the answers that they want. In each discipline, researchers ignore the simple explanation while advancing the interesting explanation that in turn advances the preconceived notion.

We can say the same for those who promote cryptozoology, gambling systems, mind reading, paranormal beings, astrology,[55] etc. The believers have the desire to become the experts; disbelievers have no real interest in the matter. Thankfully, you will occasionally find rationalists dedicated enough to devote some time to explain that glowing spherical objects in ghostly photographs are just illuminated dust particles, memories of alien abductions are the result of sleep paralysis, and tales of vengeful gods who demand to be worshipped are remnants of ancient folklore. These rationalists, who have studied with great interest but without preconceived notions, are the ones who offer natural explanations for unusual phenomena.

There is every compelling reason to believe that average people who take the time to learn both sides of the debate, and who did not enter with interest in the paranormal, will agree with the naturalistic explanations offered by skeptics. The skeptic, because he has no emotional investment in Bigfoot, will eventually conclude that the creature is based upon myth since the evidence does not support the claims of the believer. Despite the opinion of the objective skeptic, and with no good evidence in favor of the existence of Bigfoot, the believer is going to continue believing what he wants to believe, thanks in part to dubious evidence and crippled thinking skills. The Bigfoot enthusiast will not listen to reason because he convinced himself long ago of the veracity of his beliefs. Otherwise, he will have to accept that he wasted his life on nonsense–and who wants to come to terms with that?

To someone who has never heard of the Judeo-Christian God or the American Bigfoot, the nature of each should be no different. Since no special privilege has been bestowed incessantly upon either entity, debunking the existence of one should be no more difficult than debunking the existence of the other. Intelligent believers in each, however, often pose a problem because they are extremely gifted at coming up with ridiculous scenarios that maintain their increasingly ridiculous proposals. Likewise, intelligent apologists are quite skillful at making an argument seem valid when a critical eye can tell that it is not. I see the solution to this problem, not as a matter of debunking those ridiculous explanations that believers offer, but rather as a matter of exploring the best options to make them appreciate the underlying reasons for their beliefs. Once this is accomplished, the foolishness of the defense should eventually become apparent. Appreciating the absurdity of the Judeo-Christian God is a simple task for an outsider; similarly convincing a crowd who has believed in a talking snake since they were children proves much more challenging.

There can be a tendency within us to make the erroneous assumption that a large volume of repetitious material that defends a certain proposition somehow increases the validity of the proposition. Many Christians have made the mistaken assumption that there must be something legitimate about the religion due to the large number of books promoting and defending it. This outlook borders on the logical fallacy of arguing by numbers. Of course, we should apply the same rule to disbelievers and non-Christian authors. If a million people repeat what I have written in this book, the statements are no more valid than they were when I wrote them. The validity of the statements rests entirely upon how well someone can demonstrate them as factual.

The importance of this point is that religious veracity is not a matter of deciding which major world religion with widespread publication is the right one. Circumstances independent of the veracity of those religions' claims created the current distribution of observation. Fundamental beliefs in aggressive conversion, rapid changes in social structure, and localized advances in information technology all certainly play a role in the availability of literature that supports a particular viewpoint on a global debate.[56] All things equally considered, any of the ancient religions might be correct. It is not logically sound to disqualify a belief system from consideration as the correct one just because a very small population observes it. Conquering and converting for several centuries might very well increase the number of adherents, but these methods do not increase the likelihood of the conquerors having the correct religion. Since the number of followers of a religion has never been (and probably never will be) empirically demonstrated to correlate with the veracity of that religion, Christianity is just as likely to be true from the onset as Jainism, for example. Again, there are religious scholars of every belief system who contend that they can prove the veracity of each of their respective religious beliefs. There is simply no consensus among unbiased scholars as to which, if any, makes the most reasonable claims. It is a great intellectual dishonesty to think that your religion has "something to it" simply because it has the highest number of authors who support its veracity.

There is further difficulty in accepting the veracity of Christianity based partly upon these books. While I have already demonstrated the illogical methods through which the overwhelming majority of experts come to accept the divinity of the Bible, it is also worth noting that many Christian authors obtain doctorates and other titles from diploma mills in part to increase their audiences' perception of credibility.[57] Petty and Cacioppo offer a study in which an audience "agreed more with statements attributed to respected and trusted sources, such as Abraham Lincoln, than with the same statements when they were attributed to nonrespected, nontrusted sources, such as Vladmir Lenin."[58] Cialdini reports that people will even view someone as *taller* when they have an official title because height is often associated with reliability.[59]

People are persuaded to a greater extent, quite understandably, by a person who they perceive to have more expertise on a subject.[60] It would be reasonable to assume further that people would similarly find an argument more persuasive when written by someone who lists their formal title as opposed to someone who omits it. I would never argue that it is a bad practice to consider arguments more heavily when they are from authorities, but many diploma mill graduates have taken advantage of this finding. I can think of no better illustration than a recent episode of *The Simpsons*, in which creationists have gone to court in order to fight for the opportunity to teach their nonsense in public schools. When a witness for the plaintiffs is asked for his title, he trumpets, "I have a Ph.D. in Truthology from Christian Tech" to the awes of the jury.[61] Due to such widespread manipulation, I have decided to omit my formal title, gained from eight years of post-secondary education, from the cover of the book. I will let my arguments stand on their own merit.

Petty and Cacioppo elaborate on the effectiveness of one-sided messages targeted toward those with confirmation bias. Such communications are effective on those who have made pre-determined conclusions on the issue in question and those who know very little about it. I have found that a solid majority of religious believers fit both descriptions quite well. Two-sided message, on the other hand, are often persuasive to audience members who are well-versed on the issue and have the intellectual curiosity to be persuaded in either direction. Furthermore, commercial advertisements (in our situation, apologetics) often utilize one-sided messages on an audience when the product (correspondingly, the religion) is well-liked, widely consumed, has few competitors, and enjoys loyal customers.[62] All four qualities can easily be applied to Christianity in America.

Dissonance

As we have seen, people will often acquire their religious beliefs in illogical fashion, primarily through childhood indoctrination, and justify those beliefs using illogical methods, notably by relying on faulty sources. The reality, however, is that from time to time, conflicting information will be unavoidable. Human beings passionately strive to remain free from internal conflict because there is a strong tendency to maintain consistency among the elements of our cognitive systems. This motivation is inseparable from Bob's uneasy feeling that drove him to explain the video of his mother prostituting. It is provoked by cognitive dissonance, which the mind has the innate tendency to eliminate as quickly as possible.

The founder of Cognitive Dissonance Theory compared the psychological drive to physiological hunger.[63] Just as hunger is a motivation to eat and rid oneself of the hunger, dissonance is a motivation to explain inconsistency and rid oneself of the dissonance. Explanations, therefore, work toward satisfying dissonance just as nutrients work toward satisfying hunger. He suggested three modes that we use to rid ourselves of cognitive dissonance.

1) An individual can alter the importance of the original belief or new information. Suppose that you believe in the Judeo-Christian God. If someone presents evidence that contradicts your belief, you can alleviate the dissonance by deciding that the existence of God is not important to you or that the new information on his existence is irrelevant because the debate falls outside of human understanding. Encountering the former is rare, but we see the latter on occasion when

discussing aspects of religion, particularly when an apologist for biblical inerrancy finally surrenders to the idea that the Bible might not be perfect. As one can decide that an inerrant Bible is not a necessity for believing in God, the question of inerrancy becomes moot. Note that this avenue does not necessarily resolve the discrepancy, but instead relegates it to a matter of non-importance–a move that successfully eliminates the uneasy feelings.

2) An individual can change his original belief. Suppose again that you believe in the Judeo-Christian God. If someone presents evidence that contradicts your belief, you can also alleviate the dissonance by deciding that the information is correct and your previous belief was premature. We almost never see this in matters of religion because of the perceived level of importance that childhood indoctrination has placed upon Christianity. Someone who cares very little about religion, on the other hand, is more likely to be persuaded by the veracity of the argument.

3) An individual can seek evidence that is critical of the new information. Suppose yet again that you believe in the Judeo-Christian God. If someone presents evidence that contradicts your belief, you can also alleviate the dissonance by convincing yourself that the new information is invalid. Needless to say, this is what we usually see in matters of religion. Since religious people do not want to trivialize or change their beliefs, finding information that supports the original belief and/or information that brings the new evidence into question is the quickest method to eliminate the cognitive dissonance. Therefore, cognitive dissonance primarily drives confirmation bias. We will thus consider this phenomenon for the remainder of the section.

It makes perfect sense for an individual to want to study the issue in question when a conflict arises, but unfortunately, we often fall victim to confirmation bias and use illogical reasoning to rid ourselves of the conflict when it manifests on important issues. In situations where the information cannot support our decisions, such as the undeniable reality that we have based our religious affiliations primarily on environmental cues (without any real knowledge of other religions), we often resort to methods that will increase the attractiveness of our decisions and decrease the attractiveness of the unchosen alternatives.

Petty and Cacioppo cite a number of studies in which subjects utilize the practice of spreading the attractiveness of two contrasting decisions, even when there are no objective facts on which to base the reevaluations of the alternatives. People simply become increasingly sure of their decisions after they have made them by "rationalizing one's choice of alternatives, [which] serves to reduce the cognitive dissonance produced by foregoing the good features of the unchosen alternative and accepting the bad features of the chosen alternative."[64] When it comes to religion, a believer will defend his faith and attack the alternatives in part simply because he has already rendered a decision on the matter.

Furthermore–and this is where the strength of the motivation kicks into overdrive–Petty and Cacioppo explain that the effects of cognitive dissonance and the subsequent practice of confirmation bias increase as the positions between the two beliefs diverge and the perceived importance of establishing a position grows.[65] Could any two positions be in sharper contrast than the existence and nonexistence of God? Could any dilemma be more important to the Christian than whether or not God exists? It naturally follows that questions on the issue of God's existence provoke the most cognitive dissonance within those who are deeply involved in the issue. As this debate generates the greatest amount of cognitive dissonance, it naturally follows that people are increasingly willing to accept explanations that alleviate the uncomfortable feelings and decreasingly willing to consider disconfirming arguments. As the uneasiness becomes more powerful, people become more willing to surrender to whatever arguments are offered–just as when hunger becomes more powerful, people become more willing to eat whatever food is offered. This will subsequently lead to highly illogical justifications for maintaining highly important beliefs.

Imagine the contrasting levels of cognitive dissonance generated in the following two scenarios of a married economist with a 5 percent failure rate on private financial predictions:

For the only time in his life, the economist publicly proclaims the wisdom of investing in a certain mutual fund, based on his professional understanding that the value of the fund will increase quickly and dramatically. However, his trusted private detective friend tells him that he is almost certain that he spotted a secret earnings report, which stated that the value of the fund will immediately fall 50 percent. A moderate amount of cognitive dissonance is generated in this individual because his failed understanding might cost him his reputation as a reputable economic forecaster. The economist has three options for eliminating the dissonance: he can convince himself that the decrease in value is irrelevant to his status; he can accept that he is not really an economic expert; or he can convince himself that the new information presented to him by his friend is wrong, and he is therefore still an economic expert. It is clear that the last avenue yields the most desirable results. From our understanding of confirmation bias, he will likely want to confirm his original belief by finding a way to convince himself that his friend is wrong.

In addition, after having been faithfully married to his wife for twenty years and having absolutely no reason to distrust her, our economist is told something else by his trusted private detective friend. The detective is almost certain that he spotted the economist's wife in a hotel room with another man while on an unrelated assignment. A large amount of cognitive dissonance is generated in this individual because his perception of being a good husband is of higher personal importance than his perception of being an expert in the economy. He has three options for eliminating the dissonance: he can convince himself that his wife's infidelity is irrelevant to his standing as a good husband; he can decide that she cheated because he has not been a good husband; or he can convince himself that the information presented to him by his friend is wrong, and he is therefore still a good husband. It is clear that the last avenue again yields the most desirable results. From our understanding of confirmation bias, he will likely want to confirm his original belief by finding a way to convince himself that his friend is wrong.

The economist is now battling with two pieces of discomforting news. The issue now becomes which conflict he will be more likely to resolve by accepting the idea that his friend was mistaken. Since the perceived difference in his potential career status is not as important as the perceived difference in his potential husbandry status, I would strongly argue that he will likely sooner believe that his friend was mistaken on his second claim than his first, even though this judgment is contrary to his own field of expertise.[66]

The economist will pursue methods to invalidate the new information, not based on the unlikelihood of the new information, but rather on how much he dislikes the new information. If our subject were a completely rational individual who stuck to the facts, it should be much harder for him to accept the information on the investment than the information on his wife. He is wrong on economic forecasts only 5 percent of the time, and given the nature of his unique declaration, he no doubt committed an extraordinary amount of time to researching the mutual fund. Being faithfully married for twenty years barely makes him an average husband, and studies have shown that over one-half of all American marriages likely experience some sort of infidelity.[67]

Because of his greater bias for wanting confirmation of his wife's fidelity, he will seek reasons, many of them highly unlikely, for the new information to be erroneous. Being convinced of a comfortable belief is of much higher priority than coming to an objective conclusion based solely on the facts. Despite the possibility of tangible evidence pointing to the conclusion of his wife's infidelity, he still may not be fully convinced. He may need to hear his wife's confession personally to believe the story–and even then, he may briefly remain in a state of denial. The new information on his economic prediction, on the other hand, he will likely not take so personally. The stronger the conviction in question, not necessarily the more unlikely the possibility, the stronger the resistance against contradicting evidence will be.

Now imagine the level of dissonance he would feel after receiving information that is contradictory to his core religious beliefs that have served him throughout life. These solid ideas tell him that there is no good reason to accept the existence of his god. His parents and grandparents are not in heaven; the man who kidnapped his missing child might never be punished; no one is really listening when he prays out of desperation; complete justice is an idealistic fantasy; eternal happiness does not exist. While one-half of all people will experience marital infidelity, at least two-thirds of all people in the world have the wrong religion.[68] Thus, the likelihood of an expert botching a once-in-a-lifetime economic prediction is low (5%), the possibility of experiencing marital infidelity is relatively high (50%), and the prevalence of being born into an incorrect religion is widespread (67+%). Nevertheless, he becomes increasingly less willing to believe the outcomes even as the chances of those outcomes become increasingly probable. Cognitive dissonance, due to individual preference, will cause him to accept increasingly unlikely explanations as long as he uses them to prevent having to accept increasingly undesirable consequences. When cognitive dissonance becomes more and more involved in thought processes, decision making is driven less and less by the facts.

The methods chosen to eliminate cognitive dissonance in unfamiliar territory do not necessarily need to be complex, especially when tensions are high and stress inhibits proper judgment. While some bewildered people will quickly manufacture outlandish explanations to eliminate the feelings from the dissonance, others will simply appeal to the positions of authorities. Very rarely will people decide to undertake a meticulous fact-finding exercise in order to understand the best reasons for each position when their most sacred beliefs are being questioned.

Many people with whom I discuss the Bible in person will put the method of appealing to authority into practice as a first line of defense. If I cite a foundational problem with their religion, such as why an all-knowing creator cannot co-exist with free will,[69] they will often report later that they received satisfaction after finding a wealth of material in books or webpages that justified their original beliefs. Perhaps they came across an individual with some sort of degree who runs a website chocked full of articles that offer a long, complex argument as to why my suggested difficulty is nothing to worry about. The previously troubled Christians might not peruse, comprehend, or even read the entire argument offered on that website, but the mere fact that the article exists for public review satisfies them that there is a reasonable answer to my suggestion. Never mind the fact that anyone can probably cite an authority who agrees with a particular position, especially when it comes to interpreting religion. Due to the innate bias to confirm what we already believe, the article surely is not going to be scrutinized or tested against a rebuttal. The Christians were interested in feeling comfortable with their beliefs, not in dispassionately evaluating them. While such actions will successfully alleviate the uncomfortable feeling accompanying the realization of conflicting information, the individuals experiencing these emotions have not actually rectified the problem. To the Christians, the invalid dispute is now gone; to everyone free of emotionally predetermined conclusions, the conflict still requires a logical and justifiable resolution.

Eliminating the cognitive dissonance is of foremost importance. People want to feel reassured that they are correct in their beliefs, especially when there is a lot of emotion, personality, history, and identity at stake. If those Christian were actually interested in the truth, they would analyze the article critically and thoroughly to see if it adequately addressed the points of my suggestion. But they are not questioning; they are defending. We have all taken the easy way out at some point, but freethinkers appreciate the intellectual dishonesty in such an approach and have already made a decision to follow the truth wherever it leads.

To evaluate the idea that involving topics arouse high levels of illogical thinking, consider a series of real world examples of religious followers being confronted with what ordinary people would consider damning evidence against their beliefs. The following is from Leon Festinger's *When Prophecy Fails*:

> The group was a private and cohesive band of individuals who believed that the world would end by flood before the sun rose on 21 December. This belief was based upon a "message" received from aliens on the planet Clarion by the group's leader, Mrs. Keech. The aliens also indicated that they would use their flying saucer to save the members of the group on the eve of the flood. Following the flood, the group would be returned to earth to create a better world.
>
> The eve of the great flood arrived. The eve turned to night, then to early morning. The aliens and flood failed to materialize, and the group was downcast. Suddenly, Mrs. Keech received another "message" from the aliens saying that the world had been spared because of their faith. Hearing this, the group members rejoiced, reaffirmed their faith in their purpose, and set out to

> recruit new members for the group. The undeniable disconfirmation of their beliefs left them not only unshaken, but more convinced of their truth than ever before. As illustrated in this case, people sometimes think, feel, and act in ways that don't appear plausible. People sometimes hold or change attitudes *despite* the objective facts.[70]

This report is from an article published in the Journal of Abnormal and Social Psychology:

> A southwestern evangelical Christian group believed that there was soon to be a devastating nuclear attack. One hundred three members of the group descended into bomb shelters so that they might survive the attack and build a better civilization. After forty-two days and nights in the bomb shelters, the members surfaced, accepting the fact that no nuclear attack had occurred as expected. But rather than accepting the obvious conclusion that they had erred in their prediction, group members proclaimed that their beliefs had been instrumental in stopping the nuclear attack.[71]

Consider a third story in which followers of a popular American religion are unconvinced that their beliefs are a sham, even when smacked in the face with hard evidence.

Joseph Smith purportedly translated The Book of Mormon, the holy text of the Latter-Day Saints, from golden tablets provided to him by an angel. He did not perform the translation by looking at the ambiguous text on the tablets, which incidentally no one else ever laid eyes upon, but rather by burying his head in his hat, staring at a rock that he placed inside, and using a spiritual medium to transcribe what he saw on the rock.[72] After completing 116 pages of translation, Smith loaned the pages to his scribe who either destroyed or lost them. The scribe was replaced, and the lost pages were never retranslated. Smith claimed that God forbade him to retranslate the lost pages because the ones who stole the manuscript planned to publish an altered version in order to discredit his ability to translate the golden tablets. Instead, Smith translated an abridged version out of the hat.

To anyone who was not indoctrinated with Mormon beliefs, it is clear that Smith could not retranslate the tablets because he could not remember the nonsense that he had made up and rattled off as he went along. The Church of the Latter-Day Saints commonly explains the obvious fraud by declaring that the decision was made by God and therefore unquestionable. Apologists for the Book of Mormon can no doubt defend this position to the satisfaction of its adherents, but because the rest of us were not indoctrinated to accept the veracity of Smith's translation, we see right through the smokescreen. The Mormons simply see the matter as a judgment from God, and this explanation is perfectly satisfactory to them because they are already believers. Outsiders, however, see the matter as God never having made such a declaration because Joseph Smith was lying or delusional. This defense is very similar to the Christian belief that arguments provided by nonbelievers are resolved by citing "the incomprehensible and mysterious ways of God." Where the Mormon chooses not to question God's decisions regarding the Book of Mormon, the outsiders (Christians and other non-Mormons) see their reasoning as an absurd alibi. Correspondingly, where the Christian chooses not to question "the incomprehensible and mysterious ways of God," the outsiders (non-Christians) see their reasoning as an equally absurd alibi.

The explanations offered by Mrs. Keech and Joseph Smith relieve the uncomfortable dissonance generated in the believers immediately after external elements showed that the facts were inconsistent with their beliefs. I imagine that even most of the Christian audience is asking how the doomsday cults and Mormons could be so foolish as to not acknowledge the obvious, but I say to this Christian audience that the evidence against your own beliefs is every bit as strong. Jesus' failed return prophecies (not to mention his resurrections and demonic exorcisms, among other absurdities) are no more deterring to Christians than alien/nuclear absences are to doomsday cults or translational hoaxes are to Mormons–simply because believers have accepted the veracity of each respective suggestion as the essential foundation for each respective belief. Just as the cult members used wild explanations for the failures of their outlandish predictions, Christian apologists offer lengthy speculations that the failed textual prophecies of Jesus returning to earth in the near future were a product of misunderstanding or mistranslations. Others even believe that Jesus already fulfilled the predictions sometime in the first century.[73] Never mind that there is no rational evidence for either suggestion; all that matters is maintaining an internally justifiable belief in the Bible's veracity. Anyone who has not been socially indoctrinated to accept the Bible's veracity sees the clear mistake. The apologists for each belief were likely aspiring for the plausible or probable, but they reluctantly settled for the tenuously possible.

Consider a similar topic that arouses almost as much nonsense as religion–politics. One study performed just prior to the 2004 US Presidential Election enabled researchers to empirically demonstrate, using MRI scanning, that people who were strongly loyal to one candidate did not use areas of the brain associated with reasoning to resolve contradictory statements made by their candidate. The supporters instead relied upon regions of the brain associated with emotion to justify their personal allegiance with their candidate.[74] I could continue to cite similar studies that demonstrate irrational behavior from highly involved individuals for the remainder of this book, but I hope this will be sufficient to establish my point that people do not utilize dispassionate critical thought when justifying their most important beliefs. Human beings are highly emotional creatures who shun logic when something challenges our personal values.

In addition to Cognitive Dissonance Theory, there are two other compatible and/or complementary theories currently floating amongst persuasive psychologists that may explain additional reasons why people provide illogical defenses for their beliefs. Impression Management Theory suggests that people increasingly stick by their decisions because consistency leads to social reward and inconsistency leads to social punishment.[75] In this case, a Christian may be inclined stick to his beliefs because his peers may frown upon an inconsistency if he changes his mind and decides, for example, that the Bible is not without flaw and that donkeys consequently have never talked.

Psychological Reactance Theory suggests that people increasingly stick by their decisions when others threaten the opportunity to express those decisions freely.[76] It is my opinion that this explains, in part, the boom of Christian beliefs in Rome during the infant years of the movement. While most religions were readily accepted and incorporated into Roman culture, Christian followers gained the disdain of authorities by refusing to worship emperors and attempting to convert others into doing the same. It should be obvious that this upset a number of Roman officials.

A lengthy discussion of the persecution and laws against Christianity in the Roman Empire is beyond the scope of this text, but consider two examples. Nero is often believed to have burned and crucified Christians for their beliefs.[77] Diocletian, in addition to burning and torturing Christians for their beliefs, ordered the destruction of Christian scriptures and places of worship.[78] Even for someone who knows next to nothing about persuasive psychology, it's not difficult to imagine how people would become more dedicated to and firm in their beliefs when faced with such violent opposition. Petty and Cacioppo point out that people in such a situation are "driven to respond by performing the threatened behavior; counterarguing, often covertly, the reasons for and benefits of the restriction; and changing attitudes toward the various alternatives, particularly revealing more favorably the threatened or eliminated alternative."[79] It is obvious that under such circumstances, any group will respond by dropping their relatively minor differences and uniting for a common cause. Others outside the group may then naturally desire what the authorities have forbidden and investigate the beliefs of the persecuted.

As the Roman Emperors openly punished people for observing Christianity, the findings of modern psychology indicate that this may have had the opposite effect of what the Emperors intended. We cannot ignore the ramifications of affecting people's desires by denying them from what they might otherwise be indifferent to or requiring them to do what they might have done anyway. Cialdini reports several cases of outrage and increased rebellion in cases requiring residents of a town in Georgia to buy firearms, the banning of laundry phosphates in Miami, and the banning of speeches on university campuses.[80] In addition, there are the more popular cases of Prohibition in 1920s America, pornography regulation on the internet, the banning of certain books from libraries, and the scorn of religion in the Soviet Union. Thus, the overbearing punishments for observing the Christian religion in all certainty generated more interest in it and support for it. Furthermore, the ostracizing of Christians in the Roman Empire was a sharp reversal of religious freedom, a course much more likely to lead to revolt than the perpetual absence of religious freedom. Cialdini explains:

> It is not traditionally the most downtrodden people–who have come to see their deprivation as part of the natural order of things–who are especially liable to revolt. Instead, revolutionaries are more likely to be those who have been given at least some taste of a better life. When the economic and social improvements they have experienced and come to expect suddenly become less available, they desire them more than ever and often rise up violently to secure them.[81]

The Justification Of Contradiction

Now that we have a rough explanation for why individuals hold their misguided beliefs, let us see how conditioning, bias, and dissonance come into play when defending those beliefs. We will do this with three examples of an apologist supporting his inerrancy beliefs by attempting to eliminate the presence of contradictions and inconsistencies in the Bible. Contrary to the opinion of the religious community, the average disbeliever does not base his decision to disregard the Bible on the presence of contradictions. After all, the Bible could be 100 percent free from contradiction, detectable error, historical anomaly, female oppression, animal cruelty, etc., but this does not mean that God has returned dead men to life, made donkeys talk, or that he is beyond ethical judgment for drowning the entire world. In my first book, I made the retrospectively unfortunate decision of offering a long list of major contradictions without elaborating much on why the presence of contradictions was important. Not that the long list is a bad thing of which to have a good appreciation, but it can get quite boring for people who are not interested in knowing everything about an admittedly boring book. Instead, I hope to illustrate the existence of contradictions with three examples and demonstrate what lengths defenders of the Bible will go to in order to maintain their predetermined perceptions of the Bible's divine perfection.[82]

The first contradiction example involves a discrepancy of at least ten years between two gospel accounts on when Jesus of Nazareth was born. The more popular account of Matthew has King Herod alive at the time of Jesus' birth.[83] We know from several reputable historical sources that Herod's reign ended in or before 4 BCE.[84] Thus, according to Matthew, Jesus must have been born in or before 4 BCE.[85] However, Luke says that Mary was still with child during the time Quirinius was conducting a census as Governor of Syria.[86] According to relatively meticulous Roman history, Quirinius could not have carried out this census until at least 6 CE. Thus, according to Luke, Jesus must have been born in or after 6 CE. In order for the two accounts to be harmonious, Jesus had to be born before 4 BCE and after 6 CE: a contradictory feat that is impossible even for a supernatural being. The two accounts provide a ten-year discrepancy in need of a difficult resolution. This is the equivalent of two people disagreeing today on whether Theodore Roosevelt or Woodrow Wilson was president of the United States when Bob Hope was born. The potential importance of Bob Hope, however, is nothing compared to that of the alleged son of God.

While it is true that we have increasingly accurate records in our modern society, it should not have been insurmountably difficult for biblical authors to remember a specific year when an individual was born because they tended to base their dates relative to concurrent events. If the author of Luke wanted to convey the year that we now understand as 4 BCE as the year of birth, he could have just as easily said that Mary was still with child during the time that Quintilius, not Quirinius, was Governor of Syria. Such a comparative detail can hardly become exaggerated by the passage of time. If, on the other hand, someone whimsically created the supernatural birth story decades after its setting and neglected to attach a definite time period, which is what we have very good reason to believe actually happened, we could anticipate such discrepancies. It is also important that we not forget that the gospel writers had the advantage of divine inspiration for maintaining consistency. What modern technology in timekeeping could possibly be more helpful in preventing complications in your writings than an omnipotent god's assistance? Nevertheless, Christians would like the world to believe that Jesus was born during the distinctive incumbencies of King Herod and Quirinius.

To rectify this insurmountable problem, Christians initially proposed, without justification but much desperation, that Quirinius was a Syrian Governor twice. As the argument goes, in order for Luke to be consistent with Matthew, Quirinius held this phantom governorship sometime before 4 BCE. Here's what we know from Roman history: Quintilius was Governor from 6 BCE to 3 BCE; Saturninus was Governor immediately before that from 9 BCE to 6 BCE; Titius was Governor immediately before that from 12 BCE to 9 BCE; and Quirinius, the Governor mentioned in Luke, didn't obtain consulship until 12 BCE, making him ineligible to hold Syrian Governorship before that time. Furthermore, no one ever held the Governorship of Syria twice; Josephus and Tacitus, the two most important historians from the early Common Era, never mentioned Quirinius holding the post twice; censuses of provincial inhabitants were few and far between, making the "coincidence" of there being a census during Quirinius' tenure far less likely; and there would be no reason for Quirinius to conduct a census prior to 6 CE because Judea wasn't under Roman control until that time.[87]

Most Christian apologists have come to abandon this argument for good reason. Nevertheless, since the indoctrinated Christian often deems the Bible flawless before he ever opens it, he is convinced that there *must* be a self-satisfactory solution somewhere. A rational person would simply conclude that the text was in error, but the consequences of doing so are too detrimental to the inerrancy fundamentalists. Thus, the apologists must find a new "solution"...

> *The word* Governor *(Greek* hegemoneuo) *should have been translated as holding a command rather than specifically holding governorship.*

In a vacuum, this is certainly an acceptable translation. However, many contextual problems still exist with this wild explanation. There is still no reason for Quirinius to conduct a census prior to 6 CE because Judea wasn't under Roman control until that time; it makes little sense for the author of Luke to relate the era to an otherwise irrelevant figure when he could have just as easily mentioned the true Governor of Syria; Quirinius was assigned to fight in Galatia, not Syria, from 6 BCE to 1 BCE; such a rendition is in sharp contrast to the direct meaning of the passage and only derived *ad hoc* to superficially satisfy the contradiction; and secular scholars agree that the grammar of the passage does not support such a rendition.[88]

While this wild suggestion cannot be 100 percent invalidated using hard logic, it is only reasonable, given the overwhelming evidence, to conclude that the passages are contradictory. However, if you begin with the premise of biblical inerrancy, instead of dispassionately testing the book and arriving at that conclusion, it is only reasonable to believe that the apologetic suggestion is correct.[89] This is where premature conclusions and confirmation bias certainly come into play. In the minds of the believers, wild scenarios become more likely than reasonable conclusions. Tenuous possibilities that maintain inerrancy are more acceptable than probable explanations that do not. If the situation were reversed, and the doctrine of inerrancy required the meaning of Matthew to change in order to match what the text plainly states in Luke, you could bet your last dollar that the apologists would find a way to have King Herod in power ten years after his death.

The Bible has a definite inconsistency on whether God looks favorably upon those who pray in public. Most churches observe public prayer in accordance with the (supposedly) divinely inspired author of Timothy who says, "I will therefore that men pray every where, lifting up holy hands."[90] However, Jesus specifically told his followers to refrain from this behavior: "And when thou prayest, thou shalt not be as the hypocrites are: for they love to pray standing in the synagogues and in the corners of the streets, that they may be seen of men. Verily I say unto you, They have their reward. But thou, when thou prayest, enter into thy closet, and when thou hast shut thy door, pray to thy Father which is in secret; and thy Father which seeth in secret shall reward thee openly."[91] I will be the first to grant that the people who pray in public are not hypocritically doing so just to let others see them, but they are still violating a direct order given by Jesus to avoid prayer in public. Jesus was very clear in his desire of not wanting his true believers to have commonalties with the hypocrites who pray in public for counterfeit reasons. This is why he specifies that his followers should pray in secret.

A lesser-known online apologist[92] has raised a vehement objection to the idea that there is a contradiction about public prayer in the Bible. It is his position that Jesus is speaking in Matthew 6:5-6 against public prayer *for the purpose of being noticed*, but this is obviously not what an objective reader without a strong confirmation bias would conclude. Jesus was quite clear in the passage that he wanted people to pray in private. The whole notion of praying in public did not sit well with him because that is how the people who wanted to be seen chose to pray. Since Jesus wanted his believers to be nothing like the hypocrites, he ordered them to go into a state of privacy when they wanted to pray. It does not matter whether or not your prayers are genuine when praying in public, it is the act of praying in public that Jesus forbids in this passage. Pray privately, and you will be rewarded publicly. That is distinctly how Jesus said prayer should work.

It should be clear to dispassionate readers that the apologist has completely misunderstood and/or misinterpreted this passage, possibly through no conscious fault of his own, when he states that Jesus' command is "an instruction against public prayer, done for the purpose of being noticed." The command is in fact "an instruction against public prayer, because others do it for the purpose of being noticed." If Jesus wanted to say, "Don't pray in public for the purpose of being noticed, but it's okay to pray in public if you aren't doing it for that reason," he would have said so. He did not. The apologist prays in public, has probably always done so, has always noticed others doing so, sees nothing wrong with it, and consequently feels that uncomfortable drive to make the text say something other than what it plainly says.

Although he does not need to attack my interpretation of the contrasting verse, he chooses to take that route as well. It is his position that First Timothy 2:8 is not a direct instruction for prayer. While this much is no doubt true, the author nevertheless expresses his *hope* that men pray *everywhere*. That desire would necessarily include him *hoping* that men would pray in public. One cannot logically satisfy the hope of a divinely inspired author of the Bible wanting us to pray everywhere, as the author of First Timothy expresses, without praying in public, which Jesus forbids.

Consider the dilemma in this fashion: A person reading only First Timothy would believe it was okay to pray in public, but a person reading only Matthew would know that Jesus forbade it. A person reading both would understandably become confused. This is a terrific example of the Bible's inconsistency on a very important issue. The two passages are in no way complementary. If you merely believe in a somewhat divinely inspired Bible, not necessarily an inerrant one, ask yourself this question: If the authors of the Bible were divinely inspired, why does God inspire one man to record an encouragement for people to pray everywhere while he inspires another to strictly forbid it?

The interesting part of our exercise here is that the patent inconsistency is not even a major issue for Christians who have managed to gain a more progressive style of thought. It's simply a matter of one fallible man making the mistake of saying something that he probably should not have said. However, this glaring inconsistency *is* a big deal to the apologist who defends the idea of inerrancy and cannot allow a single contradiction in the Bible. Thus, the text must be twisted in some fashion to fit with the premise of inerrancy.

The apologist later published a rebuttal to my response, and he took two indefensible steps while doing so. The first blunder is that he tries to make it sound as though I need First Timothy 2:8 to mean that we have to pray non-stop in every place under every circumstance. The apologist sarcastically proclaims, "Like this means Paul envisions people stopping while climbing down ladders, or doing surgery, or skiing down a slope, to pray!" I suspect the apologist knows on some level that I only need the passage to show that "praying everywhere" means that prayer must not necessarily be done in private. I can think of no reason why he would elect to make such accusations if he has any academic or intellectual integrity.[93] The apologist continues, "[Jason] Long merely tries to strain 'everywhere' into a physical location for the act of prayer, when the clearest meaning is that 'everywhere' modifies 'men' and that men are to then follow some mode not specified in Timothy." This is a new argument that he did not bother to offer originally, but I suspect that on some level he saw the bankruptcy in his original position and felt the necessity to make a new one.

So we must now consider if the author meant to convey that he wanted "men everywhere to pray" as the apologist and the editors of 25 percent of the major Bible versions suggest–or "men to pray everywhere" as I and the editors of 75 percent of the major Bible versions suggest.[94] How exactly does the apologist determine that "the clearest meaning is that 'everywhere' modifies 'men'?" We do not know because he provides no argument–only an assertion that it is "the clearest meaning."

On the other hand, we are on solid ground to argue that the passage is a clear declaration of prayer *policy* because it tells not only *where* to pray, but also *how* to pray: "lifting up holy hands, without wrath or doubting." I have even taken the time to consult three experts in ancient Greek, all of whom assure me that I have translated the verse properly.[95] According to them, the phrase *everywhere* (Greek *en panti topo*) is the recipient of the infinitive verb *to pray* (Greek *proseuchesthai*) and that it can, without question, only be rendered as "men to pray in every place." Furthermore, the literal English translation, "I want therefore men to pray in every place," is also consistent with the 405 CE Latin Vulgate of the New Testament (*volo ergo viros orare in omni loco*). I could belabor this relatively meaningless point further, but this is not the verse of the contradiction to which the apologist objects. Therefore, I will leave it up to the readers to consider the matter further. At the very least, however, does the realization that the issue is open to debate not smell of human fallibility in the writing? Could an all-powerful god not inspire an author to provide writing that is beyond dispute?

The second blunder in his response is that he accuses me of ignoring a supposed qualifier in Matthew 6:5 that allows public prayer. However, he is the one who completely ignores the meaning of Matthew 6:6, which is the verse with Jesus ordering people to pray in private because hypocrites pray in public. The apologist states, "Either 'that they may be seen of men' is missing from Long's Bible; or else he thinks that extended pointless rambling will cover his error. None of this negates the presence of the clear qualifier of why: '*to be seen of men*.' Thus public prayer for an altruistic purpose is not forbidden, no matter how much Long wishes to pretend that the qualifying phrase is not present."

The apologist attempts to convey to his audience that his assertion is so unquestionably accurate that the only remaining explanation for my position is that my Bible is missing words. However, I am not the one who circumvents what the text clearly states. Jesus does not say it is okay to pray in public as long as it is not "to be seen of men." He explains that hypocrites pray in public to be seen of men, then gives *very specific instructions* to pray in private in order not to be like the hypocrites. If the verse means what the apologist wants it to mean, Jesus' entire exercise of ordering his followers into privacy before praying is useless, irrelevant, and without meaning. He would have just ordered them not to pray for hypocritical reasons and left it at that.

Suppose I state, "Politicians help impoverished people in the open to gain public approval. Don't be like them. When you help impoverished people, do so anonymously because God can still see you and will reward you with public approval." In no way can one honestly twist this to mean that I am endorsing or condoning the act of helping people in public as long as it is not for the purpose of public approval. I am giving a *direct command* to help people anonymously just as Jesus gave a *direct command* to pray in private. If Jesus had not given the specific order to go into private, one might be able to interpret the text to support the apologetic argument successfully, but such an overreaching agenda certainly does not reflect reality. It does not even rise to the level of tenuous possibility, much less probability or plausibility. Again, if Jesus wanted to say, "public prayer is okay as long as you aren't doing it to be seen" as opposed to "pray in private," he would have said so. He did not. The matter is not open for serious debate, but even if it were, does the opportunity for misinterpretation not smell once again of human fallibility in the writing?

Let's now consider one of the most popular contradictions in the Bible. Shortly before the crucifixion, Jesus tells Peter that he will choose to disavow any knowledge of Jesus on three occasions. After these events manifest, a cock will crow to remind him of Jesus' words. In the books of Matthew, Luke, and John, Jesus warns Peter that all three of his denials will take place *before* the cock crows.[96] In these three accounts, the situation unfolds exactly how Jesus predicted. The cock crows after, and only after, Peter's third denial is made in accordance with what Jesus states, "the cock *will not crow* until you have denied me three times."[97] However, the details are different in Mark. Here, we see Jesus warning Peter that he will deny their friendship three times before the cock crows *twice*.[98] Of course, this is exactly how the events play out in Mark.[99] The cock crows after the first denial and again after the third denial. At face value, this is an undeniable contradiction without a rational explanation. If Mark is correct, the cock *must* have crowed after the first denial–even though Jesus said, in the other three gospels, that it *would not* crow until after the third denial. If these three gospels are accurate, Mark is wrong because the cock could not have crowed until after all three of Peter's denials. How does the apologist handle this one?

> *What it runs down to, in terms of weight of evidence, is that 14:30 and 14:72 are likely to have been part of Mark originally, whereas the key verse in 14:68 ("and the cock crew") is not, and was likely added to make the fulfillment of Jesus' prediction more exact.*

In other words, God allowed someone to alter his perfect, divinely inspired word by adding a non-existent crowing. Mark 14:68, which takes place after the first denial but before the next two denials, reads, "But he denied, saying, I know not, neither understand I what thou sayest. And he went out into the porch; and the cock crew." The apologist asserts that the last part of the verse, "and the cock crew," was "added to make the fulfillment of Jesus' prediction more exact." When there can be no other solution, he claims that the Bible says something God did not want it to say. If a phrase gives him trouble, the apologist throws it out and justifies his best reason for doing so.

Since the apologist argues by assertion instead of argumentation, I will have to speculate on his reasoning. The duplicate crowing in Mark 14:68 (along with segments of dozens of other verses) do not appear in one of the two oldest (currently) discovered complete New Testament manuscripts. This fourth century manuscript, Codex Vaticanus, stands in contrast to other early extant manuscripts that contain both crowings, as well as all major English translations that chose to include them. As the apology stands, God apparently lets the majority of the world think for centuries that there was a crowing after the first denial–even though there really wasn't. In short, the apologist is hardly arguing for weight of evidence, but more likely for the sake of maintaining inerrancy.[100]

This is confirmation bias in its finest hour. The apologist does not thoroughly scrutinize the Bible before drawing a conclusion on its infallibility; he does not consider for one second that the text might have an otherwise insignificant error; he begins with the premise of its infallibility and subsequently offers ways around its errors in order to remain consistent with his premise. What book could we not hold as infallible by employing such disingenuous methods? Practices like these render the idea of an inerrant text meaningless.

> *That said, what of the fact that the other gospels do not say "twice"? Strictly speaking, there is no contradiction in action, since of course if Peter denied before the cock crowed once, he also did it before the cock crowed twice!*

And the same would be true when the cock crowed three, four, or seventy-two times, but the prediction in Mark says that the cock would crow *twice* for what later appears to be a clear textual reason. This apologist's defense, on the other hand, is the rationalization we receive after he has removed whatever is inconvenient for his cause.[101]

> *In that light, I would suggest that Mark offers the original verbiage of the prediction (as might be expected, if Mark is recording from Peter), while the other gospels contain a modified and simplified oral tradition that follows the usual oral-tradition pattern.*

If the author of Mark was indeed getting his information from Peter,[102] how is it that Peter's guidance provided a more thorough account for the author of Mark than God's divine inspiration did for the authors of Matthew, Luke, and John? God had to have known that, when combined, the gospels create a mess of the denial story. Is this subsequent confusion what we would expect from divine inspiration–or is it what we would expect from variance in fallible human memories?

A different apologist would later extend this argument by asserting that the second (and now only) crowing in Mark referred to the second crowing of the day, which was also the first crowing after the three denials. This apologist convinced himself that the first crowing of the day was a standard middle-of-the-night crowing that Matthew, Luke, and John decided not to count, even though most early manuscripts of Mark specifically tell us that the first crowing was after the first denial. This explanation is an *ad hoc* assertion for the sake of inerrancy that has never amounted to anything more than mere speculation. The supporting passage typically referenced is Mark 13:35, which states, "Watch ye therefore: for ye know not when the master of the house cometh, at even, or at midnight, or at the cockcrowing, or in the morning." It is my position that one must shun intellectual integrity to argue that the cockcrowing in this passage is referring to the middle of the night. Having grown up on a farm, I would not deny that a cock often crows throughout the day and night, but it has never been established that it crowed just once in the middle of the night and that this was understood to be the day's first crowing. The cockcrowing should clearly be interpreted via its normal context as the early morning period that divides the nighttime from the daytime. The apologist also argued that the post-denials crowing was the second daily crowing, which is the supposed symbolic start of the day, and that this crowing is apparently what most people (but not Jesus) counted as the first (not the second) crowing of the day.[103] Therefore, the post-denials crowing can be counted as either the first crowing (due to supposed "modified and simplified oral tradition") *or* the second crowing (due to supposed local understanding that the middle-of-the-night crowing was actually the first) and can then alternate between the two explanations as gospel circumstances require.[104]

Some apologists have argued instead that the cock crowed twice in succession following the third denial and that the second crowing was an "attention-getter."[105] Other apologists have suggested that the first crowing actually *did* take place after the first denial, but that it shouldn't count because Peter didn't hear it.[106] Still others regard the expression of the cock crowing twice as a local idiom that was not to be taken literally.[107] Not all of these wild speculations can be right, but they can all certainly be wrong.

If we are to simply brush the textual connotations off as a disparity due to the simplified oral tradition found in three of the four gospels, why not just say that the story details themselves are different due to the same shortcomings of oral tradition?[108] Mark is internally consistent on the matter. Matthew, Luke, and John are internally consistent and consistent among each other on the matter. The only problem is that Mark is not consistent with the other three. The simplest answer is that the author of Mark made a simple error. The apologist, on the other hand, would have his audience believe four propositions: 1) Three of the gospels are "modified and simplified oral traditions" that do not fully explain the details. 2) The fourth gospel mentions that the cock crowed a second time without mentioning that the cock crowed a first time because the post-denials crowing just happened to be the second crowing of the day.[109] 3) The audience understood that the true first crowing was in the middle of the night. 4) God allowed someone to tamper with Mark 14:68 after he inspired a perfect record of what actually happened, thus misleading Christians for centuries. The apologist readily admits that oral tradition is fallible, played a role in the formation of the current text, and was responsible for details being left out, yet the apologist will not allow the skeptic to use the same reason, the fallibility of oral tradition, to explain the error *already in the text*–simply because the apologist predetermined that the original manuscripts, which he has never seen, were free from error.

> *Within this context, this is not considered a "contradiction" or "error"–no ancient reader would have thought this!*

A different apologist once offered me this explanation for why gospel writers attributed Old Testament sayings to the wrong prophets.[110] Since other readers of the day thought the misattributions were factually correct, and since no ancient reader would have called the authors on their mistakes, no errors were apparently committed. I hope even the most novice of readers can appreciate the absurdity of such an argument. It does not matter what ancient readers reached as a consensus. What matters is whether the recorded facts are consistent with reality. If they are not, they are in error. I do not care whether ancient readers would have considered the cockcrowing stories contradictory; I care whether we can regard all four as consistent with reality. Explaining why no ancient reader would have thought of something as a contradiction is pretty much admitting the contradiction and explaining the reason for it. I ask again, what book could we not hold as infallible by employing such disingenuous methods? Inerrancy would lose all meaning.

Incidentally, it is not my intention to have you think that I am arguing that all of the apologetic positions are unattainable; I am arguing, given the weight of the evidence, that they are unlikely.[111] The apologists, on the other hand, will not grant the opposing viewpoint the slightest possibility of being correct because it is tantamount to admitting that the text *might* be errant–and this would still invalidate their predetermined, emotionally bound premises. I will close the topic here to let the readers decide which explanation is more likely, and which party is more objective.

These three examples are a small part of a larger set of biblical incongruities. God's holy word contains contradictions of every kind from cover to cover within accounts of important events, rules for worship, how to get into heaven, the nature of God, historical records of birth and rule, and the teachings of Jesus.[112] An impartial ear can even translate many of the common apologetic justifications for these problems as the Bible saying something it doesn't mean or meaning something it doesn't say. Honestly accepting the existence of such contradictions would destroy the ideal quality of the book that many set out to explain by any means necessary. Intellectually dishonest, inconsistent, biased, thoroughly conditioned apologists, on the other hand, feel that as long as they put out a nonsense scenario that tenuously satisfies the contradiction, it's up to everyone else to prove otherwise. This is a very implausible attempt at holding the Bible to be perfect. Since anyone can do that to any book, the practice is not logically permissible. If all else fails, remember, apologists often brush aside unexplainable objections as "the incomprehensible and mysterious ways of God." Smith describes this phenomenon rather well:

> While it is true that the Christian will never find a contradiction between the propositions of reason and his religious beliefs, this is true only because he will never permit such contradictions to exist. The apologist reduces all contradictions to apparent contradictions, which he claims are ultimately reconcilable…If there exists a conflict between reason and religious dogma, we are assured that this *apparent* conflict results from our insufficient understanding of divine truths. Whenever consistency, logic, or science became uncomfortable for the Christian, he can safely retreat into his incomprehensible God and argue that our problems are a consequence of man's puny understanding.[113]

The textual contradictions exist for a reason. First of all, as I have said many times before, there was no true divine inspiration from God guiding the authors to write their material. Each person wrote through his own limited interpretations and experiences because no one honestly expected the collection of books to grow in popularity to their current state. In addition, no one had any way of knowing which books were going to be enshrined in the Bible and which ones were destined to face omission. It would have been too daunting of a task for the authors to check every historical record for contradictions with their compositions. Instead, it is likely that most authors simply tried to keep a steady theme set by preceding authors. Reasonable, freethinking people accept this conclusion. Indoctrinated apologists who cannot appreciate the psychological forces driving their misguided beliefs continue to promote their unlikely resolutions.

It is my hope that one day, when a biblical apologist proposes some wild explanation for what is obviously a textual error, I will be able to reach his audience's intellect by simply pointing out that the apologist used the same methods of reasoning to conclude the veraciousness of a talking donkey and a literal resurrection. But as long as the human mind finds conflicting information uncomfortable, troublesome issues steeped in deep emotional investments will rarely be rectified by the use of such an otherwise obvious argument.

You must be careful of dishonest or irrelevant counterarguments used by Christian apologists. Although there is an enormous amount of Christian material claiming to debunk skeptical arguments, you have a duty to ask yourself some uncomfortable questions regarding these works. Can you better describe the apologetic arguments as wild scenarios rather than probable solutions? Do the arguments originate from a biased researcher with a deep emotional investment or an obvious agenda to prove something one way or another? Do the arguments resort to the use of fallacious logic to reach a desired conclusion?[114] Do the arguments take biblical passages out of context or use a premise that is contradicted by what the Bible plainly says? If you have answered *yes* to any of these questions after considering an apologetic explanation for anything that you have read, keep looking. I encourage you to read books on Christianity by both secular *and* religious authors. Think dispassionately about the issues, and you will no doubt discover which group acts as its own worst enemy by grasping at slippery straws to support its erroneous viewpoints. Don't fall into the trap described by Smith:

> Volumes are written on the subject of God, pro and con, but fresh material is rarely presented. The Christian presents the standard arguments for the existence of God, and the atheist presents the standard refutations of these arguments. The Christian responds with a flurry of counter-objections, and the atheist retaliates.
>
> Meanwhile, the average bystander becomes confused and impatient. He has observed arguments, but he has not been told why these arguments are important. He has witnessed disagreements, but he has not been presented with the basic conflicts underlying them. While this person may have absorbed a smattering of divergent theories and ideas, he lacks an overall perspective, a frame of reference from which to integrate and evaluate the particulars that have been thrust upon him. Consequently, he frequently dismisses the

> philosophical investigation of theism as too abstract, remote and irrelevant to merit his attention. He will leave philosophy to the philosophers; and, while they construct endless debates, he will rely on what he has been taught, or on what his friends believe–or on what his "common sense" and "intuitions" tell him.[115]

Even if you have heard an argument that you think solidly disproves something I have written, I hope you will choose to bring it to my attention. I would certainly like to be able to respond to any claims made against the ones in this book. I may be able to more clearly explain the problem or, perhaps, correct my own mistake. You see, no author is truly infallible.

Leaving Superstition Behind

The decision to denounce the Christian faith and leave the comfortable confines of the religion has a strong correlation with at least three factors of extreme importance: low levels of exposure, high levels of intelligence, and high levels of self-esteem. From my anecdotal observations, I noticed that individuals who left Christianity were less indoctrinated, more intelligent, or more confident about themselves than the average person. Once I made this discovery, I noticed that those who had all of the aforementioned qualities tended to question the Bible's veracity at an exceedingly early age, while those who had only one or two of those qualities took a while longer. I strongly feel that a general point exists where a certain level of intelligence, influence, and self-esteem reach the threshold necessary to allow someone the opportunity to become a freethinker.

Christians probably would not deny that a strong influence persuades a person to remain active in church. From what we have considered thus far on indoctrination, it's only logical to conclude that a lack of the same influence increases the chances a person will leave the faith. The intelligence and self-esteem elements to my hypothesis, on the other hand, are surely insulting and certainly difficult for Christians to swallow. For this reason, I will now begin providing a defense for my position.

Petty and Cacioppo point out that influential messages are much more likely to persuade individuals with a lack of self-esteem compared to those with normal or high self-esteem.[116] As misfortune would have it, one of the central tenants of Christianity targets such an audience. The very foundation of the religion is built upon the suggestion that we are insignificant creatures compared to the creator of the universe and that it is not possible to carry out a meaningful existence without accepting the biblical belief system. Jesus even points out that we are not worthy of following him if we place the love for our parents or children above our love for him.[117] However, once we accept the biblical teachings (and only after doing so), we become worthy of God's gift of eternal life. Such ideas are no doubt appealing to those with little or no self-confidence and self-worth, but they probably carry less weight with someone confident of his own abilities and intelligence. Smith has something pertinent to say on this topic:

> It is not accidental that Christianity regards pride as a major sin. A man of self-esteem is an unlikely candidate for the master-slave relationship that Christianity offers him. A man lacking in self-esteem, however, a man ridden with guilt and self-doubt, will frequently prefer the apparent security of Christianity over independence and find comfort in the thought that, for the price of total submissiveness, God will love and protect him.[118]

There is a vast wealth of experiments that effectively demonstrate the idea that intelligence and religious disbelief go hand in hand. The first meta-analysis of all such studies conducted since 1927 was published in 1986. It showed that nearly three-fourths of all investigations considering a correlation between intelligence and religious affiliation have found that the proportion of self-proclaimed atheists, agnostics, and deists increases dramatically as you move up the scale in school grades, exam scores, and IQ tests. The remaining one-fourth of the studies shows no correlation, while zero reviews suggested that people in organized religion are more intelligent than those with secular beliefs.[119] A more recent meta-analysis, published in 2002, reveals that the percentage of studies confirming this position has risen to over 90.[120] Another recent major poll[121] suggests that individuals who have graduate degrees, live in regions of the country where standardized test scores are higher, or belong to the male gender are less likely to believe in the Judeo-Christian God.[122]

It is important to note that when I speak of a study confirming a position, I am not talking about a "more than likely" conclusion, but rather that each study on its own typically has a confidence standard of 95 percent or greater. In other words, the likelihood of such results occurring by chance for each individual study was less than 5 percent in each individual instance. When meta-study analyses review the compounded results of multiple tests, the likelihood of obtaining these results by chance decreases exponentially. The apparent conclusion to draw from the data is that people who are more intelligent tend to disbelieve religions based upon books that include things like a talking donkey. Come to think of it, could we honestly name one single issue on which intelligent people are less likely to be correct than unintelligent people?

I recently came across the updated demographics and related statistics for the American MENSA[123] chapter while browsing the internet. I wasn't too surprised at what I found. Almost 20 percent positively identify belonging to the unreligious designations (atheist, agnostic, and Unitarian[124]) compared to just over 1 percent of the general American population. Roughly 49 percent consider themselves Christian, compared to 76 percent of the general American population.[125] In other words, those who belong to MENSA are several times more likely to have no affiliation with religious beliefs and almost 40 percent less likely to be a Christian. Likewise, 93 percent of members of the United States National Academy of Sciences, a group composed of the country's most prominent scientists as voted on by their peers, do not believe in a personal god.[126] Less prominent scientists disbelieve in a personal god at a rate of only 60 percent, but 60 percent is still much higher than the 5-10 percent for the American public at large.[127] The British equivalent of the NAS, Fellows of the Royal Society, only has a 3.3 percent rate of belief in a personal god.[128] In other words, members of the NAS are roughly ten times more likely to disbelieve in a personal God, and perhaps even thirty to fifty times more likely to positively identify with atheistic beliefs.

You will of course hear the religious apologists offering subsequent defenses for the benefit of their fellow religious followers. They will often assert that the figures from these organizations are not truly representative of the intelligent part of the population. Members of MENSA, they claim, typically fall within the less religious ages, but how does their overly optimistic math account for such an enormous difference? Members of the NAS and FRS, they claim, work in fields that ignore the supernatural and explain the universe strictly in natural terms, but how do the apologists not spot the irony in such an explanation?

Who would have ever thought that MENSA, comprised of people with IQs in the top 2 percent, would increasingly disassociate itself from a religion based on a dead man coming back to life? Who would have ever thought that the NAS and FRS, comprised of people who have the best understanding of the universe, would disbelieve fantastic stories of magical creation written thousands of years ago? In all seriousness, the most important thing we can take from these studies and observations is that the more intelligence a person has, the less likely he is to believe in the divinity of a book with a talking donkey. Dawkins adds:

> The efforts of apologists to find genuinely distinguished modern scientists who are religious have an air of desperation, generating the unmistakably hollow sound of bottoms of barrels being scraped. The only website I could find that claimed to list 'Nobel Prize-winning Scientific Christians' came up with six, out of a total of several hundred scientific Nobelists. Of these six, it turned out that four were not Nobel Prize-winners at all; and at least one, to my certain knowledge, is a non-believer who attends church for purely social reasons.[129]

While we should be confident that people with higher intelligence are less likely to believe in the Judeo-Christian God, this still does not explain *why*. One suggestion could be that it takes critical thinking to appreciate indoctrination and confirmation bias. Another could simply be that intelligent people are less gullible. Petty and Cacioppo, who may have the best answer, report that individuals with below average intelligence are especially susceptible to influential messages when such communications are readily comprehensible.[130]

To satisfy ourselves that the religious communications are indeed easy to understand, we must remember that the premise of Christianity is quite simple: God is the creator, obey his word, and follow his son. That's pretty much all most Christians know about their religion–and what person couldn't understand a premise as simple as that? However, the precise details of the movement, laid out over 800,000 words in the Bible, are quite involved and often ignored due to the tedious complexity of learning the complete message. Petty and Cacioppo correctly point out that such individuals would likely yield to the ideas of such a complex document, if only they were capable of comprehending the text in its entirety. Intelligent people, on the other hand, are less susceptible to influential messages and may be able to offset certain amounts of indoctrination during childhood by silently developing counterarguments for the religious assertions.

Even though people with higher intelligence tend not to accept religion, one cannot deny that many still do. If we are to extrapolate the demographics of MENSA into the American population, there are still three million people in the country with an IQ over 130 who consider themselves Christians. Granted that we have no way of knowing exactly how many of these people believe in the more absurd biblical accounts, such as the six-day creation, Noah's flood, and Jesus' resurrection, we should still feel confident that hundreds of thousands of people with vastly superior intelligence believe that these events actually took place.

The question is still *why*, and the best answer, in my opinion, comes from Shermer within the very argument that he became famous for coining: "Smart people believe weird things because they are skilled at defending beliefs they arrived at for non-smart reasons."[131] The phenomenon applies wonderfully to religion itself, which is exactly the institution I think that he had in mind. Believing in otherwise absurd stories simply because they are part of a religion bestowed upon you by your parents and other influences in your society obviously qualifies as believing in something for "non-smart reasons." The intellectual breakdown arrives from such gifted people inventing extremely clever (but equally absurd) reasons why they think their beliefs are correct.

Most of my former Christian friends and I once did the same thing. We invented absurd extrabiblical rationalizations for biblical problems. After all, we were beginning with the premise that the Bible is true and molded all considerations around that central idea. The ease with which smart people can interpret the facts is powerful. More than anything else, we wanted to avoid just admitting that we didn't believe it anymore. Intellectually, it would have been much easier and much more satisfactory, but the absurd suggestions that we conjured were our way of being able to say (not to mention convincing ourselves) that we believed–while at the same time not appearing foolish for accepting such ridiculous claims at face value. Even in the confines of solidarity, I could not be realistic about my beliefs for one key reason: *It is never easy to be honest with yourself about the Bible when a mind-reading god is always present.* Simply *thinking* that God did something wrong might be as discomforting to someone as *saying* that a potentially abusive authority figure did the same. As Smith succinctly put it, "We are told that God is monitoring us at every moment, and that he has complete knowledge of our innermost thoughts and feelings. If the notion of an omnipresent voyeurist does not create a high level of nervous tension and anxiety, not to mention guilt, nothing will."[132]

This point about God reading our minds is not by any means something we should take lightly. I have intended for it to be salient to skeptics and compassionate toward believers. This obstacle to reasoning, perhaps more than any other, prevents people from thinking rationally about religion. If Big Brother is listening, he knows you are having doubts about his authority and existence. Such ideas supposedly do not go unnoticed and perhaps unpunished. Guilt certainly follows. People who were never indoctrinated with a religious belief often fail to appreciate the consequences of this dilemma.

I'm afraid that I don't have much advice to give to those who are battling with intellectual self-honesty–other than to point out the inherit unfairness of a system in which an all-powerful being mistreats anyone who has the intellectual curiosity to arrive at his existence through reason rather than through faith. Perhaps you can tell God that you are going to set his existence aside for a moment and partake in a series of exercises that are designed to determine if the Bible is really his word. Ask for forgiveness in advance if you feel you must, but if the evidence for God is as strong as the religious experts would have you believe, should it not find you rather easily?

To be thorough, I should point out that there are also very unintelligent and illogical reasons why some people leave religion, such as God missing a deadline to respond to a request in a certain way. Unfortunately, I have had a few individuals write and tell me that this applies to them. Such people give God a deadline to meet, leave the religion once the deadline passes without the evidence, and will usually return when they receive an acceptable result–because the deadline is no longer a factor as to whether God exists since the positive evidence for some arbitrary individual goal has now manifested itself. Others may simply dislike their religious denominations. These self-professed former atheists experienced a very shallow form of secularism that mirrors the very shallow form of Christianity widely practiced today. In other words, they just decided to be atheistic without researching the veracity of the system in depth, which of course is not within rational grounds for a positive atheistic belief. They relied instead on individual preferences and anecdotal observations.

The individuals who return to religion after initially professing disbelief typically describe their former selves as being coldhearted and self-obsessed, but such personal traits are more about foolishness and moral depravity than they are about the absence of religion. Perhaps these people would like to share what valid reasons they had for abandoning freethought and embracing a particular religion, especially the religion that they just happened to begin with. What made them leave the religion? Did they do in-depth dispassionate analyses of the presented historical inaccuracies, contradictions, absurdities, and cruelties of the Bible; or did they have an emotional experience that caused them to abandon belief in God? More times than not, those who leave a religion and rejoin do not offer logical reasons for rejoining, which naturally leads us to believe that they probably did not leave for logical reasons either. People who undergo such transformations usually attribute them to "traumatic, life-changing experiences." Petty and Cacioppo offer five major studies to support the idea that rapid conversion often follows an emotionally traumatic event in a person's life.[133]

Since we can see that childhood indoctrination, threats of punishment, cultural isolation, biased argumentation, cognitive dissonance, low self-esteem, and low intelligence lead people to illogical conclusions about religion, the question should now become how to undo the effects of some of these phenomena. One of the primary findings of persuasive psychology is that, outside of the rare instances of instinctive and biochemical factors, people are tied to their opinions through emotional and/or logical deduction. In other words, people believe that certain concepts are true for emotional and/or logical reasons. Therefore, in order to instill a new belief into an individual, we must remove the existing belief by appealing to people through the exact avenues by which they have derived their beliefs.

Let us consider a hypothetical scenario in which we are entrepreneurs who have just opened a business on the top floor of an old city skyscraper. Everything is set to go, but there is one major problem with which we need to contend. The only business consultant in the entire city refuses to take the elevator to such a high elevation because he has deduced that something tragic could possibly take place at that height.

Since our first impulse is to conclude that the man has a fear of heights, let us first consider that this is in fact the correct scenario. We must now ask ourselves whether this man has a fear of heights for emotional reasons or for logical ones. Barring the presence of a series of tragic events that have taken place while the consultant was in similar structures, it is a reasonably safe assumption that the man has a fear based on emotion. This should be nothing new to us because we realize that phobias are typically emotional fears often attributed to isolated events that took place at an impressionable age.[134] Therefore, the next logical step here is to ascertain why the consultant is afraid of heights. If he cannot articulate a legitimate reason and relies instead on such explanations as "I just get scared when I look out," we know we have made a safe assumption that the man holds his belief for an emotional reason.

How do we eliminate this fear? Should we bring in the experts who built the structure to ensure him that it won't fall? Should we show him the evidence that demonstrates the skyscraper was constructed according to proper building codes? Should we show him the statistics of how unlikely it would be for a tragic event to take place at that height? None of these measures would likely work because the logic falls on ears that are deaf to reason. The man has an emotional fear of heights, thus we cannot appeal to his senses through pleas of logic. As he is perfectly aware that millions of people go into tall buildings every day and return to the ground unharmed, what good would it do to tell him what he already knows? Instead, we must appeal to his emotion. One such recommendation would be to have the man ascend the building slowly, allow him to look outside on each floor, and let him adjust to his surroundings each time until he feels comfortable progressing up the skyscraper. Such methods are how psychologists often remove unreasonable fears in their patients.[135]

Let us now consider a situation in which the man thinks that the building will fall because he believes that old skyscrapers are not as safe as the newer ones. Instead of having an emotional fear, our business consultant has formed what he believes is a logical reason to avoid ascending the building. Do we use the same measure as we did in the previous scenario? Will having him slowly ascend and allowing him to adjust to his surroundings alleviate his fear? No. Why would such a tactic fail to work? The man has a *logical* fear, thus we cannot appeal to his senses through pleas of emotion. We must show him the evidence that the building was constructed according to code. We must bring in the experts who built the structure to ensure him that it will not fall. Such methods are how we appeal to logical intellect in order to remove unreasonable fears from reasonable people.

Religious beliefs, like the beliefs of the consultant, must also be held for emotional and/or logical reasons.[136] With this in mind, how should someone free of indoctrination approach the practice of convincing others of their false beliefs? As before, we must delve into the history of the individual's beliefs to find the avenue from which they originate. I would be confident that if we undertook this exercise in a large group of people, almost the entire sample would have built their beliefs upon *emotional* reasons. Remember four conclusions we reached earlier: 1) Children are introduced to the emotional components of Christianity before the logical ones. 2) Notions of God being perfect, Jesus loving us, and heaven being for the saved are consistently instilled in children long before they are approached with evidence and arguments that weigh the genuine or fraudulent nature of such claims. 3) Smart people believe dumb things because they are very gifted at coming up with ideas that support their irrational viewpoints. 4) Apologists are masterminds at creating quasi-logical reasons for the defense of their emotional beliefs.

If our tentative conclusion is accurate that religious beliefs are primarily built on emotional grounds, we now know the avenue that one should take to change the incorrect beliefs held by Christians. This discovery, of course, does not destroy the layers of conditioning that one will have to fight through, nor does it remove the individual's propensity to invent absurd justifications to eliminate cognitive dissonance. It does however demonstrate the near-certain futility in trying to convince someone that the gospels are unreliable by pointing out factual discrepancies like the year of Jesus' birth. People with emotional ties will emotionally cling to the gospels' veracity in this instance while the apologists' absurd "Quirinius was a governor twice" or "Quirinius was a co-governor" explanations alleviate their cognitive dissonance.[137]

Life, however, is rarely as black and white as we can make it in hypothetical scenarios. Often we find emotional and logical reasons for religious belief closely intertwined. The apologists who purport that they have all the answers have in reality weaved a tangled web of what they believe are logical defenses for the foundational beliefs and emotional attachments acquired from the most persuasible stage of human development. While simply clearing the emotional attachments before destroying the perceived logic may work for ordinary individuals, this tactic will surely not work on those who have come up with clever ways to convince themselves that their beliefs are solid. With a network of logical and emotional bonds to wade through in order to reach the apologist, how does one even begin? For the answer, I believe we should revisit the business consultant scenario offered earlier.

Let us now consider a hypothetical situation in which the consultant has a combination of emotional and logical reasons for not wanting to visit us at the top of the skyscraper. Not only has he developed an emotional fear of heights beginning at a young age, he has also convinced himself of the legitimacy of his fear by reinforcing his decision with a network of misinformation built upon logical inaccuracies. Now the man has created a wall of what he perceives are legitimate reasons as to why his emotional fear is a sensible one. How do we handle this situation?

Since we wish to invoke clear thinking in order to get people to drop their misplaced beliefs, we must decide whether emotion or logic is the biggest initial obstacle of instilling rational thought. This choice should be obvious since emotion is often irrational, and logic is closely related to rationale itself. In short, we cannot begin appealing to logic when emotion is in the way. We must defuse as much irrationality as possible before we can begin to utilize reasoned arguments in support of our position. We cannot simply usher the man to the top of the building by allowing him to adjust to his surroundings because there will come a time when the logical fears of being higher than floor three will be outweighed by the emotional fears of being higher than floor ten. The amount of success in this initial step of tackling emotion will vary from person to person, but through much time and effort, we might be able to force the man to make enough concessions on his emotional beliefs to eliminate enough emotional irrationalism so that we can illustrate how his logical fears of floors four through nine are misplaced. If this much easier step of tackling logic proves fruitful, then we simply lather, rinse, and repeat.

Admittedly, this is much easier said than done when it comes to matters of high personal importance, such as politics, patriotism, and religion. When some of the constructs of emotional beliefs include "God is perfect," we find that locating a sword sharp enough to put chinks in perfect armor can be difficult. Not all is lost, however, because we know that it is possible to intellectually reach people who believe that God is perfect; communities of former believers would otherwise not exist. Consider what the Chinese disingenuously accomplished against American prisoners in a POW camp during the Korean War:

> Prisoners were frequently asked to make statements so mildly anti-American or pro-Communist as to seem inconsequential...But once these minor requests were complied with, the men found themselves pushed to submit to related yet more substantive requests. A man who had just agreed with his Chinese interrogator that the United States is not perfect might then be asked to indicate some of the ways in which he thought this was the case...Suddenly he would find himself a

> "collaborator," having given aid to the enemy. Aware that he had written the essay without any strong threats or coercion, many times a man would change his image of himself to be consistent with the deed and with the new "collaborator" label, often resulting in even more extensive acts of collaboration.[138]

Petty and Cacioppo offer what I believe to be an obvious and more reasonable course of action for adjusting an individual's religious beliefs:

> The theory of reasoned action makes it clear that any influence attempt–whether the goal is to change an attitude, norm, intention, or behavior–must always be directed at one or more of the individual's beliefs. The beliefs that serve as the fundamental determinants of the variable that one is trying to change are called *primary beliefs*. The beliefs that the influence attempt is designed to change are called *target beliefs*. For example, a persuasive message will be successful in changing someone's attitude about smoking to the extent that the target beliefs the communication is designed to change correspond to the primary beliefs that serve as the foundation of the person's attitude toward smoking.[139]

In other words, we attack the notion that God inspired the Bible by attacking the reasons people *believe* that God inspired the Bible. Where one should ideally begin this task is debatable when the targets are unwilling to offer a reasoned answer, but I strongly feel that attributing human authorship to the Bible is the proper avenue to take. This course of action does not invalidate the premise that God is perfect because it makes room for such possibilities as God allowing humans to write their own history and God not concerning himself with perfection of every detail. These ideas seem harmless enough on the surface, but they begin to provoke questions with bigger impact potential, such as why God would choose such avenues when they lead to increased doubt and logical ambiguity.

The Handicapping Of Skepticism

To this point, we have explored a few of the reasons why skeptics are at a nearly insurmountable disadvantage when trying to educate a religious audience on the hard reality of their belief acquisition. The overwhelming majority of religious followers were indoctrinated during childhood by certain aspects of their environment to accept those beliefs. Parents who unknowingly condition their children to shun logic and reason when confronted with testable and observable Bible-debunking evidence perpetuate the domination of Christian beliefs. Contributors to our environment deceitfully teach us that certain things are unquestionably true, and such nonsensical ideas begin at an age at which we have yet to behave or think in a rational manner. The same ideas are also continuously reinforced in an isolated Christian environment until they accumulate to a degree at which conditioning trumps rational inquiry, bias influences judgment, cognitive dissonance leads to absurd rationalizations, intelligence becomes increasingly unimportant, and religious beliefs render common sense impotent. When confronted with evidence against conditioned thoughts, the logical and emotional components of which can be hard to discern and address directly, people will seek out only evidence that supports their beliefs. Uneasy feelings from cognitive dissonance weaken the faculties for critical thought and will allow the believers to accept highly irrational reasons for their beliefs. Quite simply, people hold beliefs that are fundamental to them even thought there is no conclusive evidence for those beliefs.

As if all of these obstacles were not enough to discourage a freethinker from assisting others, the practice of persuading an audience through critical analysis is further handicapped from the beginning by the very nature of skepticism. There are a number of reasons why this is so.

The practice of skepticism entails the exploration of any possible argument that would debunk preconceived notion. While some of the arguments are often strongly supportive of a skeptical position, many are only moderately convincing yet still valid. In contrast, the shallow counter-solution that "God works in mysterious and incomprehensible ways" is widely applicable and hardly attackable. The inclusion of the moderate arguments against Christianity weakens the perceived credibility of the person presenting them. Petty and Cacioppo explain that "providing a person with a few very convincing arguments may promote more attitude change than providing these arguments along with a number of much weaker arguments."[140] In effect, people are prone to believe that if they can argue against a moderate message, they would probably be able to spot the fallacies of the other messages if they considered them long enough. This can be an unfortunate aspect of human psychology because the addition of lesser arguments onto a pile of already strong arguments should only add credibility to the position and not affect the veracity of the stronger arguments.

People are motivated to defend their beliefs from attacks, particularly when they are forewarned of a speaker's intent, and even more so when the belief is closely linked with identity.[141] Not only are religious beliefs effectively synonymous with identity for a number of people, religious followers have been inoculated from skeptical arguments because they have been forewarned and exposed to weak or patently ridiculous arguments that are allegedly offered by disbelievers. This "poisoning of the well" modifies individuals to be more resistant to attitude changes toward the position that they already believe to be fundamentally weak. Examples might include the supposed atheism of harsh dictatorships, lack of morality in an atheistic worldview, absence of atheists in foxholes, atheism requiring enormous amounts of faith, atheists being unhappy, atheism being a childish form of rebellion, atheists being mad at God, etc. You can even find such ridiculous assertions within the Bible.[142] If it were not for these inoculations, Christianity might otherwise be vulnerable to adjustment due to its cultural nature as a truism: a belief that is widely accepted, rarely defended, and consequently malleable.

The targeted audience for the skeptic is often very large, and people tend to be decreasingly persuaded by messages as the size of the potential audience grows.[143] Petty and Cacioppo report that subjects are often motivated by strong arguments and discouraged by weaker arguments if the subjects are under the impression that the communications were intended to be heard only by a small number of people. In contrast, when subjects believe that a larger number of people are hearing the exact same arguments, the perceived difference in quality between the strong and weak arguments shrinks dramatically. In such a situation, listeners perceive weaker arguments as stronger, perhaps because the subjects feel that the arguments must contain merit since they are going to be heard by a wide audience; and stronger arguments are perceived as being weaker, perhaps due to the perceived decrease in personal importance. The difference would normally be a wash, but in mainstream culture, where arguments against Christianity are far superior to arguments in its favor (as anyone will attest as long as you replace the word "Christianity" with someone else's religion), skepticism is at a disadvantage because there is less perceived difference in the strength of weak arguments for Christianity and strong arguments against it.

There is no pressure from society to understand or defend against the position of skeptics. Petty and Cacioppo report that subjects are often motivated to understand an issue when they are led to believe that, as a part of the study, they would have to discuss the issue with someone who took a contrasting position.[144] Without this pressure, subjects are less likely to consider the position of the opponent. Since people do not have true interest in evaluating their innermost beliefs, those who have been conditioned to believe in a book with a talking donkey will never actively seek someone to challenge this position.

Society has painted a nasty picture of atheism and skepticism in general. Even though I left Christianity several years ago, the words still carry a sort of negative connotation with me–in the same sense that the meaningless word *alaria* sounds soothing while *peklurg* sounds irritating. It is of little question that people who do not believe in God are the least trusted minority in America.[145] Petty and Cacioppo report that the likeability of the message's source plays a major role in the message's capability of persuasion.[146] The disparity in the amount of attitude change resultant from identical messages provided by a likable source and an unlikable source is comparable to the disparity in the amount of change resultant from identical messages provided by an expert source and nonexpert source. In other words, you can obtain the same amount of perceived credibility by being likable as you can by becoming an expert. This is an enormous blow to objectivity, but I suppose we have to write it off as human nature and find some way to work around it.

Human beings are unbelievably gullible and illogical creatures. The ability to think skeptically is not innate; it requires practice. One-half of America believes that a person can use extrasensory perception to read another person's mind.[147] Nearly the same amount believes we can communicate with the dead.[148] Otherwise sane individuals have been known to send death threats to meteorologists, not for inaccurate predictions, but for the actual weather conditions.[149] Among other feats of incredible sheepishness, Cialdini reports that people are more likely to buy unusual items when priced higher, more likely to buy items with coupons despite no price advantage, more likely to respond to requests when empty reasons are given, more likely to agree to absurd requests if preceded by ones of greater absurdity, more likely to consider people intelligent and persuasive if they are attractive, and less likely to take an enemy prisoner during warfare if the potential captive offers them bread.[150] If people are so prone to follow foolish patterns under such poor assumptions in order to help guide them through this complex world, should we be at all surprised when people hypothesize the existence of a personal god in order to explain intelligent life, distant galaxies, childbirth, universal physical constants, starving children, crimes against humanity, natural disasters, and suicide bombers?

Human beings have an innate tendency to search for patterns and simple explanations in order to make sense of the world. Such a practice results in an incorporation of elements that fit into an understandable answer and a neglect of elements that do not. Psychologists often use this phenomenon to explain the reason people believe in clairvoyance, horoscopes, prayer, and other such foolishness. In a sense, we remember when these methods "work" and forget when they do not. With respect to religion, people will often remember "answered" prayers but forget or rationalize the unanswered ones. Have you ever noticed how people will trumpet abundances of miracles when there are a few survivors of an accident or natural disaster yet say nothing about the many people who died? It's the same principle. Dawkins alludes to this:

> [Pope John Paul II's] polytheistic hankerings were dramatically demonstrated in 1981 when he suffered an assassination attempt in Rome, and attributed his survival to intervention by Our Lady of Fatima: "A maternal hand guided the bullet." One cannot help wondering why she didn't guide it to miss him altogether. Others might think the team of surgeons who operated on him for six hours deserved at least a share of the credit; but perhaps their hands, too, were maternally guided.[151]

It is very easy to claim that prayer healed a person dying of a terrible disease, but quite another to prove it. Study after study demonstrates that prayer has no effect on patients when they are unaware that they are being prayed for.[152] On the other hand, when subjects *do* realize that they are being prayed for, two results tend to reoccur:

1) Patients typically improve from holistic methods, such as laying on of hands, meditation, compassionate care, etc. This is nothing new. Medical researchers have well established that the mind can work wonders and inexplicably heal the body. The problem with crediting God for the healing, other than the fact that it only works in concert with the patient's knowledge of being prayed for, is that the results appear across the religious/irreligious spectrum.

2) Patients sometimes take a turn for the worst due to what some believe is a form of performance anxiety. They may stress over the need to get better in order to not let the people who are praying for them

down. Perhaps they might also start dwelling on the severity of their conditions because the physicians are using drastic, unorthodoxed measures like prayer to assist them.[153] People use prayer as their way of appealing to God and use God's will as an explanation for why certain things happen. Since we can easily discredit the idea of prayer serving as a simple pattern for the complex natural events of the world, its usefulness should be self-evidently ridiculous.

Suppose we *really* wanted to test the power of prayer and see to it that no confounding variables from the temporal realm would be present. To begin the study, we gather a group of fifty atheists and a group of fifty Christians who volunteer to have an extremely lethal dose of bacteria injected intravenously. Following the injection, we provide the fifty atheists with a regimen of broad-spectrum antibiotics to counteract the infection. We then isolate the atheists in a secret location and tell no one that they are involved in the experiment. Essentially, they do not exist to the rest of the world. Likewise, we isolate the Christians in a secret location but refuse them the antibiotic regimen. News of the fifty Christians injected with the lethal bacteria will then be broadcast over the entire Christian world. The report will ask everyone to pray to God for their facilitated recovery from the infection so that deductive reasoning will force the world to acknowledge the one true religion because of the unquestionable and verifiable power of God and prayer. Because no one knows about the atheists in isolation, no one is specifically praying for them. All they have are antibiotics, while the Christians have the power of prayer from hundreds of millions of certain volunteers and the omnipotence of God. After two months, we will end the experiment and see which group has the most survivors.

Whether or not Christians are willing to admit it, I think everyone knows which group would fare better in this study. No semi-rational Christian would *ever* sign up for this deadly experiment even with the added promise of a great monetary compensation for the survivors. They know that God isn't *really* going to answer the divinely directed requests of hundreds of millions of Christians because God only seems to answer prayers in some mystical and unobservable fashion. Deep down, these Christians may even realize that they cannot consider prayer dependable. Some Christians reading the results of this hypothetical experiment would simply appeal to authorities who assert that there have been studies demonstrating just the opposite. Other Christians would manufacture reasons such as "God doesn't like being tested"[154] or "People didn't have enough faith."[155] They will avoid the rational conclusion that prayers are only "answered" by placebo effect. They will avoid admitting that tragic events or unbelievable coincidences are the result of complex natural factors. They will avoid admitting that prayers have answers just as often as problems have solutions.[156]

Messages favoring the veracity of Christianity and religion in general typically arrive through more persuasible channels than those that support a nonreligious viewpoint. Petty and Cacioppo report that psychologists have repeatedly found face-to-face appeals to have a greater impact than appeals through mass media.[157] Let us suppose that an ordinary Christian has begun having doubts about the existence of God. What course of action does he take? I have previously noted that, due to confirmation bias, religious doubters will first seek out testimonies and other pieces of evidence that would support the school of thought to which they already belong. These would include discussions with the preacher, family, friends, and possibly members of a church group. If, in the rare interest of intellectual honesty, the doubter wants to hear arguments from those with contrasting beliefs, where does he turn? To an atheist lecturer? To his atheist family members? To his atheist friends? To an atheist church group? Chances are that he has none to which he can turn. Instead, he will likely rely on the mass media, more specifically, a paperback written by Richard Dawkins, Sam Harris, or perhaps even this admittedly inferior piece of work. In doing so, the freethought literature must be superior enough to overcome not only indoctrination, dissonance, and the Christian message itself, but also the difference from the perceived level of superiority attributed to face-to-face communication.

It has been said that people are persuaded more by the actions of others than by any proof we can offer.[158] Although it's not exactly a traditional face-to-face appeal, Cialdini reports the findings of a study in which socially withdrawn children were individually shown a twenty-three minute film of other socially withdrawn children deciding to join social activities, much to the enjoyment of the other children in the video.

> The impact was impressive. The isolates immediately began to interact with their peers at a level equal to that of the normal children in the schools. Even more astonishing was what [researcher] O'Connor found when he returned to observe six weeks later. While the withdrawn children who had not seen O'Connor's film remained as isolated as ever, those who *had* viewed it were now leading their schools in amount of social activity. It seems that this twenty-three-minute movie, viewed just once, was enough to reverse a potential pattern of lifelong maladaptive behavior. Such is the potency of the principle of social proof. [159]

Cialdini offers an additional example of how people are prone to follow others marching, almost literally, off a cliff:

> The People's Temple was a cultlike organization that began in San Francisco and drew its recruits from the poor of that city. In 1977, the Reverend Jim Jones–who was the group's undisputed political, social, and spiritual leader–moved the bulk of the membership with him to a jungle settlement in Guyana, South America. There, the People's Temple existed in relative obscurity until November 18, 1978, when four men of a fact-finding party lead by Congressman Leo J. Ryan were murdered as they tried to leave Jonestown by plane. Convinced that he would be arrested and implicated in the killings and that the demise of the People's Temple would result, Jones sought to control the end of the Temple in his own way. He gathered the entire community around him and issued a call for each person's death in a unified act of self-destruction.

> The first response was that of a young woman who calmly approached the now famous vat of strawberry-flavored poison, administered one dose to her baby, one to herself, and then sat down in a field, where she and her child died in convulsions within four minutes. Others followed steadily in turn. Although a handful of Jonestowners escaped rather than comply and a few others are reported to have resisted, the survivors claim that the great majority of the 910 people who died did so in an orderly, willful fashion.[160]

There are two additional difficulties in getting equal attention from the doubting Christian if the doubter seeks Christian reassurance from group discussion. Petty and Cacioppo explain the handicapping that arises from both.

Numerous investigations have shown that the arguments generated by people in a group are learned by and can change the attitudes of the other people in the group. Because people are often persuaded by the arguments that others in a group discussion generate, an interesting phenomenon may occur as a result of a face-to-face discussion–*group polarization*. That is, people's attitudes after group discussion are often more extreme than the attitudes held prior to discussion. The group polarization effect is most likely to occur when most group members are on the same side of the issue, and group members have *different* reasons for favoring that side of the issue. Thus, during discussion most group members will hear arguments on their own side of the issue that they had not considered previously.[161]

The undeniable reality that a group of Christian apologists will have different (often contradictory) interpretations of biblical texts, ideas, and philosophies, yet they all arrive at the same conclusion (that the Bible is the word of God), is often quite convincing due to the phenomenon of group polarization.[162] Mainstream religious skepticism, typically differing only in relatively quibbling details and possible methods of conveying rational thinking to the believers, has no such foundational polarity. Rational people accept the facts, follow where they lead, and roughly end up around the same place. When a religious social group support is available, an individual hears all the varying reasons to believe in God and tends to become a more ardent follower than ever when no one in the group is convinced by the evidence that is driving his doubts. The individual is then prone to settle on an explanation that he deems to be a reasonable solution to his original dissonance.[163]

The second difficulty in having a doubting Christian turn to a group is that it is a "well-known finding in social psychology that when people are confronted with the opinions of others who disagree with them, there is considerable pressure to go along with the group."[164] Billy Graham, for one, has been known to arrange an army of revival volunteers with instructions on when to create the impression of a spontaneous mass outpouring.[165] Furthermore, social proof is such a strong psychological force, it has been found that not only are people much more likely to commit murder or suicide following similar stories broadcast in the media, the individuals who do so share traits with the original subject to a much higher degree than you would anticipate by chance.[166] This phenomenon, termed *The Werther Effect*, is even strong enough to evoke racially motivated violence following heavyweight championship fights. Whether black or white, members who are the same race as the victor of the fight tend to commit more homicides against people who are the same race as the loser of the fight.

This group pressure, however, goes well beyond the level of importance placed on the actions and judgments of one's peers. Individuals whose opinions are facing group opposition "are motivated to think of the arguments that might have led these other people to hold their discrepant views."[167] Knowing that others have chosen differently stimulates individuals in the minority to generate explanations for the divergence of opinions. So not only do people feel the need to conform in such a situation, they are also actively convincing themselves that their new opinions are probably wrong.

The realization that rational skepticism is not as interesting, promising, or comforting as optimistic romanticism is perhaps more formidable than any other obstacle. It's only human to believe in things that make us happier. If you have admired a book since childhood because it says that your lost loved ones are waiting for you in heaven when you die, it's going to take an extraordinary amount of work to convince you that the talking donkey also found in the book might mean that the book is not proper evidence for such an optimistic idea. Consider this final story told by Cialdini, which is one of the best examples of religious foolishness I have ever heard. It is worth including in its entirety because it contains a great deal of the psychological processes that we have assessed.

> One night at an introductory lecture given by the transcendental meditation (TM) program, I witnessed a nice illustration of how people will hide inside the walls of consistency to protect themselves from the troublesome consequences of thought. The lecture itself was presided over by two earnest young men and was designed to recruit new members into the program. The program claimed it could teach a unique brand of meditation that would allow us to achieve all manner of desirable things, ranging from simple inner peace to the more spectacular abilities to fly and pass through walls at the program's advanced (and more expensive) stages.
>
> I had decided to attend the meeting to observe the kind of compliance tactics used in recruitment lectures of this sort and had brought along an interested friend, a university professor whose areas of specialization were statistics and symbolic logic. As the meeting progressed and the lecturers explained the theory behind TM, I noticed my logician friend becoming increasingly restless. Looking more and more pained and shifting about constantly in his seat, he was finally unable to resist. When the leaders called for questions at the completion of the lecture, he raised his hand and gently but surely demolished the presentation we had just

heard. In less than two minutes, he pointed out precisely where and why the lecturers' complex argument was contradictory, illogical, and unsupportable. The effect on the discussion leaders was devastating. After a confused silence, each attempted a weak reply only to halt midway to confer with his partner and finally to admit that my colleague's points were good ones "requiring further study."

More interesting to me, though, was the effect upon the rest of the audience. At the end of the question period, the two recruiters were faced with a crush of audience members submitting their seventy-five dollar down payments for admission to the TM program. Nudging, shrugging, and chuckling to one another as they took in the payments, the recruiters betrayed sings of giddy bewilderment. After what appeared to have been an embarrassingly clear collapse of their presentation, the meeting had somehow turned into a great success, generating mystifyingly high levels of compliance from the audience. Although more than a bit puzzled, I chalked up the audience response to a failure to understand the logic of my colleague's arguments. As it turned out, however, just the *reverse* was the case.

Outside the lecture room after the meeting, we were approached by three members of the audience, each of whom had given a down payment immediately after the lecture. They wanted to know why we had come to the session. We explained, and we asked the same question of them. One was an aspiring actor who wanted desperately to succeed at his craft and had come to the meeting to learn if TM would allow him to achieve the necessary self-control to master the art; the recruiters had assured him that it would. The second described herself as a severe insomniac who had hopes that TM would provide her with a way to relax and fall asleep easily at night. The third served as unofficial spokesman. He also had a sleep-related problem. He was failing college because there didn't seem to be enough time to study. He had come to the meeting to find out if TM could help by training him to need fewer hours of sleep each night; the additional time could then be used for study. It is interesting to note that the recruiters informed him as well as the insomniac that Transcendental Meditation techniques could solve their respective, though opposite, problems.

Still thinking that the three must have signed up because they hadn't understood the points made by my logician friend, I began to question them about aspects of his argument. To my surprise, I found that they had understood his comments quite well; in fact, all too well. It was precisely the cogency of his argument that drove them to sign up for the program on the spot. The spokesman put it best: "Well, I wasn't going to put down any money tonight because I'm really quite broke right now; I was going to wait until the next meeting. But when you're buddy started talking, I knew I'd better give them my money now, or I'd go home and start thinking about what he said and *never* sign up."

All at once, things began to make sense. These were people with real problems; and they were somewhat desperately searching for a way to solve those problems. They were seekers who, if our discussion leaders were to be believed, had found a potential solution in TM. Driven by their needs, they very much wanted to believe that TM was their answer.

Now, in the form of my colleague, intrudes the voice of reason, showing the theory underlying their newfound solution to be unsound. Panic! Something must be done at once before logic takes its toll and leaves them without hope again. Quickly, quickly, walls against reason are needed; and it doesn't matter that the fortress to be erected is a foolish one. "Quick, a hiding place from thought! Here, take this money. Whew, safe in the nick of time. No need to think about the issues any longer. The decision has been made and from now on the consistency tape whenever necessary: 'TM? Certainly I think it will help me; certainly I expect to continue; certainly I believe in TM. I already put my money down for it, didn't I?' Ah, the comforts of mindless consistency. I'll just rest right here for a while. It's so much nicer than the worry and strain of that hard, hard search."[168]

THE CONFLICT BETWEEN CHRISTIANITY AND SCIENCE

While an understanding of human psychology demonstrates that the focus of an individual's religious dedication is heavily reliant upon mere chance, the presence of observable and falsifiable scientific evidence is perhaps the most compelling reason for concluding that Christianity itself fails to contrast with hundreds of other false religions. Because scientific findings clearly yield many conclusions that are contradictory with direct statements from biblical authors, we can safely say that the Bible is an imperfect book containing flaws of human origin. Due to the overwhelming amount of scientific errors the book possesses, you should have great comfort in deciding that there was no divine inspiration or intervention during its creation. Furthermore, the vast categories of errors contained in the Bible demonstrate that the mistakes are not confined to a single author or field of study, a realization that should devastate the foundation and intent of the book as a whole. We need look no further than Genesis to find an extraordinary number of bogus claims: the universe was created in six days only six thousand years ago; an ocean remains aloft in the sky; plants and light existed prior to the sun, moon, and stars; DNA can be altered by placing peeled branches in front of mating livestock; populations of centuries-old humans can inexplicably mushroom within a matter of years; the entire world was killed in a flood; and heaven was in danger of being breeched by a manmade tower. For the Christian readers wise enough to disregard Genesis as ancient mythology, let's not forget that the New

Testament claims that seizures and blindness were caused by demons and that stars were small enough to fall to the earth.[169]

In my first book, I made another questionable decision of offering a summary treatise in defense of all the scientific disciplines that support the finding that the earth is billions of years old. This is perhaps a less than ideal way to go about the matter. I could have simply offered the basic foundations of a number of scientific disciplines that support a young earth, referenced supporting studies, and briefly stated the conclusions of those findings. All of that could have been done in a fraction of the time that I spent elaborating on the sciences, but I was falsely under the impression that people were more likely to accept a principle if you took the time to explain it to them. I was wrong. People will either accept facts, or they will not.

Instead, I will now simply say that several fields of scientific study are founded on the principle that the earth is billions of years old and that no evidence has ever brought any of these foundations into question. According to experts in the scientific community, the age of the earth is in no more question than the basic shape of it. The percentage of today's scientists who believe that the earth is only a few thousand years old is less than 1, a distribution yielded almost certainly because the dwarfed minority holds their position out of dogmatic desperation. I often wonder if *any* questioned premise in *any* scientific discipline is in less dispute than the age of the earth.

These self-proclaimed scientists in the minority are determined to make all evidence fit with a young earth while ignoring the completely overwhelming juggernaut of counterevidence working against their predetermined conclusions. Such research methods are very unscientific and blatantly dishonest because a true scientist does *not* start out to prove something one way or another. Such researchers should always remain impartial and undecided before considering *all* of the available evidence to make a rational and logical decision that is *independent* of their hopes and beliefs. Instead, they surround themselves with so-called scientific evidence and call evolution a religion because they understand that science is the driving force in our education system.[170] Confirmation bias has no place in progressive scientific discovery.

Before I begin answering the specific Christian responses to critical interpretations of the Bible's reliability on scientific matters, the complete incompatibility between mainstream science and literal biblical fundamentalism makes it necessary to divide Christian views into three distinct categories based on their approach toward science. Since this incompatibility is indisputable and Christians do not even attempt to deny it, they must avoid cognitive dissonance by altering their view of science, the Bible, or both. While it is certainly possible for Christians to hold positions that are not necessarily entirely within a single distinction, they incorporate their opinions on the matter of science and the Bible from one or more of them.

The core beliefs of each category are as follows: 1) Science, when properly applied, is a valid discipline that validates a literal reading of the Bible. We often refer to individuals in this group as Young Earth Creationists. 2) Science is a valid discipline that invalidates a literal reading of the Bible, which is instead often figurative, allegorical, or metaphorical in nature. This position, often termed Old Earth Creationism, does not dispute mainstream scientific findings and consequently takes the most time to dissect. Whereas Young Earth Creationists twist scientific evidence to fit with the Bible, Old Earth Creationists twist the Bible to fit with scientific evidence. 3) Science is not a valid discipline and consequently cannot be applied to interpretations of the Bible. This position is so absurd that I would hesitate to address it if so many readers had not already tried to advance it. I'll begin with arguments from category one.

True science helps to validate the Bible.

I have received a number of similar statements from high school students who are reporting that they are convinced that there are major problems with biological evolution, based on the things they have heard or read outside of the science classroom. Sadly, I believe that this phenomenon is indicative of the low critical thinking ability found in the general high school population. Sagan put the problem best, "If we teach only the findings and products of science–no matter how useful and even inspiring they may be–without communicating its critical method, how can the average person possibly distinguish science from pseudoscience?"[171]

I do not wish to pick on high school students in particular, but this is the point in the educational experience where people tend to have already drawn their conclusions on many key issues in life. This is why it is of the utmost importance to teach students critical thinking, a discipline rarely touched upon when I was in school. I can only hope that these individuals are curious enough in college to discuss the creation/evolution "debate" with reputable biology professors and to discuss religious beliefs with social psychologists who specialize in persuasion and the formation of beliefs.

Some of the more conservative state governments are even considering bills that allow high schools to teach the Bible as an elective. Now this may come as a shock to some, but I think that teaching the Bible in school can actually turn out to be a positive thing for society. Comparative religion would be even better. As Dawkins requested, "Let children learn about different faiths, let them notice their incompatibility, and let them draw their own conclusions about the consequences of that incompatibility."[172] My optimism for this plan is only in principle, however, because I highly doubt that any teacher will keep his job if he remains objective. I have always said that if more people read the Bible, less people would believe it. If the teacher simply got up there and addressed the scientific mistakes, historical inaccuracies, and moral bankruptcy among the writers, along with the apologetic solutions for these difficulties, some students might actually begin to think critically about what everyone hastily accepts as unquestionably authentic. In reality, teachers would probably forget to leave their biases at home, and the vast majority of teenage students are probably already lost to the ideas of their childhood indoctrination.

The suggestion that the Bible is lacking a realistic scientific foundation is nothing less than a colossal understatement. The Bible has failed fair, impartial, and universally applicable tests in multiple fields of science. If God truly is the inspiration behind this purportedly divine declaration to the world, he shows absolutely no interest in its understandability or accuracy in astronomy, cosmology, zoology, botany, anthropology, geology, ecology, geography, or physiology.[173]

In fact, the Bible handicaps those who use their "God-given" talents of reason and logic to settle blatant biblical problems. Nothing can be more detrimental to the authenticity of a biblical claim than contradictory phenomena that we readily observe and experience. With no other evidence to consider, these clues from natural manifestations should *always* override what we might hope to be correct explanations for unignorable discrepancies. Such is the power of science and reason. They are the impartial pursuit of answers to questions, not the biased search for supplemental evidence to predetermined answers.

The presence of erroneous biblical claims throughout Genesis is one of the most popular reasons why many Christians continue to turn their backs on a literal interpretation of the creation tale. If we were to allow other religions the same amount of leniency, could we ever possibly determine which one is making the legitimate claims? Due to the overwhelming amount of observable, testable, and falsifiable evidence, we can comfortably denounce the proclaimed authenticity of the Bible solely on its erroneous, pseudoscientific claims. Those who accept these findings yet still believe that the Bible is of divine origin are either unaware of what the Bible says or were driven by cognitive dissonance and confirmation bias to seek out absurd ways of bringing science and the Bible into congruency.

> *Scientists date the earth layers based on the fossils in that layer, which are in turn dated by the layer in which they were found. The earth's antiquity is therefore based on circular reasoning.*

Some people genuinely think that our best and brightest are truly dumb enough to use such fallacious logic. I realize that dismantling Young Earth Creationist arguments is like taking candy from a baby, but since I encounter this assertion at least once a month, I'm going to address it anyway. Scientists accepted the idea of dating layers of the earth well before the evolution of species was a scientific discipline.[174] Scientists independently reached methods for the dating of layers and the dating of fossils, and the results of both processes are in agreement with a third process, radiometric dating.[175] Is it merely a coincidence that fossils found deeper in the ground have undergone more radioactive decay and have a less evolved structure? The stupidity of Young Earth Geology is so astounding that I will not give its specific qualms against mainstream science an air of respectability beyond this paragraph. If you are similarly convinced by such nonsensical disputes, I can only encourage you to seek out and read mainstream scientific publications.

> *There's a great book recently published* [title omitted] *which outlines in a VERY science-friendly way, both naturalistic and supernaturalistic theories of life's origins. It then uses current peer-reviewed journal publications to assess the state of our knowledge with devastating effect to proponents of naturalistic origins. Life as we know it is not just improbable, it is physically impossible.*

I have completely lost count of all the book suggestions and appeals to authority that readers have offered me over the past few years. First, it is hardly conceivable that we should consider a book dealing with supernaturalistic theories to be science-friendly when the very act of using the existence of the supernatural directly violates scientific principle. Natural ideas are theories; supernatural ideas are constructs. One is testable; the other is not. Would we suggest that a hypothetical book, which happens to suggest how invisible pink unicorns could have created the world in the supernatural realm, is science-friendly simply because it does not violate any known scientific laws? We should make no such suggestion because it begs the question of the supernatural when there is no good reason to consider it. Substitute God for the invisible pink unicorns, and all of a sudden, it's supposed to sound feasible to a monotheistic-centered society. It's a small wonder that the authors of the recommended book do not submit their claims to the scientific community and win a Nobel Prize by becoming the people who overthrew the cornerstone of modern biology.

The supposed boundary between non-life and life is not even as definitive as we were taught years ago; in fact, it is completely arbitrary.[176] Studies of abiogenesis[177] have demonstrated transitions from nothing to atoms, atoms to molecules, molecules to amino acids, amino acids to proteins, and proteins to prions, all without the need for supernatural intervention.[178] In fact, scientists have already created a fully functioning synthetic cell from scratch and expect to create an actual organism by 2017.[179]

It is also quite absurd to suggest that something is "impossible" unless it's on the basis that it is logically impossible. After all, God could have supernaturally created life using naturalistic methods in the exact way described by biologists, thereby rendering the argument useless. I wonder how the conclusion that life as we know it is "physically impossible" leads to the "possible" supernatural explanation. For whatever conclusion that drives us to the supernatural, why can we not say that it applies to the natural? I have absolutely no problem with the existence of an impersonal higher power that is distantly controlling the universe, but I have many problems with these pitiful supposed proofs that do nothing but attack aspects of the natural and beg the question of the supernatural. Confirmation bias greatly affects the authors of the vast majority of these books, and what good are the scientific opinions of those whose sole intent is to advance the scientific validity of the Bible?

> *The chances of evolution being true are the same as the chances of a tornado going through a junkyard and assembling an airplane.*

This little gem is otherwise known as the argument from improbability. The act of invoking it displays a complete lack of comprehension regarding natural design. I could write an entire book dealing with just the responses from readers who *literally* do not understand the first thing about evolution. I would suggest some reading material to them if they cared to learn, but most of them make it obvious from the onset that they have no desire to review anything that contradicts what they have merely accepted as the truth since childhood. These individuals often challenge me to name something that produces something other than its own "kind," which is an utterly ridiculous proposal since there is no such objective scientific designation as a "kind." Young Earth Creationists often use similarly vague terminology in defense of the feasibility of gathering animals for the biblical flood, but they have never been able to decide what constitutes a discrete "kind" and how the immediate outliers are objectively disqualified from belonging to the "kind." The arbitrary boundaries always suit the user.

To make the issue disturbingly worse, this "kind" argument is not even close to reflecting how evolution by natural selection works. The challenge is the same old "an orange will always be an orange" straw man that creationists have been proposing for years. Forcing an organism to undergo changes to make it in incompatible with organisms farther up the hierarchy is not how the products of time and genetic mutation eventually manifest. One need not demonstrate that two members of one species can create an offspring belonging to a new species; one need only demonstrate that two different species are the product of a common ancestor, slowly separated by genetic mutation in the past. These things take time. There are far better primers for learning about evolution than what I can propose in a few paragraphs, but since there may be some readers who have no interest or intention on reviewing the matter further, I could not forgive myself if I had a chance to educate them briefly and did not do so.

All known cellular organisms contain DNA, which determines genetic makeup, which in turn gives the organisms their traits and appearances. DNA, however, often does not copy itself perfectly during reproduction because random amounts of genetic mutation take place on random generations for a number of reasons. Evolution, in its simplest terms, is the change of these traits and appearances over time. This change in the DNA is responsible for the transformation of organism traits and appearances. Some mutations are harmful while others are beneficial. If an organism is born with a harmful mutation, it is less likely to survive and pass the harmful mutation on to its offspring. On the other hand, if an organism is born with a mutation that is beneficial to its survival, it is more likely to survive and pass the mutation on to its offspring. In this manner, organisms constantly improve in their likelihood of adaptive survival over time.

Let us suppose that there is a population of a certain species living within a specific area. If one segment of the population chooses to migrate to a different area, the population splits itself into two groups. If these groups remain isolated from each other, they will only reproduce within their respective gene pools. The genetic mutations within each group will be random, and those mutations will almost certainly be different from one group to the other. As time progresses, the mutations will accumulate and the genetic makeup of the two groups will begin to diverge from one another. While a thousand years of reproduction might only produce a very small difference in their DNA, several thousand years might produce a difference large enough so that the two groups would no longer be capable of reproducing with each other if they elected to converge. We would now have two new distinct but closely related species, and the original species would no longer exist. This phenomenon, responsible for the creation of different types of organisms, is what we call speciation. Over the course of a billion years, one would expect to see enough divergence to produce a hierarchy of life similar to the one to which we belong.

We call this entire process of mutation and reproduction the *Theory of Evolution*, but it is anything other than a theory in the popular sense. In scientific terminology, the word *theory* does not imply in any way that there is some sort of uncertainty on the existence of a process. A theory is simply a tentative explanation on the observance of facts. It is a fact that gravity is a part of our universe, but the explanation of why all objects are attracted to one another is called *Gravitational Theory*. It is a fact that microorganisms often cause disease in higher organisms, but the explanation of how this process works is called the *Germ Theory of Disease*. It is a fact that organisms have undergone speciation for billions of years, but the explanation on why associated phenomena take place is called the *Theory of Evolution*. Evolution is a fact; the explanation of evolution is the theory.

Responding directly to the airplane analogy, there is never a specific result to which evolution is leading. Humans were never a "goal" of evolution–in sharp contrast to the apologetic implication that the airplane was the "goal" of the tornado. Moreover, there is no one "tornado," but rather a seemingly endless series of reproductions and mutations that remain only when beneficial. In short, "We believe in evolution because the evidence supports it, and we would abandon it overnight if new evidence arose to disprove it. No real fundamentalist would ever say anything like that."[180]

The eye could not have evolved since all of the parts are required for vision.

As many times as others have destroyed this argument for irreducible complexity, I will address it briefly for readers who have not heard it before. We will also revisit a similar concept later. The offered claim is patently false, and most apologists know better than to suggest it. A defective or incomplete eye is better than no eye at all. Any organism with a genetic mutation that is beneficial enough to be remotely light sensitive is more likely to survive and pass that trait on. As beneficial visual mutations accumulate, the vision improves. Some species have relatively primitive vision compared to our own; some species have relatively superior vision compared to our own. Logic forces the apologist to admit that our own eyes are "unfinished products" when compared to those of a hawk or some other organism with superior vision. This is a necessary admission that is obviously contrary to his intention. For more reasons than we need to delve into here, many biologists often light-heartedly point out the poor nature of the eye's "design" as evidence of a poor "designer."

> [Random bankrupt creationist claim found in a book suggestion omitted]...*This is one of the many ways the fossil record and modern geology lean toward a young earth.*

No, this is one of the many ways that creationists present false/inaccurate/partial scientific information that they probably do not fully understand in an attempt to make their pre-determined beliefs seem valid. This is also one of the many ways that uncritical minds are fooled into believing what they read because the author appears to have great knowledge on the subject. Creationists at the most widely consulted pseudoscientific websites do not even recommend the argument that this individual offered. That is one of the reasons I omitted the claim; the other is that I do not wish to turn this work into a lengthy list of rebuttals against arguments that no unbiased scientist would seriously consider.

Why should I read a book suggested by someone who does not take the time to confirm scientific material presented by an author who holds an opinion against the overwhelming majority in the field we were discussing? Why should I read a book that even the Young Earth

Creationist community does not hold in any esteem? The problem here, in addition to confirmation bias, is a total failure to investigating the claims. Reading introductory material on earth science, speaking with geologists, or discussing evolution with professors who teach entry level college sciences will show how popular creationist claims are bankrupt. Since people don't bother to do any of these, the public often views creationism as a viable alternative to a grounded scientific discipline. Unfortunately, there seems to be an innate tendency for people to be fooled by partial or fake evidence. According to Cialdini, people can behave by automatic response, evidenced by the response from canned sitcom laughter.

> We have become so accustomed to taking the humorous reactions of others as evidence of what deserves laughter that we, too, can be made to respond to the sound and not to the substance of the real thing. Much as a [recorded] "cheep-cheep" noise removed from the reality of a chick can stimulate a female turkey to mother, so can a recorded "ha-ha" removed from the reality of a genuine audience stimulate us to laugh. The television executives are exploiting our preference for shortcuts, our tendency to react automatically on the basis of partial evidence. They know that their tapes will cue our tapes.[181]

Young Earth Creationism is just another discipline found on a long inventory of pseudosciences. There is even a brand of pseudoscience quickly gaining popularity in my primary field of study called homeopathy, which offers a terrific illustration on how someone can manipulate information before presentation. Homeopathy is the principle that a disease can be cured by giving very small amounts of a substance that produce symptoms similar to the ones produced by the disease. According to homeopathy, as you further dilute the concentration of the medicinal substance that you administer to someone, the active ingredient will accomplish an increasingly desirable result. Mainstream pharmacologists (who all realize that homeopathy is bunk) understand that most drugs work on production inhibition or under enzyme-receptor theory. We know that as you increase enzymes levels introduced to the body, more receptors will become stimulated and produce greater effects. We also know that as more inhibitors are introduced to working processes, fewer enzymatic goals will be accomplished. These are currently undeniable facts of science; and the field of nonsensical homeopathy is in direct contrast to these foundational theories of medicine.

Substances that follow the principles of homeopathy cannot actually work to any appreciable degree if they are not present in sufficient concentrations.[182] Manufacturers of homeopathic products can even legally sell their products in the US as long as they carry a warning that the Food and Drug Administration does not evaluate their claims. As an alternative, you will find many supporting studies referenced on the product labels that support their claims. So if the products do what the manufacturers say they do, and there are studies to support their claims, why do these products not go through the FDA approval process? The answer is very similar for both homeopathy and creationism.

The FDA serves as the governing body that orders drug manufacturers to present all relevant evidence for review–not just evidence favorable to the manufacturer. If you run enough studies, according to the statistical laws associated with chance, you will eventually get a result that you want.[183] One of the shortcomings with our administration of scientific research is that there are no governing bodies controlling what studies are published and advertised to consumers. The best that the scientific community can do is separate journals that publish only peer-reviewed findings from ones that will publish anything offered. Creationists do not publish in peer-reviewed journals because those involved in the appraisal process know that their methods are too flawed for other scientists to consider seriously. This observation came to light in the 1987 United States Supreme Court Case Edwards v. Aguillard, which decided that teaching creationism in public schools is unconstitutional because it a religious belief that cannot be factually supported.[184]

In addition to bogus claims designed to derail the credibility of evolutionary biology, I have also received my fair share of urban legends that someone started in order to make the religious believer more comfortable with his faith. I have actually found it curious that these stories amaze religious followers. Would a firm believer not just brush the results off as what we should naturally expect? To me, they reek of insecurities.

> *I do know that the Hubble telescope has in recent years convinced the majority of astronomers that the universe isn't billions of years old. I'm not an astronomer, but it had something to do with the number of a certain type of stars being few in number - hundreds instead of thousands.*

I have been unable to track down the origin of this myth, but would it not serve this individual well to consider the discovery's potential ramifications within the scientific community? This consequence is irrelevant however because, if you remember, the Bible defender cares not for rational thought–only comforting evidence. The Hubble telescope story is one of those comforting myths that Christians pass among each other to externally justify their beliefs. As a former Christian, I was also once guilty of only wanting to hear scientific testimony that substantiated my blind faith. Anyone who does a modest amount of research, however, will discover that there is only evidence for the contrasting position, which is that the universe is about fourteen billion years old.[185]

> *NASA found a missing day in time, which supports the story of the sun standing still in Joshua.*[186]

According to the researchers at snopes.com,[187] this myth has been around since 1936 when the author Harry Rimmer virtually invented the story when allegedly referencing another work written in 1890. As for the growing popularity of this tale, I could not possibly provide a better explanation than those who already addressed it:

> To those who've given over their hearts to God and the Holy Word, this is a *deeply* satisfying legend. Faith is, after all, the firm belief in something for which no proof exists, a quality that can leave believers — especially those who find themselves in the midst of

> non-believers — feeling unsatisfied. As steadfast as their certainty is, they cannot prove the rightness of the path they tread to those who jeer at their convictions. And this is a heavy burden to shoulder. A legend such as the "missing day explained" tale speaks straight to the hearts of those who yearn for a bit of vindication in *this* life. Being right isn't always enough — sometimes what one most longs for is sweet recognition from others... Our willingness to accept legends depends far more upon their expression of concepts we want to believe than upon their plausibility. If the sun once really did stand still for a day, the best evidence we'd have for proving it would be the accounts of people who saw it happen. That is what the Bible is said to offer. Some of us accept that, and some of us don't.[188]

Didn't you hear that a large group of scientists got together and determined that evolution wasn't true?

The Discovery Network's Science Channel recently ranked evolution as the greatest scientific discovery in the history of humankind.[189] Viewers considered it more important than the discovery of cells, the discovery of penicillin, the Germ Theory of Disease, Mendel's laws of heredity, Newton's laws of motion, and Einstein's Theory of General Relativity, among others. People who believe such rumors have no idea how significant it would be for the mainstream scientific community to repeal the foundation of biology. Since such a bald assertion would never convince a rational person without sufficient evidence to support it, I shall not give it the air of respectability by providing further comment. Some of us will accept that, and some of us will not.

Defenses of the Noachian Flood and Young Earth Creationism almost always go hand in hand. If you are gullible, stupid, ignorant, or indoctrinated enough to believe in one, you will almost certainly believe in the other. If you think one is false, then it pretty much follows that you are going to reject the other as well. Stories like the one of Noah's ark and countless other absurdities probably reclaim more victims from Christianity than skeptical critiques ever could–and for good reason. First and foremost, the stories in the first five books of the Bible are patent nonsense. However, if you wish to throw common sense out the window and put the matter to other tests for validity, there are still plenty of reasons to disbelieve just about everything you find in the earliest biblical writings.

An increasing number of modern scholars have all but concluded that the first five books of the Bible, traditionally considered to have been written by Moses (a supposed eyewitness to the majority of the events), are actually a combination of several different legends by several different authors written several centuries after the setting. There are a number of reasons why we believe this is so. The east side of the Jordan River is referred to as the "other side" when Moses never crossed over into the west side. The dates of conquests of cities do not match the dates yielded by archaeological digs. There are many contradictions and repetitions in close proximity to one another. Different names for God are used. Lists of people who were born after Moses died are recorded. The text speaks of Moses in the third person, even going as far as calling him meek and superior in the same verse–which is hardly plausible as a self-declaration. Moses died and was buried in the final chapter. Camels were already domesticated in the stories even though secular historians believe they were not domesticated until centuries later. Names of pharaohs are omitted. Future names of cities are provided. Moses has knowledge of certain matters that no one from the period would have had.[190] Furthermore, the entire book of Deuteronomy is likely a forgery "discovered hidden in the Temple in Jerusalem by King Josiah, who, miraculously, in the midst of a major reformation struggle, found in Deuteronomy confirmation of all his views."[191]

The overwhelming majority of secular scholars (and many progressive religious scholars) agree that the final biblical version of the flood account culminated long after the deaths of Noah and Moses, perhaps around the time of the Babylonian Exile. During this troubling period for the Israelites, their priests likely embellished the historical event with supernatural attributes, possibly as a way of manufacturing propaganda to intimidate their captors and console their fellow captives. In essence, the Israelites may have wanted to increase their own power by frightening others with a deity angry enough to decimate even his own people. If the mystery behind Noah's ark has this much simpler explanation, why should we not apply the same reasoning to the remaining ridiculous, unverifiable, supernaturally based accounts found throughout the incredulous Old Testament? Even if we ignore all this evidence and instead suppose that Moses was an eyewitness to the events he records during his life, Noah's ark still predates him by several centuries. Thus, when considering whether the story of Noah's ark is a literal occurrence, we must realize that the story was written between one thousand (traditional dating) and two thousand (scholarly dating) years after it happened.

A little known but important piece of information about the Noachian flood is that the extremely similar Epic of Gilgamesh in the Sumerian legend predates Noah's story by at least one thousand years in the written form and perhaps five hundred years for the setting.[192] The similarities between the two tales are so remarkable that we cannot write them off in good conscience as mere coincidences. In the earlier flood legend, Utnapishtim receives instructions and exact dimensions on how to construct a large ship to avoid an imminent flood (as does Noah in Genesis 6:14-16), takes animals and his family aboard to preserve life on earth (as does Noah in Genesis 6:19-7:1), lands the ship on a mountain after the flood has stopped (as does Noah in Genesis 8:4), releases a dove and a raven from the ship in order to aid his search for dry land (as does Noah in Genesis 8:6-11), and burns a sacrifice after the flood for the gods who find its odor pleasing (as does Noah in Genesis 8:20-21). Because several additional minor parallels exist, I would encourage everyone to read Tablet XI of the short epic in its entirety in order to appreciate fully the similarities between the two legends. Since the Gilgamesh tale is the earlier version of the two, we can only surmise that the authors of Genesis copied the Epic of Gilgamesh or inadvertently patterned the story of Noah's ark on an even more ancient flood legend that we have yet to discover.

This fact alone is sufficient for unbiased people to conclude that Noah's ark is a story borrowed from another culture, but this does not stop uninformed criticisms from rolling in.

> *We know that the biblical story of Noah's Ark is true and that the Sumerian Epic of Gilgamesh is false because the latter lacks the details and simplicity of the biblical account.*

To which I shall respond by declaring that this guy has it backwards. That is to say, we know the Sumerian version is the correct one because the Bible lacks the vagueness and complexity of the Sumerian account. Now of course this is a terrible argument I've just made, but it only goes to show what straws people will grasp at in order to avoid having to admit that their religious stories are wrong. How does the inclusion of what one person arbitrarily considers graphic details and simplicity make one story true over another? The individual offering this argument simply declares the biblical story true and attempts to discredit other stories based on how they differ from the one that he arbitrarily declares to be the winner. To restate the individual's argument in a more realistic fashion: the epic disagrees with the Bible, so the epic is wrong. Such a suggestion is not even coherent enough for us to consider the presence of confirmation bias. Why does the individual not want to address the issue that the Bible has no less than five major parallels with the older story? If the biblical flood is true, how is it that the Sumerians knew exact details of the future centuries before it happened? Why does the individual not want to address extant written records from other civilizations straight through the flood era? Why does the individual not want to address any of the logistical problems with the voyage?[193]

> *Noah's Flood didn't mean the whole world was flooded.*

It is painfully obvious upon in-depth analysis that the story burdens itself with a number of significant logistical problems, not to mention the presence of historical records from a number of civilizations that fail to mention their demise.[194] For this reason, many apologists will attempt a hopeless defense for it by suggesting that the tale was speaking of a local flood. This notion, however, clearly contradicts the text, which states that all the mountains of the earth are covered.[195] Although the Hebrew word in the text used for earth, *erets*, has an ambiguously additional meaning of *land*, we can still easily determine the author's intended connotation for this specific passage. How else would God's flood annihilate every living thing on earth, as this was his stated intention, unless the elevated water extended well beyond the Middle and Near East? How else could the ark travel hundreds of miles to Ararat without water high enough to reach out and spill into the oceans? Liquids seek their own level and do not stand in one area without complete confinement. Since the barriers required for this magical constrainment are not present, we can only conclude that a local flood scenario is not only logically impossible but also entirely incompatible with the biblical text.

Recent archaeological evidence, on the other hand, has shed some light on the possible origins of the ancient global flood legends. A couple of researchers have gained notoriety for arguing that the Mediterranean Sea had likely become swollen with glaciers during the most recent ice age.[196] If this proposal is truly representative of past conditions, it is quite likely that the water pressure increased to the point where a fine line of earth previously serving as a barrier between the Mediterranean Sea and the land currently under the Black Sea collapsed. Such a scenario would then allow a violent surge of water to rush inland and create the Black Sea. Needless to say, this feasible natural process would result in widespread devastation in areas now buried under hundreds of feet of water. As a further consequence, survivors who witnessed the aftermath of the tragic event would certainly spread their consistently diverging, consistently exaggerating stories to neighboring regions.

The story's utter ridiculousness is probably why many polls indicate that an increasing number of *Christians* no longer claim a literal belief in the Old Testament and are moving toward the relatively rational category that we're going to consider next.[197] It is evidence that Christians are capable of believing anything, no matter how ridiculous, because God can *do* anything, no matter how ridiculous. Sure, one can easily explain the logistical problems of the whole fiasco by appealing to the use of miracles: God made all the water appear and disappear; God prevented all the water from becoming too hot; God collected the animals and put them into hibernation; God kept the ark afloat; God repopulated the earth with life; and God erased all evidence of the flood. By invoking the miracle clause, however, Christians are using unverifiable events that *any* person can insert into *any* scenario in order to maintain the legitimacy of *any* religion. To rectify all of these problems in such a deceitful manner is to go against the whole purpose of constructing the ark in the first place. Applying such implausible explanations would also mean that God intentionally misleads people who rely on their logical and observational talents that he himself gave them for deducing answers to readily apparent problems. Searching for the truth behind Noah's ark isn't a matter of coming up with any solution for a problem that makes the story fit, but rather discovering the most likely solution to the problem so that we have the most likely answer.

The intent of the story is sparkling clear. A global flood wiped out all life on the planet with the exception of one human family. Like every other global deluge story that came before and after Noah, the biblical flood is a lie. The source of the entertaining tale was most likely a tremendous flood that a series of individuals would later embellish to fantastical proportions. When taken literally, the tale of Noah's ark is an insult to human intelligence and common sense. If the story did not appear in the Bible, as is the case for dozens of other flood legends, no one would be giving it a second thought. Christianity, and every other ancient religion for that matter, emerged in an era of mysticism where people readily believed that miracles happened every day.

Fast-forward two thousand years. Some of the more liberal Christians have come to this realization and formed a new camp of belief. They interpret, according to their beliefs, where there otherwise need be no interpretation. This is the quintessence of the next group.

The belief in a symbolic or figurative Bible is synonymous with moderate or liberal Christianity. Harris has something very poignant to say about this before we start:

> The problem that religious moderation poses for all of us is that it does not permit anything very critical to be said about religious literalism. We cannot say that fundamentalists are crazy, because they are merely practicing their freedom of belief; we cannot even say that they are mistaken in *religious* terms, because their knowledge of scripture is generally unrivaled. All we can say, as religious moderates, is that we don't like the personal and social costs that a full embrace of scripture imposes on us. This is not a new form of faith, or even a new species of scriptural exegesis; it is simply a capitulation to a variety of all-too-human interests that have nothing, in principle, to do with God. Religious moderation is the product of *secular* knowledge and scriptural *ignorance*–and it has no bona fides, in religious terms, to put it on a par with fundamentalism. The texts themselves are unequivocal: they are perfect in all their parts. By their light, religious moderation appears to be nothing more than an unwillingness to fully submit to God's law. By failing to live by the letter of the texts, while tolerating the irrationality of those who do, religious moderates betray faith and reason equally. Unless the core dogmas of faith are called into question–i.e., that we know there is a God, and that we know what he wants from us–religious moderation will do nothing to lead us out of the wilderness.[198]

I have studied a considerable number of figurative interpretations surrounding Genesis and have found them to be desperate attempts to reconcile the Bible with scientific data. There are a number of descriptive terms floating around for this method, but they all basically assert the same thing: God intended for us to interpret Genesis figuratively. If there is something definitive in the original language to support this position (as opposed to forcing puzzle pieces to fit with known data), let those who object to a literal rendition present a valid reason for a figurative one. This will be difficult to do because the intent of the creation story is clear.

We still have no good reason to conclude that the authors' intentions were anything other than to convey that God literally created the earth over a six-day period about six thousand years ago. No amount of textual manipulation can change what the original text states; and no unbiased hermeneutic[199] endeavors have created any reasonable support for the position of the moderate and liberal Christians. Moreover, there was no *reason* for the author to be figurative. It is merely because the text is inconsistent with reality that people suggest a figurative interpretation. An unbiased eye can see that the authors display no more historical knowledge than any of their contemporaries. Thus, there is nothing in Genesis to distinguish the Bible's creation myth from any other ancient creation myth.

> *You seem to read the Bible as though it were a scientific or historical document, as though it were measurable and logical. You provide no reason why you read it in this manner.*

No, I do not read it as a scientific or historical document; I read it as a book of information. If I am to accept that God wrote or inspired the book, I expect the information to be accurate. When the science or history is woefully inaccurate, I tentatively conclude that an omniscient being had nothing to do with it. Many of the latter books in the Old Testament, however, I *do* read entirely as attempts at history because they are widely acknowledged to be such. Hence the designation given by biblical scholars: *the historical books.* I consider the Old Testament to be within the measurable bounds of scrutiny and logic because the events described within either happened or not. These are the standards by which I measure the Bible. Is logical soundness too much to expect from an omnipotently inspired book that demands a lifetime of adherence?

I analyze it in this manner for the same reason that I read any other book of reports in this manner–it is either true or false. Trying to place a book on some different plane of esoteric thought by begging the question of its divine nature is wrong for so many reasons, primarily because we can do it for any work. What book cannot maintain its inerrancy by simply being deemed figurative whenever it fails tests of scientific scrutiny? I once ran across a terrific point on the internet written by a skeptic and former English professor:

> A very basic principle of literary interpretation is that the words in a written text should be interpreted literally unless there are compelling reasons to assign figurative meaning to them, but a desire to make the text inerrant is not a compelling reason to assign figurative meaning, because that approach is based on an unverifiable claim that biblical writers were divinely inspired in what they wrote, and so they could not have made mistakes.[200]

Do you suppose its many stories were ever intended as literal actual accounts?

Let those who disagree demonstrate how they can separate fact from fiction, literal from figurative, metaphorical from allegorical, etc. To my knowledge, no one has ever been able to develop a reliable method or formula to do so. Intense hermeneutic studies consistently yield inconsistent conclusions because the problem with biblical interpretation is that the interpreters can interpret by utilizing a seemingly endless variety of disciplines. If we are simply going to hold the Bible to some sort of common sense litmus test when deciding what is literal, as the one asking this question seems to suggest, we must immediately rule out Jesus' resurrection as a historical account. Why conclude that the fish swallowing Jonah is clearly figurative while a man returning to life after being dead for over a day is clearly literal? Since the vast majority of Christians will never make this concession, we should see an enormous problem with the suggested arbitrary approach. After all, moderate and liberal Christians, who are willing to accept scientific and logical conclusions, will attempt to shrug off the absurdities by claiming that the statements are merely figurative; fundamentalists Christians, who will not accept obvious scientific and logical conclusions, attempt to invent their own non-testable solutions. The best answer freethinkers can provide–that primitive minds spread fantastic stories in a time when humans understood virtually nothing in the universe–goes unheard by all religious parties.

> *Aesop's fables contain no actual occurrences yet they contain a deeper meaning: colloquially- a moral.*

This is a false analogy because Aesop's fables are set in a fantastical environment and are clearly intended to be works of fiction that convey an underlying meaning. The Bible, on the other hand, is an attempted history of the Ancient Near East that intertwines documentation of a specific god's earthly actions with stories of talking animals and other such absurdities. If moderate Christians have valid arguments that the Bible was clearly intended to be figurative or colloquial, let them present those arguments. Better yet, let them present those arguments to the fundamentalist Christians who have valid arguments that the Bible was clearly intended to be taken literally. Once again, we see that apologists cannot agree among themselves what the Bible is supposed to be, yet they all expect non-believers to accept their contradictory positions toward the same conclusion: that the Bible is the word of God. If this does not demonstrate that the apologetic conclusion of the Bible's divine origin was made before the gathering of evidence, nothing will.

> *Most people understand that the bible is full of allegories, metaphors and symbolism.*

Not really. For every person who believes that a certain story is allegorical, metaphorical, or symbolic, I guarantee that I could find another person who believes it is entirely literal. I further guarantee that each person could use hermeneutics to find textual justification for their respective positions. What does this say? How can one definitively determine literal from figurative? Is the resurrection of a dead man allegorical, metaphorical, and symbolic? If not, why not? "Most people understand that the *resurrection* is full of allegories, metaphors, and symbolism." How is that statement less valid than the one above? Dawkins elaborates:

> Modern theologians will protest that the story of Abraham sacrificing Isaac should not be taken as literal fact. And, once again, the appropriate response is twofold. First, many many people, even to this day, do take the whole of their scripture to be literal fact, and they have a great deal of political power over the rest of us, especially in the United States and in the Islamic world. Second, if not as literal fact, how should we take the story? As an allegory? Then an allegory for what? Surely nothing praiseworthy.[201]

The fact of the matter is that those who argue that the Bible is an allegorical, metaphorical, or symbolic book belong to a generation that has merely retreated from the position of their predecessors. Apologists for religion have changed over the years, just as apologists for other pseudoscientific disciplines have incorporated new interpretations for more recent evidence that debunks their disciplines. The first ghost photographer was found to be a fraud when living people started showing up in his pictures, but this doesn't discourage the field from forming new explanations for subsequent ghost photographs.[202] The first spirit-rapper confessed that the otherworldly sounds in her sessions were the popping of a joint in her big toe and not communications from the dead, but this doesn't discourage the field from continuously pressing the validity of subsequent ghost whisperers.[203] The first footage of Bigfoot was admitted to be a hoax by the man who made the suit and the man who wore the suit, but this doesn't discourage the field from forming new explanations for subsequent films.[204] The first verifiable crop circles were made by two men who confessed to having invented the whole idea in a pub, but this doesn't discourage the field from forming new explanations for subsequent crop circles.[205] Abductees alleged that the first space aliens told them that they came from Mars and Venus, but once scientists determined those worlds to be inhospitable to life, abductees talked of subsequent abductors hailing from far away solar systems.[206] In this same manner, once science destroyed a literal reading of the Bible, the book retreated into the realm of symbolism and other such explanations. Sagan explains the consequences:

> The religious traditions are often so rich and multivariate that they offer ample opportunity for renewal and revision, again especially when their sacred books can be interpreted metaphorically and allegorically. There is thus a middle group of confessing past errors–as the Roman Catholic Church did in its 1992 acknowledgement that Galileo was right after all, that the Earth does revolve around the Sun: three centuries late, but courageous and most welcome nonetheless.[207]

> *The Catholic Church has never made any assertion to the effect that the Bible is literally true.*

I placed this hilarious statement after Sagan's quote for an obvious reason. What the Catholic Church does and does not do is irrelevant to whether or not the Bible is literally true. Is the Catholic Church the ultimate authority on the Bible? Hardly. Does all of society base its opinions on the Catholic Church? Hardly. More importantly, the Catholic Church once arrested Galileo, one of the greatest scientists who ever lived, for presenting scientific hypotheses that were contrary to literal statements of the Bible. I'm pretty sure that the Catholics did not go around arresting people for making scientific discoveries that contradicted figurative stories. I am certainly not going to delve into the history of the Catholic Church because any reasonable person knows what a deplorable history the institution has made for itself. One hundred years after Darwin publishes *On the Origin of Species*, a Pope declares that evolution might be true. Centuries after the Catholic Church persecuted Galileo for his scientific discoveries, another Pope offers an apology. The reader apparently believes that these admissions somehow help the Catholic Church's credibility in the argument for figurative interpretations. I disagree.

> *The stories of the Old Testament are clearly, and have been understood as such since their inception, origin stories that reveal a religious truth.*

Then why is it that no one has been able to support this assertion with a satisfactory argument? Then why is it that fundamentalist Christians claim to be able to support a literal reading of the stories? Then why is it that Christians cannot agree on what is figurative and what is literal? How could one even begin to argue such a ridiculous notion when we have overwhelming evidence that people held the exact opposite as true throughout the Middle and Dark Ages? Even *today*, many studies show that a large portion of Americans believe the stories to be literally true.[208] Nevertheless, let us step back and look at the big picture for a moment. What can we say about a god who inspired a book that inspires so much confusion? I ask readers to take the time to consider the ramifications of this question.

> *The word* begat *often skips generations, so the dating for Creation is wrong.*

There are a few passages that liberal Christians cite to support this view, but those passages are easily explained by none other than the fundamentalist Christians. As these specific arguments are far too detailed to dwell on here,[209] I will simply move on to the overall absurdity of the notion that the biblical genealogies skip generations. We can obviously denounce the idea that they are allegorical, metaphorical, symbolic, or summary in some fashion because there is no reasonable explanation as to why the authors would record them in this manner. Mills elaborates beautifully:

> If we are to interpret these names and numbers metaphorically, then I suppose that the telephone book–which is also a list of names and numbers–is also a collection of deeply profound metaphors. And anyone who can't appreciate this 'fact' is a narrow-minded literalist incapable of elevated, metaphorical abstraction…When viewed in isolation, the Genesis genealogies themselves posit no miraculous events or supernatural Beings. If we cannot interpret these mundane genealogies literally, then we cannot interpret *anything* in the Bible literally. These same creationists,

> however, demand that we interpret literally the existence of God, Jesus, the Holy Ghost, the Devil, Angels, Heaven and Hell. All miraculous events portrayed in the Bible are likewise to be interpreted in a strictly literal sense: Jesus literally turned water into wine–literally cast out demons–literally walked on the Sea of Galilee–literally placed a magic curse on a fig tree–literally rose from the dead. Apparently, it's only the Genesis genealogies that we are suppose to interpret metaphorically.[210]

Yours is indeed a curious exercise, ignoring so many hermeneutical tools that are well established in critical literary analysis.

I do not ignore the process of hermeneutics; I often delve deep into it in order to see if it has merit. On the other hand, I ignore *ad hoc* interpretations of passages to explain errors when they conflict with the clear intentions of the passages. As one can use hermeneutics to find a way to interpret the Bible to mean whatever he wants it to mean, and just about any Christian will agree with this assessment, what good is the process? There is an enormous problem with applying hermeneutics to a widely interpretable piece of work. If ten people undertake the practice, you are likely to get ten entirely different conclusions–yet they all somehow support the divinity of the Bible. And we all saw it coming. Harris even undertakes an interesting exercise in which he uses hermeneutics to find the meaning of life hidden in a recipe for fish cakes. He elaborates on his discovery:

> That such metaphorical acrobatics can be performed on almost any text–and that they are therefore meaningless–should be obvious. Here we have scripture as Rorschach blot: wherein the occultist can find his magical principles perfectly reflected; the conventional mystic can find his recipe for transcendence; and the totalitarian dogmatist can hear God telling him to

> suppress the intelligence and creativity of others. This is not to say that no author has ever couched spiritual or mystical information in allegory or ever produced a text that requires a strenuous hermeneutical effort to be made sense of. If you pick up a copy of Finnegans Wake, for instance, and imagine that you have found therein allusions to various cosmogonic myths and alchemical schemes, chances are that you have, because Joyce put them there. But to dredge scripture in this manner and discover the occasional pearl is little more than a literary game.[211]

Often enough, I have encountered entire pages that have been written on a single *word* in the Hebrew text.[212] Therefore, the question we should be asking is whether a person can use hermeneutics to offer a *valid* and *likely* reason for a particular interpretation. Again, I say to Christian apologists, demonstrate a way that will consistently allow us to determine what is figurative from what is literal. And one more time, tell us what kind of perfect god would allow an imperfect book that can be so widely interpreted? Thomas Paine was perhaps the first to point out this absurdity when he wrote in *Age of Reason*:

> It has been the practice of all Christian commentators of the Bible, and of all Christian priests and preachers, to impose the Bible on the world as a mass of truth and as the word of God; they have disputed and wrangled, and anathematized each other about the supposed meaning of particular parts and passages therein; one has said and insisted that such a passage meant such a thing; another that it meant directly the contrary; and a third, that it meant neither one for the other, but something different from both; and this they call *understanding* the Bible.[213]

Before we move on to the final camp of religious opinion on science, I want to share two examples of individuals using hermeneutics while arguing that we should interpret certain verses figuratively. The first set of assertions is from a professional apologist while the second is relatively amateurish. Since the arguments for hermeneutical interpretations are often long and tedious, the majority of such instances are not very well suited for this book. I could have included a number of similar examples I have received, but these two arguments are probably the most representative examples of *ad hoc* reasoning. To begin, recall the earlier urban legend about NASA finding a missing day in order to support an unusual event in the tenth chapter of Joshua.

> Then Joshua spoke to the Lord in the day when the Lord delivered up the Amorites before the sons of Israel, and he said in the sight of Israel, "O sun, stand still at Gibeon, And O moon in the valley of Aijalon." So the sun stood still, and the moon stopped, Until the nation avenged themselves of their enemies. Is it not written in the book of Jashar? And the sun stopped in the middle of the sky, and did not hasten to go down for about a whole day. And there was no day like that before it or after it, when the Lord listened to the voice of a man; for the Lord fought for Israel.[214]

Since a number of apologists have come to appreciate the scientific repercussions of such an event, a number of suggestions have been offered as to why the Bible apparently says something it does not really mean.

> *The Book of Jashar is poetical, so the event is probably metaphorical. Therefore, verses twelve through fourteen likely refer to the hailstorm because the verses are also non-sequential.*

Assuming that Jashar is poetical, I will again ask how we can separate the literal from the figurative. Have poetic works not been written about historical events? It is absurd to suggest that the event "is probably metaphorical" because the story can be found in a book of poems. Extant copies of the book no longer exist, but if we knew that it contained mundane historical accounts as well, would those accounts be metaphorical like the *begats* in Genesis? If one can simply assert that a passage is figurative when it conflicts with science, we can regard any book we wish as infallible.

The key problem with such a solution is that the passage was written several centuries before the start of the Common Era. It is extremely likely that no one, especially no relatively primitive Hebrew, had any idea that the earth's motion around the sun prevented a cosmic collision. Since the archaic minds in the book's original audience could not appreciate the potential catastrophes from what was being purported, there was no reason to consider the passage figurative at that time. Nothing but our advanced scientific understanding would prompt anyone to think that the passage is anything but an attempted literal accord of what took place on the battlefield that day. The explanation is therefore a thinly veiled *ad hoc* attempt at maintaining inerrancy. Where the apologist suggests a metaphorical meaning based on a mention in a poetic book, I could much more sensibly suggest a literal meaning based on consistency with contemporaneous scientific understanding.

> *The Hebrew word for the idea of standing still* (damam) *can also mean being silent. Likewise, the Hebrew word for the idea of being stopped* (amad) *can also mean being inactive. Therefore, the sun and moon only became dark and stopped producing heat.*

The problem with this proposal becomes apparent when the author declares that the sun "did not hasten to go down for about a whole day." If God simply silenced or inactivated the sun, as the apologist suggests, why did the author mention anything about the *movement* of the sun when God never affected its movement? Is it not odd that God does something to the sun and moon in one verse that supposedly means *inactivated* rather than *stopped*, yet in the very next verse, the author comments on the *movement* of the sun?

Decide which interpretation makes more sense: 1) Joshua tells the sun and moon to be still, the sun and moon stood still, and the sun did not go below the horizon for quite a while; or 2) Joshua tells the sun and moon to be silent, the sun and moon became silent, and the sun did not go below the horizon for quite a while. The apologetic explanation is clearly inconsistent with the text. This is why all twelve major biblical versions do not translate the passage in such an intellectually dishonest fashion.[215]

Furthermore, what advantage could a darkened sky give Joshua over his enemies, and why is this advantage not stated or well understood from the text? A prolonged day, on the other hand, would obviously allow him enough time to defeat them since it was already near the end of the day when the battle started. The most likely conclusion is obvious, but since apologists do not favor likely conclusions when they conflict with predetermined beliefs, it has been suggested that, based on the author's word choice, the sun not hastening to set is a poetic observation for its irrelevance during the rest of the day. Thus, we are right back to the original problem of how such inane reasoning can make any book infallible.

We must also ask ourselves why God would allow such an erroneous translation to be present in all of the versions for the masses to read, while only a select few who practiced deeply involving hermeneutics would ever understand the supposed true meaning of the passage. This is where the common sense litmus test strikes a deathblow to the apologist.

> *Joshua needed the sun to stop producing heat because his army was fatigued from having just marched for most of the day.*

Then why does Joshua also ask for the moon to be silent? Since the moon does not produce heat, this argument is either invalid or unnecessary. If you are making pleas to the sun and moon, and we accept that the presence of light is the problem for battle, it is useless to offer a non-textual conjecture. Otherwise, we are to accept two stretches of the text instead of one, and one highly unlikely scenario is more likely to be consistent with reality than two of them.

> *The miracle in Joshua isn't widely recorded by other cultures because it could have been a divinely induced hallucination or local distortion of reality.*

In other words, when science is against you and the metaphorical argument has no solid textual support, invoke the miracle clause. Why not just accept the obvious interpretation of the text and save the miracle clause for God temporarily suspending the universal laws of motion? That way, you do not have to offer ridiculous interpretations that contradict what the text plainly states. Since one miracle is as easy as the next once you invoke the supernatural clause, it would make much more sense to just claim a miracle from the beginning rather than offer an unlikely interpretation of the text that still requires a miracle to complete it. With that said, I'll now move on to the second example of hermeneutics in action.

> *The light at the beginning of Genesis, which seems so at odds with the creation of the natural celestial lights a number of verses later, was not any natural light that we know of, but rather the eternal light of the world: Christ. When we fast-forward to the book of Revelation, towards the very end of the Bible, it makes it clear that Christ is the "Alpha" and the "Omega," as he was there from the very beginning.*

Let us decide if we can adequately apply this suggestion to the text by considering the appropriate literary passage in Genesis. The idea initially seems to work fine in Genesis 1:3, but by also replacing the idea of "light" with "Christ" two verses later in Genesis 1:5, we would make Christ a twelve hour period of the day, which is a completely nonsensical suggestion. If we simply accept what the Bible plainly says in context, however, we realize that Genesis 1:3-5 talks about the creation of natural light that is different from darkness. The periods divided by the light are called night and day, which comprised the first day on earth.

Let us also consider the Revelation account. If Christ were the "beginning," as the reader suggests, Christ would have to be the earth or heavens, both of which were present from the beginning. The light clearly was not. Sure, we can force Christ to fit into parts of the stories, but the hermeneutical interpretations become nonsensical when we attempt to apply the remainder of the argument into passages where we should certainly extend them. Since making Christ a twelve hour period of the day was clearly not the Genesis author's intent, and since light cannot be the "alpha" due to not being present at the beginning, the suggestion that "light" refers to "Christ" is erroneous *ad hoc* reasoning.

When science cannot be used to support the Bible, and the Bible cannot be twisted to fit science, many have found comfort in jettisoning the process of gathering data altogether. While science does not disprove the existence of God in the supernatural realm, it quickly demonstrates the presence of scientific errors in a book that is supposed to be inspired by and representative of a certain god. If we are to just throw our hands up and declare that science cannot test the feasibility of God's existence, we may as well just say that natural science is not an instrument to investigate ProtoGod, the entity that is more powerful than and creator of God. One could imagine infinite aspects of the supernatural, such as the fictitious ProtoGod, and claim that each one is superior to science because science cannot touch it. For this reason, one should have a good natural reason for believing in a specific aspect of the supernatural. If Christians are going to presume the existence of entities in the supernatural realm that cannot be falsified by science (and consequently declare science unfit to test these presumptions), I should be allowed to presume the existence of a supernatural creature as well. If one wishes to appeal to supernatural explanations, I should be allowed to say that ProtoGod killed God and made the universe herself.

As this suggestion is quite absurd to say the least, I hope readers see how hiding behind the esoteric cloud of the supernatural does nothing to help the case of those who hold such positions. Science only explains things in the natural realm, such as earthly phenomena reported in the Bible. The Judeo-Christian God leaves the supernatural realm and enters into the natural one when he commits actions in the Old Testament that have a direct impact on the earth. We can then test such claims. When we have evidence leading us to conclude tentatively that the occurrence of such phenomena would be consistent with other known factors, we would also have sufficient reason to consider the plausibility of the related supernatural assertions. However, decades of relevant scientific study demonstrate that we have no reason to believe such events ever happened.

You cannot learn anything unless you first convince yourself that what you are being told is true.

This horrible assertion does not really have anything to do directly with the conflict between science and religion, but I thought it was rather indicative of the poor thinking skills maintained by those who put no stock in scientific scrutiny. A person is not required to accept something as true in order to learn from it. Critical thinkers will listen to an assertion, regard it is a possibility (or a hypothesis), weigh evidence for and against the assertion, consider the position of unbiased authorities on the assertion, and draw a tentative conclusion on the assertion. All of this is a learning process in which we do not convince ourselves that what we are being told is true until we are ready to make such a conclusion based on what we have learned since the assertion was offered.

We shouldn't trust science because it violates its own rules.

I always find it amazing how Christians will support any type of science when it supports the Bible or some other position that they hold in life, but science quickly "violates its own rules" when the results of scientific study begin contradicting the Bible. I wonder if the person who offered this advice would refuse antibiotics because they are products of self-violating scientific research. I wish this individual would elaborate on how we should not apply a method of empirical study that is willing to change its tentative conclusions when disproved by further analysis. After that, I would not mind an explanation on how studies of the Bible (the gathering of information and forming of explanations on the material) are not utilizing the scientific method itself.

This apologetic suggestion is simply an absurd justification for choosing alternative avenues of acquiring knowledge (namely, faith) and has been credulously offered so many times in the past that I have lost count. Believing something based on evidence is rationalism; believing something because it is written in a book is dogmatism. Sagan once masterfully warned, "Because science carries us toward an understanding of how the world is, rather than how we would wish it to be, its findings may not in all cases be immediately comprehensible or satisfying."[216]

Science is the pursuit of answers–not a dogma of predefined ones. I may as well just invent a religion myself, have it explain all possible answers by inserting an all-powerful entity into the mix, and declare it superior to the process of gathering data since all the answers are already explained by my religion. This notion is so absurd that I hesitate to elaborate further, but I will point out that it is often consistent with certain parts of biblical doctrine. Proverbs 3:5 is perhaps the most well known example: "Trust in the Lord with all thine heart; and lean not into thine own understanding." It seems obvious that the author is saying that we are to put faith above reason when they appear to conflict, yet he does not explain how we should know where to place our faith without the utilization of reason in making that decision. Sure, one could cite a contrasting verse like the one that says the pursuit of knowledge is a just cause,[217] but this only serves to demonstrate the drastic inconsistencies offered among authors who are also supposed to be divinely inspired. If a proposition requires faith to survive, no matter what the hypothesis might be, the likelihood of that proposition being true weakens considerably.

Atheists must have faith in reason.

I would only say that atheists must *rely* on reason because it is the only testable method that they have in their arsenal. We can best describe faith as believing in something despite the lack of evidence or the presence of evidence to the contrary. Opinions based on reason can be tested; opinions based on faith cannot. Logic does not fail, and reason always triumphs in the end. If we hold a ball in the air and release it, reason tells us, based upon experience, that it will fall to the ground; faith tells us, based upon what we were indoctrinated with during childhood, that it will perhaps fly into the sky every billionth trial. Smith elaborates:

> The ploy to vindicate faith through skepticism is a failure twice over: it is useless and fallacious. Let us suppose, for the sake of argument, that the atheist is required to have "faith" of some kind, such as faith in the laws of logic. As a barest minimum, the atheist can give an intelligible meaning to his "faith" by specifying what he has faith in, the object of his faith. Such is not the case with Christian faith in the existence of God...Theologians are unable to provide a coherent and consistent description of God; so faith in God, aside from being unjustified, is also unintelligible. The Christian may just as well claim to have faith in the existence of square circles. Because the concept of God is incoherent, the primacy of faith, even if true, is stripped of its major impact. The Christian can never reduce the beliefs of an atheist to the same depths of irrationality as the concept of God.[218]

Science is not to be trusted because scientists cannot agree on the details of things like dinosaur extinction.

I am going to take issue with this statement, even though a keen mind may immediately realize that I make the same claim of not trusting the Bible because the apologists cannot agree on the details of events like the biblical creation. Most importantly, there is an enormous difference between scientists utilizing complementary methods to draw a conclusion with a variety of differing details and apologists utilizing contradictory methods to draw identical conclusions. The key difference is that scientific findings are not life-long emotional beliefs for absolute predetermined declarations of a perfect god. Scientific findings are designed specifically to be testable, falsifiable, and correctable. Otherwise, they join with religion as part of unquestionable dogma.

We no doubt have incorrect and uncertain information about topics like dinosaur extinction. Experts in the field readily admit this. One of the important parts on which mainstream scientists from varying disciplines all strongly agree is that dinosaurs lived millions of years ago. This finding disproves a literal interpretation of the creation story. Our only foreseeable alternative to the scientific process is to select, randomly and uncritically, a text that claims divinity and inerrancy. We turn to Sagan again, who suggested that science was unique in the fact that the spirit of its existence constantly reminded us that we could be wrong on our conclusions:

> Despite all the talk of humility, show me something comparable in religion. Scripture is said to be divinely inspired–a phrase with many meanings. But what if it's simply made up by fallible humans? Miracles are attested, but what if they're instead some mix of charlatanry, unfamiliar states of consciousness, misapprehensions of natural phenomena, and mental illness? No contemporary religion and no New Age belief seems to me to take sufficient account of the grandeur, magnificence, subtlety and intricacy of the Universe revealed by science. The fact that so little of the findings of modern science is prefigured in Scripture to my mind cases further doubt on its divine inspiration...But of course I might be wrong.[219]

Science wasn't a discipline when the various stories of the Bible were written.

This is entirely irrelevant. Since the Bible makes a number of positive claims, science can often test whether these claims are legitimate. Just because the idea of science did not exist at the time of the Old Testament does not mean that it is beyond the scrutiny of it. Since we would never make the argument that a ten-thousand-year-old story of a talking alligator is beyond skeptical review because the story predates the scientific discipline, why should we make that very argument for a three-thousand-year-old story of a talking donkey? If the Bible says that plants existed before the sun, which it does, the statement is either literally true or literally false. If one wants to argue that the statement is figurative, one must have a satisfactory explanation for the text. If one wants to argue that the story is literally true, one must have satisfactory evidence to present for critical review. The creation tale was a suitable literal explanation in the time it was written and for centuries afterwards, and there is no compelling textual reason not to take the story literally. We must have a good basis to conclude that the text was in some way non-literal–and we do not.

Can science measure the extent of an aesthetic experience? If not, does that mean that such experiences are not true?

What scientific studies can or cannot *currently* achieve is irrelevant. It is patently absurd to imply that a specific discipline is incapable of being applied to an observation just because there is currently no way for the discipline to explain what is witnessed. Even though there may be no way to measure or objectively evaluate whether an aesthetic experience happens, we can all agree that people experience such subjective phenomena since they are widely reported. Crediting a particular deity with such experiences, however, is a widely speculative and patently unscientific hypothesis because the credited deities correlate with the environments surrounding the experiences.

Can you prove scientifically that someone really loves you? Of course you cannot! You know it in your heart, mind, and soul!

There are no definite physical characteristics of love, but it is an idea that we can easily define, observe, test, and verify. We roughly define it as having an intense feeling of emotion for someone or something. Once we develop some arbitrary (but agreed upon) definition for this concept, we can observe and test whether people experience love. While the meaning of love to one person can be completely different from another person's definition, the idea remains somewhat consistent. Love is simply a term for a subjectively measurable emotion. While I do not attempt to "prove" anything, I can certainly demonstrate whether one person loves another person, as long as we come to an agreement on what type of elevated response constitutes love.

> *Since you admit that you make mistakes, you should trust the Bible since God does not make mistakes.*

Since many books are claimed to have been inspired, dictated, or written by God, I still have to trust my decision-making at some point in the process in order to determine which book is the real deal. The writer's suggestion is, in a sense, logically impossible. All humans make mistakes, even those who wrote the Bible. Suggesting that my conclusion is erroneous simply because I make mistakes is rather foolish. I believe that the earth is approximately spherical, that substances are composed of atomic particles, and that the human body uses ATP as its primary energy source. Should I drop these beliefs despite overwhelming evidence to their veracity simply because I make mistakes? Should I drop these beliefs despite overwhelming evidence to their veracity simply because I might be punished for not believing an alternative explanation? Since humans make mistakes, is it not also possible that someone could make a mistake in supporting the Bible's veracity, especially since many who believe in it have never spent one second analyzing it, studying it, testing it, or even *reading* it?

> *In spite of all the "evidence" that seems to justify the argument that "God and His Word are nonsense," it is simply wrong!*

Very well, let us abandon rational thought and instead embrace irrational personal feelings! One can change the word "God" to any deity of choice and make an equally valid argument. Personal experiences are not evidence of God because people of all faiths have personal experiences that reaffirm their beliefs in the gods that just happen to be observed in their respective societies. It is for this reason that we must not just say that a certain argument is wrong because of the way we feel. Otherwise, we are left with epistemological paradoxes across the globe. Faith entitles people to believe in whatever god they want; logic will test their reasons for that faith. Shermer described the predicament well when he said, "The lack of physical evidence matters little to true believers. They have shared anecdotes and personal experiences, and for most this is good enough."[220] Sagan elaborates:

> In a life short and uncertain, it seems heartless to do anything that might drive people of the consolation of faith when science cannot remedy their anguish. Those who cannot bear the burden of science are free to ignore its precepts. But we cannot have science in bits and pieces, applying it where we feel safe and ignoring it where we feel threatened–again, because we are not wise enough to do so. Except by sealing the brain off into separate airtight compartments, how is it possible to fly in airplanes, listen to the radio or take antibiotics while holding that the Earth is around 10,000 years old or that all Sagittarians are gregarious and affable?[221]

> *All the really vexing questions in science, philosophy, and theology always leave us alone, twisting in the wind, until we realize the way out of this existential darkness is by faith and love.*

Notice how this statement is a perfect example of the speaker concluding simply with the answer that he wants, as opposed to concluding with an answer to which the evidence leads. In other words, since the thought of there being no supernatural creator is uncomfortable to this individual, he avoids such a conclusion by presupposing that there is one. Sagan puts it best: "The question is not whether we *like* the conclusion that emerges out of a train of reasoning, but whether the conclusion *follows* from the premise or starting point and whether the premise is true."[222] I suppose that once you naively accept the existence of a genocidal god who can read your mind and punish you for not believing in him, explanations like this one just make sense.

The Bible demonstrates overwhelming evidence of authorship by fallible, divinely uninspired humans. In addition to the previously mentioned scientific flaws arising from an obvious limitation of knowledge and perspective, a seemingly countless number of preposterous suggestions can be found within the Bible. These absurdities include talking animals, miraculous war victories, contradictions in every conceivable category, hordes of failed and impossible prophecies, and an array of additional superstitious beliefs readily accepted by unsuspecting biblical readers.

The newly acquired ability to assign a much more recent date to the earliest books of the Bible through analyses of its fictitious historical accounts debunks the notion of a Moses/God authorship and assists in the demonstration of the book's human origins. With this consideration, the reasons for the Bible's flaws become readily apparent. Humans inventing stories set centuries in the past had no reason to anticipate that the fraudulent accounts would ever be unmasked, much less a reason to believe that their stories would be playing a dominant role in human culture centuries into the future. God did not tell us to kill people with other religions. God did not give us orders to take slaves. God did not intend for women to be socially inferior to men. God did not say that he created the universe only a few thousand years ago. God did not kill the entire world in a flood. There is no evidence God did anything. *Men* were the sole driving force behind the creation of the Bible's shameless nonsense.

Still, this does not stop Christians from fighting the evidence, giving into the cognitive dissonance, and explaining away the conflict using the best methods at their disposal. Some will do so by acknowledging that the Old Testament is scientifically incorrect if taken literally and must consequently be accepted as a metaphorical document. Some will selectively choose bits of science that agree with their beliefs and construct absurd justifications for the defense of such beliefs. Others will ignore science when convenient and unabashedly beg the question of God's perfection and consequent dominance over humankind's scientific endeavors. Regardless to which school of thought the Christian belongs, each is guilty of beginning with the premise of the Bible's divinity and finding ways to support only that premise. Rational unbiased students of the Bible will begin by examining the evidence in order to see if the religious person's premise is a probable conclusion.

Proofs And Disproofs

I agree with the old adage that few people doubted the existence of God until philosophers attempted to prove it. It was not long after I published my first work that proposed proofs of God's existence started rolling in. I have divided the suggestions into two distinct categories: 1) proofs of a higher power, and 2) proofs of the Judeo-Christian God. I think it is worth noting again that I do not categorically deny the existence of a higher power controlling the laws of the universe. Frankly, I would find the existence of such a power far more fascinating than anything the natural universe can offer. While I find the chances of such an existence remote, I nevertheless would enjoy a proof that demonstrated the existence of a higher power. However, I am very much irritated by the public uncritically accepting the upcoming assertions as proofs of a higher power's existence (and much more so as proofs of the Judeo-Christian God's existence).

At best, the purported proofs in the first category could only hope to demonstrate that a higher power must exist. While many readers even went so far in their original letters as to conclude the existence of the biblical deity, no semi-rational individual would ever make such a leap of faith based solely on the proof. These arguments, if true, would only demonstrate the existence of a distant power, not necessarily an intelligent or present one. This issue is irrelevant to biblical accuracy, but since so many are unable to distinguish the concept of a specific god from a nonspecific power, I will answer them all the same. The ones I elected to include are honestly the best of the lot. For each argument you see, I received probably a dozen that were ridiculous enough not to warrant a response. I chose not to include and address them in order to avoid accusations that I was defeating irrelevant straw men. The following sections are not meant to be exhaustive, but they are reasonably close.

What many of the people who offer arguments under the first category do not realize is that these conclusions would only support a position of *Deism*, which is the belief that a god or higher power is governing the rules of the universe. While this is an unsupported and unscientific position, I have absolutely no problem with this relatively benign belief. It is often comforting and quite harmless. Studies have suggested that as much as 14 percent of the US population is Deistic instead of Christian–without even knowing it.[223] Unfortunately, American society treats the issue of the supernatural as a false dichotomy: Christianity (or possibly the whole collection of organized religions) versus atheism. Believing in God (or *a* god or higher power) but not believing in much of the Bible (because of the realization that it is a man-made fallible work) is a position with which one can hardly argue without treading on philosophical grounds. For all intents and purposes, Deism is probably more in line with atheism than with theism.

> *Christians do not believe by proofs like those constructed in geometry class, but by faith and a feeling of shared love with Christ in their hearts.*

I tried to resist placing this argument in this section since it really does not belong,[224] but it perfectly illustrates how Christians cannot even agree among themselves on *major* philosophical points. The Bible is supposed to be God's unquestionable testament to humanity, but his followers cannot even agree on how to approach it. Interestingly enough, this practice has its advantages for the apologists. Petty and Cacioppo provide a wealth of studies to support their conclusion that "verification is more meaningful if it comes from a person who has different sources of information than you do."[225] The audience at an apologetic conference might be prone to think foolishly, "There must be something to the Bible since all of these defenders have different ideas and approaches yet they all reach the same conclusion." What the audience would fail to realize is that these apologists began with the conclusion and worked backwards to establish supportive foundations, many of which serve as the groundwork for nothing more than a host of *non-sequiturs.*

As far as addressing this specific reader complaint, you can replace the word "Christians" with a term for followers of any other belief system and replace the word "Christ" with a term for the object of reverence for those followers, and like magic, you have a statement that is equally valid for any religion. We could submit countless feelings from countless people who enter into countless religions and claim countless emotional transformations. This is why we do not simply shrug the issue off as a matter of faith and personal experience. Since faiths often contradict, not all faiths can be correct. Rather than delving into the comforts of our emotions, the objective and scrutinizing process we should all undertake would be an inquiry into whether we have good reason to consider the Bible to be a more valid religious document than other contemporaneous texts. The Judeo-Christian God proofs coming up later attempt to do just that.

> *We know you were intelligently designed because you did not create the universe and nature does not just happen all by itself.*

Since so many over the years seem to be impressed and convinced by this empty rhetoric, I will devote considerable time to expose its flaws. This Cosmological Argument, sometimes also known as the First Cause Argument, states that all effects have causes, except for the uncaused first cause, which we must then regard as a god. Four separate key problems, each standing on their own, sufficiently invalidate this line of argument. While reasonable justification for parts of the Cosmological Argument would be millions of times more valuable for Deism than the Bible would ever hope to be, this line of reasoning is not without its major problems.

1) Causes and effects do not belong to an established relationship in physical science. Mills elaborates:

> The so-called "Law of Cause-Effect," often employed by creationist writers and speakers, is a philosophical and theological plaything, rather than an established law of the physical sciences. Likewise, the "Law of Cause-Effect" provides no explanation to *any* scientific problem or question. Suppose, for example, that my car fails to run properly, and I have it towed to a garage for repair. I ask the service technician why my car will not operate. If the service technician replies, "It's just the law of cause-effect again," I would certainly feel that he was giving me the run-around, and that his "explanation" was totally empty. A realistic scientific explanation might be that my spark plugs are disconnected; that the gasoline therefore cannot be ignited; that the engine therefore cannot rotate the drive shaft; that the rear axle, attached to the drive shaft, cannot be rotated; and that the wheels, connected to the axel, have no current means of forward propulsion. A genuine scientific explanation, then, incorporates specific mechanistic relationships and interactions. Any argument, thus, that appeals blindly to the "Law of Cause-Effect," without filling in the blanks, is likewise an argument totally empty of scientific content.[226]

Quite the contrary to the claim that all effects require causes, the field of quantum mechanics is based on the principle of non-causality. Creation of strings,[227] creation of matter and antimatter from a vacuum, and perhaps radioactive decay are three examples of processes that we currently believe do not necessarily require a cause. This proposition, if correct, invalidates the presumption that "all effects have causes" and consequently destroys the argument. Again, Mills explains:

> During the last twenty years, astrophysicists and cosmologists–led by Cambridge University's Dr.

> Stephen Hawking–have expanded even further our understanding of mass-energy and have explained how mass-energy's seemingly bizarre properties actually solve the riddle of cosmic origins. Hawking and others have described a naturally occurring phenomenon known as "vacuum fluctuation," in which matter is created out of what appears to be perfectly empty space–i.e., out of a perfect vacuum. Scientists have discovered that even in a perfect vacuum, in which all traditionally understood forms of matter and energy are absent, random electromagnetic oscillations are present. These oscillations actually represent a form of energy now called vacuum fluctuation energy, which can be converted into matter in complete harmony with the mass-energy conservation laws. In other words, the "nothingness" of a perfect vacuum in empty space can and does spontaneously produce matter in full agreement with Einstein's long-established laws.[228]

The matter produced by this phenomenon is composed of equal positive and negative energy. Mathematically, the positive energy cancels out the negative energy so that a sum of no energy was created. It is feasible to propose that the universe itself is composed of a sum of zero energy, which according to known physical law, is no less possible than the complete absence of mass-energy from the universe. One might even consider nothingness to be unstable, and the creation of matter to be inevitable.

2) Causes and effects are universal concepts. If we assume, for a moment, that the universe has not always existed, we cannot apply supposed laws of the universe (e.g. all effects have causes) to explain how the universe came into existence. Assuming the existence of universal laws, which are of course characteristics of the universe, before the existence of the universe itself is an absurd strategy for the apologist to take. Furthermore, the practice of discussing anything that may have existed prior to the universe is epistemologically meaningless. Dictating the rules of logic outside of the universe is like supposing the properties of numbers that are greater than infinity.

3) Existence must necessarily precede cause. Moreover, something cannot cause an effect unless it first exists. Here we see that existence must be the first component of the universe. Even if there were a physical law of causes and effects, existence is first necessary. Therefore, something must exist before it can become part of a causal relationship. The question now becomes, "Exactly what is it that we should suppose first existed, regardless of whether it has existed eternally or without cause?" The much more simple explanation is that the universe is the first "uncaused existence."[229] Interjecting a creator into the mix only needlessly complicates the issue because the existence of the universe already gives us what we need.

Even if we propose that all effects except the first one require a cause, why must an infinitely complex creator need to be part of the solution? Would not even a breakdown in physical law be a much more simple explanation than the existence of an unlimited presence? While the influences and persuasions of society may not make it seem much more feasible to say that the universe would be that which first existed, the facts are what they are. There is absolutely nothing to rule out the possibility that the universe is an oscillating or eternal phenomenon.[230] Besides, since we have already established that matter can likely arise spontaneously from a zero energy state, we already have a working hypothesis. If we refuse this deduction, we not only have to explain the origin of the god, but also explain how the same reasoning for this god cannot be applied to the origin of the universe.

4) The argument contradicts itself by attempting to circumvent its own axiom that "all effects have causes" by baselessly inserting an exception: "God is the uncaused effect." An updated version of the Cosmological Argument, called the Kalam Argument,[231] changes the assertion that "all effects have causes" to "all things that begin to exist have causes" in order to erase this fourth objection. In other words, "God is an uncaused effect because he has always existed." The argument is now cleverly disguised as an *ad hoc* explanation because it deals with all things, which necessarily exist, except the hypothesized God, prejudicially excluded through special pleading, simply because this is the intent of the argument. In other words, the argument deliberately excludes from scrutiny what it hopes to prove through scrutiny. Furthermore, the updated argument still does not address the three previous points.

> *The Atheist must suppress the demands of logic. He is like the man who finds an encyclopedia lying in the woods and refuses to believe it is the product of intelligent design. Everything about the book suggests intelligent cause. But, if he accepted such a possibility, he might be forced to conclude that living creatures composed of millions of DNA-controlled cells (each cell containing the amount of information in an encyclopedia) have an intelligent cause.*

This is a variation of the famous Watchmaker Argument first presented in 1802 by William Paley. It essentially argued that a person who would conclude that a watch found in a field was intelligently designed due to its complexity and irreducibility must also conclude that human beings are also intelligently designed due to their own complexity and irreducibility. It is not a terrible argument, but there are many better reasons to conclude otherwise. I will summarize the best arguments against it and refer readers to other sources for further review.[232]

Most importantly, the creationist claim that life is intelligently designed is an unfalsifiable assertion; therefore, it lies outside of scientific scrutiny and understanding. The only indisputable products of intelligent design are the gadgets that humans create, which do not resemble natural life–supposed products of supernatural intelligent design. Objects resemble design because we have the drive to seek utility in an object, which can be found in just about anything.[233] The goal of known intelligent human design is simplicity, not complexity, which is the product of supposed supernatural intelligent design. Natural life shows many design flaws and has low tolerance for change, even though it is supposedly a product of supernatural intelligent design. Evolution by natural selection demonstrates that human beings are not irreducibly complex as the argument suggests. The presence of homologous structures among species indicates gradual descent and makes no sense under special creation.[234] Smith has the final and most salient point about incorrectly inferring design from nature:

> Now consider the idea that nature itself is the product of design. How could this be demonstrated? Nature, as we have seen, provides the basis of comparison by which we distinguish between designed objects and natural objects. We are able to infer the presence of design only to the extent that the characteristics of an object differ from natural characteristics. Therefore, to claim that nature as a whole was designed is to destroy the basis by which we differentiate between artifacts and natural objects. Evidences of design are those characteristics *not* found in nature, so it is impossible to produce evidence of design *within* the context of nature itself. Only if we first step beyond nature, and establish the existence of a supernatural designer, can we conclude that nature is the result of conscious planning.[235]

Everything in the universe strives to meet a goal.

Here we have an unusual form of the long-abandoned Teleological Argument. While it is true that there is a high degree of order within the universe, the argument does not establish that something designed the universe to be in that order. Furthermore, the idea that there is some sort of "goal" is flat-out wrong. Smith and Mills sufficiently answer this argument:

> Exactly what does the theist imagine the universe would be like if it was not guided by a master planner? What would a disordered universe be like? What would an acorn do?–grow into a stone, perhaps, and then into a theologian? If an acorn did grow into a stone, it would have to possess qualities radically different from what we now designate by the term 'acorn,' in which case it would cease to be an 'acorn' in any meaningful sense.[236]

> A miracle-working Creator could have kick-started the planets in numerous directions and orbital inclinations around the sun. Some planets could have been assigned West-to-East orbits, while others received opposing East-to-West assignments from the Creator. Still other planets could have been assigned polar orbits, traveling around the sun from North to South and back again. The Creator could also have established orbits with a middle-of-the-road 45-degree inclination, or any combination in-between. An almost unlimited array of orbital trajectories was available to the Creator. Why, then, was the Creator so strikingly uncreative in His choice of planetary orbits? Why did the Creator so camouflage his miraculous orbital designs as to precisely mimic naturally occurring orbits?[237]

Smith and Mills are elaborately stating that the universe follows rules, which is what we would expect a natural universe to do. A supernatural universe could (1) follow rules, (2) behave in an infinite number of different ways as it follows an infinite number of different sets of rules, or (3) follow no rules at all. If the universe followed no rules or made them up as it went along, we would undeniably conclude that it was supernatural. It does not. Since the universe follows a static set of rules, we are left being unable to conclude that there is a supernatural hand in play. With this in mind, what is the difference between a natural universe that follows natural rules and a supernatural universe that follows natural rules? Nothing. A supernatural universe following natural rules behaves like and is indistinguishable from a natural universe. There were an infinite number of ways that the universe could have behaved in order to establish its supernaturalistic qualities, but it just so happens to comport according to the predictability of natural law. Fancy that.

The universe is too fine-tuned not to have a Creator.

This argument is termed the Anthropic Principle. The Teleological Argument and Anthropic Principle are two sides of the same coin.

Whereas the former argues that the proof is in the fact that everything behaves according to the rules, the latter argues that the rules themselves are the proof.[238] Apparently, the apologist believes that everything has to be exactly the way it is or life could not exist. Nothing could be more baseless and speculative. Many of the examples that accompany this argument are often a matter of statistical probability. It is true that the sun "just happens" to be in a well-shielded part of the galaxy, but so are hundreds of millions of other stars. It is true that our planet "just happens" to sit within a zone of habitability relative to the sun, but how many of those hundreds of millions of stars would we expect, by chance, to have a similar planet? The point is that we are not supposed to be considering how unlikely life was to happen in this very place, but how likely life was to happen at all. Earth is our frame of reference because we can be nowhere else. We are not measuring the odds of life popping up on *this* planet, but rather *any* planet–because wherever we are, we are there to see it, and we can be nowhere else. Where intelligent life happens is where intelligent life observes itself.

Many notable apologists, such as Hugh Ross,[239] have compiled long lists of constants that must fall within a specific range for life to exist, and they state that these values are just too unlikely to happen by chance. Their primary mistake is ignoring how many of the constants are controlled by each other. A second is that many of the values have a great enough variance to render the latitude meaningless. Another is that they are biased toward carbon-based, water-based forms of life. Similar to the response provided against defenses of the Teleological Argument, the goal is not life as we know it, but rather life in some fashion–because whatever we are, we can be nothing else. We must consider frame of reference. M theory (way too complicated here) even establishes the presence of multiple universes where life is not possible. Again, frame of reference. Dawkins elaborates:

> The theist says that God, when setting up the universe, tuned the fundamental constants of the universe so that each one lay in its Goldilocks zone for the production of life. It is as though God had six knobs he could twiddle, and he carefully tuned each knob to its Goldilocks value. As ever, the theist's answer is deeply unsatisfying,

> because it leaves the existence of God unexplained. A God capable of calculating the Goldilocks values for the six numbers would have to be at least as improbable as the finely tuned combination of numbers itself, and that's very improbable indeed–which is indeed the premise of the whole discussion we are having.
>
> Hard-nosed physicists say that the six knobs were never free to vary in the first place. When we finally reach the long-hoped-for Theory of Everything, we shall see that the six key numbers depend upon each other, or on something else as yet unknown, in ways that we today cannot imagine. The six numbers may turn out to be no freer to vary than is the ratio of a circle's circumference to its diameter. It will turn out that there is only one way for a universe to be. Far from God being needed to twiddle six knobs, there are no knobs to twiddle.[240]

There are some additional points worthy of mention that shed light on the worthlessness of the Anthropic Principle. Life as we know it is rare, if not unique. If there were a supernatural creator who "fine-tuned" the universe for life, does it not make sense that the universal constants would allow more of it? Life must obey these constants. Life must evolve to fit neatly within these constants or it will not develop. If life is capable without water and carbon, we will never know because we cannot adjust the constants to test such a hypothesis. Hypothetically, would these forms of life that cannot exist think the universe is "fine-tuned" for them? Since the constants do not change to allow life, we must work with them. Evidence for a creator might arrive in the form of such hypothetical creatures existing without a natural explanation, but since the universe obeys natural law, we of course do not observe them.

Even within our own universe, 99 percent of all species that have ever roamed the planet are extinct. Does this sound like the success rate of an all-powerful, all-knowing creator? Would the extinct species think the earth was fine-tuned for their existence? As Mills points out, "Any watchmaker whose product similarly failed would be dismissed as incompetent."[241] Drop a naked man off in Siberia or the Sahara. Does he still think the planet is built around his needs? Organisms scurry to the regions of the globe in which they can most readily adapt to the environment. In short, the universe is not fine-tuned for life; life has become fine-tuned to the universe. Mills elaborates:

> It seems almost superfluous to rebut this [Intelligent Design] argument other than to ask: Which came first: the universe or mankind? If mankind came first and the universe followed later–displaying the characteristics necessary for human survival–then we might wonder about this incredibly fortunate coincidence and search for a possible Intelligent Designer of the universe. If, however, the universe came first, and life developed afterward, then obviously life was forced, like it or not, to adapt to the environment in which it found itself. Evolution by natural selection provides a completely satisfying and comprehensive explanation to the fine-tuning between a lifeform's needs and the environment in which it lives. It is only when our logic is backward that an Intelligent Designer seems required.[242]

Evolution violates the second law of Thermodynamics.

The second law states that the organization of systems within the universe moves toward disorder. Therefore, according to the argument, life is highly organized and therefore improbable through means of evolving. The problem is that while the universe as a whole moves toward disorder, not every part of it does. The sun constantly provides energy to the earth, enabling increasingly organized life to thrive on our planet. Even if we assumed a breakdown of the second law, we arrive only at the conclusion of a previously high state of energy–not necessarily any sort of intelligent being.

Near-death experiences are evidence of an afterlife.

I have no problems with the idea of an afterlife, even though I find it to be a highly unlikely product of disillusioned human optimism built upon the awareness of mortality, but so-called near-death experiences are not evidence for it. Shermer deals with the topic extensively, but I will address it briefly. There are three great reasons to conclude that this phenomenon is an internal one: (1) people of different religious persuasions experience detailed phenomena consistent with their own beliefs;[243] (2) the experience can be replicated by depriving the body of oxygen in a controlled experiment;[244] and (3) there must be an endogenous equivalent because similar experiences can be replicated by introducing chemical substances into the body.[245] Sagan explains people's hopes for an afterlife with great eloquence:

> Some of us starve to death before we're out of infancy, while others–by an accident of birth–live out their lives in opulence and splendor. We can be born into an abusive family or a reviled ethnic group, or start out with some deformity; we go through life with the deck stacked against us, and then we die, and that's it? Nothing but a dreamless and endless sleep? Where's the justice in this? This is stark and brutal and heartless. Shouldn't we have a second chance on a level playing field? How much better if we were born again in circumstances that took account of how well we played our part in the last life, no matter how stacked against us the deck was then. Or if there were a time of judgment after we die, then–so long as we did well with the persona we were given in this life, and were humble and faithful and all the rest–we should be rewarded by living joyfully until the end of time in a permanent refuge from the agony and turmoil of the world. That's how it would be if the world were thought out, preplanned, fair. That's how it would be if those suffering from pain and torment were to receive the consolation they deserve...Thus, the idea of a spiritual part of our nature that survives death, the notion of an afterlife, ought to be easy for religions and nations to sell. This is not an issue on which we might

anticipate widespread skepticism. People will want to believe it, even if the evidence is meager to nil.[246]

Since you cannot explain where we all came from, there's nothing wrong with believing we are created.

This is the quintessential example of a logical fallacy known as the *argument from incredulity* or *the god of the gaps* explanation. It insinuates that since I cannot answer such a question, a belief in a god is the only solution that makes sense. This line of thinking has appropriately been named *the god of the gaps* because people have used "God did it" throughout history as a way of explaining the apparently unexplainable gaps in our understanding. Natural phenomena, such as earthquakes, eclipses, rainbows, lightning, and star formation, were once considered direct interventions of God because there were no other suitable explanations. Supernatural intelligent design has failed as a suitable explanation many times in the past, and will undoubtedly continue to fail in the future, because it has wrongly been attributed to many phenomena now understood through natural laws. As time progresses and we understand more about our universe, the space within which God resides is becoming progressively cramped.

The fallacy of invoking such an argument should be apparent, but many still utilize this bankrupt line of reasoning. Many Christians understandably find comfort in the belief that "God did it" solves any problem without an apparent solution. The trouble that people overlook is that this proposal only creates a more difficult problem. If God created us all, who created God? If we suppose that God was created from nothing, why can we not suppose that the universe (a system far less complex than an all-powerful being) was also created from nothing? We are now finding ourselves back to the unsolved questions of the Cosmological Argument. Answering the question of life's origin by supposing that an all-powerful being created it only complicates and confounds the issue. Again, I do not discount the possibility that a higher power exists, but theorizing that one must exist based on our failure to explain the origin of the universe is patently absurd. With that said, I'll now move on to the arguments for the Judeo-Christian God.

God must have inspired the Bible because it maintains a consistent theme even though it was authored by dozens of individuals over several centuries.

Many have argued that the Bible deserves special consideration as a product of divine creation for this very reason. One of the most famous apologists of recent history, Josh McDowell, popularized this argument.[247] Adequately tackling this assertion requires much more analysis than one might initially anticipate. We must analyze two important questions while doing so: 1) Is the Bible actually consistent? 2) Does the consistency, if it exists, have a natural origin?

While the Bible might maintain a consistent theme or underlying connotation, I do not believe it maintains what most would consider appreciable consistency between the two Testaments–or even among the prophets in the Old Testament.[248] Even worse, of the dozens of books eligible for incorporation into the Bible, the canonized ones were often chosen doctrinally or specifically on their qualities of consistency.[249] As Richard Carrier beautifully summarizes,

> There was never a one-time, truly universal decision as to which books should be included in the Bible. It took over a century of the proliferation of numerous writings before anyone even bothered to start picking and choosing, and then it was largely a cumulative, individual and happenstance event, guided by chance and prejudice more than objective and scholarly research, until priests and academics began pronouncing what was authoritative and holy, and even they were not unanimous. Every church had its favored books, and since there was nothing like a clearly-defined orthodoxy until the fourth century, there were in fact many simultaneous literary traditions. The illusion that it was otherwise is created by the fact that the church

> that came out on top simply preserved texts in its favor and destroyed or let vanish opposing documents. Hence what we call "orthodoxy" is simply "the church that won."[250]

A committee composed of rabbis likely chose the majority of the books of the Old Testament around 100 CE. They tacked the historical, poetic, and prophetical books onto the end of the books of Moses, which tradition long held as valid. We do not know what methods they practiced while setting the Old Testament canon. Some Christians (unknowingly) support the decision of these rabbis while others have omitted some books from their palate or incorporated other works in accordance with the beliefs of their ancestors.

The story of the New Testament's formation, on the other hand, appears to be much more complex. With the explosion of gospel accounts in the second century, containment was an obvious priority for keeping the new religion within reasonable limits. While Tatian was the first known individual who believed in the validity of only the four now-canonized gospels, he combined them into one single gospel around 160 CE. The first man known to have offered a proposal of exactly four gospels on the behalf of the church was Irenaeus of Lyon around 180 CE.[251] His idea was to accredit only four gospels because there were four zones of the world, four winds, four forms of living creatures, four divisions of man's estate, and four beasts of the apocalypse.[252] For these embarrassingly primitive reasons, Irenaeus believed that there should only be four gospels accepted by the church.

In the world of organized religion, I find it only too appropriate that the most potentially important books in human history would have been decided in such a superstitious manner. Instead of God providing an unquestionably fitting reason for these gospel choices, we have a perfectly appropriate act of senselessness leading to the foundation of contemporary Christian faith. Yet, it is no wonder that surrogate reports, such as the Infancy Gospel of Thomas, did not make the cut when you consider that they contain accounts of Jesus striking people dead for arbitrary reasons.[253]

Just like the apologists of every world religion, I could make the same bald assertion that the Infancy Gospel of Thomas, along with

Matthew, Mark, Luke, and John, had God's inspiration to make it 100% accurate. If anyone thinks that they can find a way to invalidate my claim, I will simply generate a wild scenario that maintains the gospel's inerrancy while paying no attention to the improbability and absurdity of my proposed solution. What if Irenaeus accidentally omitted a fifth truthful gospel that contained an additional prerequisite for entering Heaven? In this case, Christians will not accept the stated extrabiblical requirement because there are four, not five, beasts of the apocalypse.

Irenaeus however is by no means a unique example. Justin Martyr, Tatian, Theophilus, Athenagoras, Serapion, Pantaenus, Clement, Origen, Tertullian, Cyprian, and Eusebius, all of whom were early leaders in the church, offer variant and equally questionable opinions on what books should be considered legitimate. The basic point I want to make is that if you asked a dozen prominent Christians in the second and third century which books were authentic, you would receive a dozen different answers. Nearly two thousand years later, every one is much surer of something that they are further removed from and, quite frankly, know nothing about.

It was not even until the middle of the fourth century that the New Testament began to reflect its current form, and even then, Revelation was still widely considered inauthentic. To this very day, a number of Christian denominations disagree about which canon is the proper one. The Samaritan Old Testament has fewer books than the Protestant Old Testament, which has fewer books than the Slavonic Old Testament, which has fewer books than the Catholic Old Testament, which has fewer books than the Eastern Orthodox Old Testament, which has fewer books than the Ethiopic Orthodox Old Testament. The original Syrian New Testament has fewer books than the original Lutheran New Testament, which has fewer books than the Protestant New Testament, which has fewer books than original Armenian Orthodox New Testament, which has fewer books than the Ethiopic Orthodox New Testament. I trust that you understand the fundamental flaw with the blatantly uncertain Christian system.

Ironically, the very reason for setting the canon was to eliminate all of the books that were deemed inconsistent with what the early church already believed. This is no different from a farmer selectively breeding crops and livestock to obtain a certain consistency, and then declaring the consistency to be from some kind of supernatural intervention. Submitting McDowell's argument is a little like opening a box of crayons, examining the colors, carefully selecting a handful, and bragging about how harmonious the colors are. I am not completely denying the existence of some underlying theme in the Bible, but allow me to rephrase the apologetic assertion in a more appropriate fashion: *We should consider a series of books, chosen specifically for their consistency, as credible on the basis that they maintain consistency.* If this is what we are expected to swallow, it is quite possibly the dumbest idea I've ever heard. Could I not also collect a series of books with the same theme, especially where later authors had access to works of the previous ones, and claim that there is something equally magical to them? Millions of medical textbooks have been written for thousands of years all with the "theme" of improving patient health, yet why do I not try to claim that there is some divine inspiration behind this?

The Bible contains many fulfilled prophecies and could have only been inspired by God.

I challenge anyone to find a single verifiable prophecy fulfillment outside of those incredibly obvious to predict. As a few notable zealots have often resorted to altering clear meanings of specific terms or taking passages out of context in order to create biblical intent in lieu of their agendas, we will take a realistic approach toward studying one popular fulfillment in question so that you can better understand why the apologetic methods of interpretation are not reliable.

The Old Testament contains a seemingly endless list of scriptures that Christians point to as references for the foretelling of Christ. Since there is no reliable evidence that anyone can predict the future to a respectable degree of accuracy, the burden of proof is on those who assert that people capable of this gift once existed. As you should already be able to tentatively conclude that the Old Testament prophets were void of this talent, you might have quickly deduced that apologists have taken these verses out of context or ran some translatory manipulation on them in order to make the prophetical proposals feasible.

From my experiences, I have noted approximately fifty passages consistently used to support the quasi-reality of a fulfilled prophecy. Since a complete list of failed and poorly interpreted philosophies is, again, beyond the scope of this book, we'll analyze perhaps the most popular claim that biblical apologists offer in defense of prophecy realizations. The example is Isaiah 7:14, which reads, "A virgin shall conceive, and bear a son, and shall call his name Immanuel." The claim of a prophecy fulfillment in the verse fails miserably due to both the context and the content of the message.

Let us consider the content of Isaiah 7:14 first. In this passage, the King James Version (among others) produces the English word *virgin* from the Hebrew word *almah*. However, the most accurate term in the Hebrew language for conveying a sexually untouched woman is *betula*. *Almah* is a general term for a young woman, not necessarily a virgin. If Isaiah wanted his audience to believe that a virgin was going to give birth to a child, he had a much better word at his disposal. One would do well to think that he should utilize this more specific term for such a unique event so that his contemporaries wouldn't first have to know that he was invoking the much less anticipated, potentially vague, and patently contradictory meaning of *almah*. Furthermore, Proverbs 30:19 is extremely detrimental to the *virgin* translation of *almah*: "The way of an eagle in the air; the way of a serpent upon a rock; the way of a ship in the midst of the sea; and the way of a man with [an *almah*]." Since the term does not necessarily mean *virgin*, one must apply critical interpretation and look for the obvious connotation of the original Hebrew word. With this responsibility in mind, virgins do not have children. Thus the claim of fulfillment in Matthew 1:23 tried to relate the Immanuel birth to Jesus by altering the obvious content of the Old Testament prophecy.[254]

A second and seemingly more overlooked clue in the passage's content is the name of the child, Immanuel. To put it in the simplest of terms, Jesus' name wasn't Immanuel. The fact that Immanuel means "God with us" does not make one iota of difference because hundreds of Hebrew names contain references to God. For example, Abiah means "God is my father," which, in my opinion, would have been slightly more impressive. The verse plainly declares that she "shall call his name Immanuel," but the supposed Messiah's mother called him Jesus.

As for the contextual misapplication of Isaiah 7:14, one must read the chapter in its entirety since this supposed prophecy is part of a larger story. Within this passage, a battle is about to begin in which Rezin and Pekah are planning to attack Ahaz. God informs Ahaz that he may ask for a sign as proof that this battle will never ensue. Ahaz is reluctant to put God to a test, but Isaiah interjects and declares that there will be a sign. God will reaffirm his reliability on the issue when a young woman gives birth to a son named Immanuel who will eat butter and honey. Before this boy can choose evil over good, the land will fall out of the grip of Rezin and Pekah.

We can continue studying context by reading ahead to Isaiah 8:3-4, where we find a prophetess who has recently given birth to a son. This is immensely more likely to be the child that Isaiah wanted us to believe he predicted, especially when you figure in the fact that Isaiah 7:14 uses the more specific term *ha-almah*, translated as *the* woman, to specify a particular woman most likely known by the author and his audience.

When you consider the most accurate translation of *almah*, the actual name of the child, the context of the message, and the contiguous birth of an ordinary child, this passage is in a different ballpark from reports of Jesus' birth from his virgin mother. Even though the case for Isaiah 7:14 appears solidly shut, we should consider two more questions: 1) If Isaiah wanted to predict a virgin birth story, would he not have drawn more attention to the most important and unique event in human history? 2) If God were truly interested in convincing more people of Jesus' authenticity, would he not have Isaiah make a more direct and less disputable prophecy? Nevertheless, the gospels make the mistake, the Church continues to preach it, and an ignorant 83 percent of Americans continue to believe in this most preposterous of claims without ever investigating it.[255]

While we should not honestly expect a self-proclaimed prophet to have the ability to predict the future with any appreciable accuracy, there should be an elevated level of expectation for those who Christians tout as divinely inspired. The Old Testament prophets are nowhere near meeting this reasonable expectation. What we *do* see is a Nostradamus-like *post hoc* set of poor explanations and analyses undoubtedly designed to invent prophecy fulfillments. After we thoroughly analyze every supposed claim of prophecy fulfillment, we can conclude that not one of the prophets truly mentions anything interpretable as the supposed arrival of Jesus. Bits and pieces extracted from here and there do not add up to a verifiable resolution.

While there are no known suitable proofs for the existence or nonexistence of a supernatural entity, there *are* suitable proofs that supernatural entities cannot logically maintain some of the qualities often ascribed to the Judeo-Christian God. For example, while we may not be able to conclude that a supernatural creator doesn't exist within our universe, we *can* definitively say that it if it exists, it is not omnipotent. Allow me to propose this timeless question: Can God create a squared circle? By definition, a square cannot have the complete attributes of a circle, and vice-versa. It is not logically possible to create such an object, thus no power exists to make one. Therefore, an omnipotent entity, like the one described in Matthew 19:26,[256] cannot logically exist. After reading a previous argument similar to this, one reader wrote…

> *The presence of logical impossibilities does not rule out omnipotence because even a supply of unlimited power cannot do the logically impossible.*

Let's take this one step at a time. By definition, omnipotence is the quality of having unlimited power. It follows then that infinite power could accomplish an infinite number of logical results. To this point, we are in agreement. However, even though the apologist's interpretation of omnipotence lies outside the ability of doing the logically impossible, we can still say that the omnipotent being lacks the power to enter into the domain of logical impossibility and offset the logical rules forbidding logically impossible actions. Since no being can enter or create a separate realm void of logic, omnipotence cannot exist. Our alternative is to declare that logic is an obstacle that God cannot overcome.

If God's defenders want to state that God can do anything as long as it is not logically impossible or self-contradictory, that is fine, hypothetically speaking, even though we never see such feats that would plunge the world into chaos and non-causality. However, this acceptance yet again excludes God from truly being omnipotent because God lacks the power to suspend the rules of logic that God himself somehow had the power to create! If God cannot undo the rules of logic, rewrite the rules of logic, and do otherwise impossible things, his powers are limited, and he is therefore short of omnipotence because logic constrains him. Furthermore, if the apologist wants to maintain his belief by deciding that logic and causality preceded God or that logic is inseparable from God, what then do we call logic itself? Just because an apologist might claim that an omnipotent god is exempt from the logically impossible, he does not make it so.

A similar conclusion we can draw from analytical thinking is that an all-knowing entity necessitates an unalterable future, which in turn necessitates an absence of free will. Thus, in order to establish a necessary relationship between omniscience and a lack of free will, we must link each to a certain future. We can reasonably assume that there will be no disagreement with the first half of the argument: God, an omniscient being, knows the future for certain. Otherwise, we would immediately have to disregard the existence of omniscience. The aspect to which many apologists would object is the notion that a certain future disqualifies free will. After all, the apologist could argue…

> *Just because God knows what you are going to do, it doesn't mean he has made the choice for you.*

Has he not? If the future is set and known with absolute certainty, I do not see how it can be changed; and if it cannot be changed, the future has already been determined. For example, if God knows I am going to be involved in a car accident tomorrow, I will necessarily be involved in a car accident. I cannot avoid getting into the car accident because God has already envisioned it happening. If I were somehow able to avoid the incident, God would be wrong, which is a violation of his omniscience. While there is not necessarily any divine "control" over my actions, I could not help but choose the actions I took that led to the car accident. God already knew what choice I would make, and since choosing otherwise would violate his omniscience, there was really only one choice to begin with. Free will would therefore be an illusion.[257]

This understanding is why, albeit on a much less sophisticated level, the Puritans believed in predestination. After all, if you are born with God knowing whether you are going to heaven or hell, what steps could you possibly take to change your destination? And one more question: If God has complete knowledge of the future, is he powerless to change it? If he can change what he knows is the future, he eliminates his omniscience. If he cannot change what he knows is the future, he eliminates his omnipotence. We have only touched the tip of the iceberg with respect to all of the logical violations that an infinite deity would create, but this should be sufficient to demonstrate that the Judeo-Christian God cannot exist in his biblically described form.

All of the most popular reasons offered for the existence of a higher power fail. If we were to continue this exercise by considering every single proof offered of a supernatural existence, we could safely conclude that while there may be valid yet untestable reasons for believing in a higher power, there are currently no valid proofs supporting its existence. This finding is especially true of the Judeo-Christian God, which is not supported by the Consistency Argument, Prophecy Argument, or any other popular argument. We can even begin to rule out the existence of the Judeo-Christian God analytically based on some of the logically impossible infinite attributes ascribed to it.

Even if we were able to prove the existence of the Judeo-Christian God or any other unknowable god, Sagan offers a valid point. If a person argues that there is a dragon is his garage–but we arrive only to find an apparently empty room due to the dragon's invisibility and incorporeality–what is the difference between this dragon and no dragon at all?[258] In the same manner, if one of these purported proofs actually demonstrated unquestionably that there is a god, what difference does it make if the god does not and cannot interact with the natural world? Furthermore, how do we define or describe this being with all of its nonattributes? What we are given is that "God exists" without explaining what God is–only what God is not. Smith elaborates on this problem:

> If God is described solely in terms of negation, it is impossible to distinguish him from nonexistence… God is not matter; neither is nonexistence. God does not have limitations; neither does nonexistence. God is not visible; neither is nonexistence. God does not change; neither does nonexistence. God cannot be described; neither can nonexistence. And so on down the list of negative predicates. If the theist wishes to distinguish his belief in God from the belief in nothing at all, he must have positive substance to the concept of God.[259]

A Comparison Of Methods

This section contains a number of the critiques I have received regarding the methods I've used or decisions I've made to draw my conclusions on the validity of the Bible. To demonstrate just how backwards I believe this proposal to be, I have also included a section containing some examples of what I think are very poor methods that apologists use in defense of their own positions. I shall let the readers decide which party makes the better case.

> *Christianity is a belief, and since it is only a belief, there is no need to fight over whether it is true.*

This is the most frequent argument I receive, and I personally believe it is because religious people understand on some level that their beliefs are mostly indefensible and completely nonsensical. I find it quite convenient that followers of a religion want to hide behind some magical esoteric cloud that only others who share such beliefs will understand. Reason can fortunately see right through this attempted evasion. Claims should not go untested simply because they are important to someone, and religions do not get immunity from examination just because they are beliefs.

Being a belief does not take a proposition outside the realm of logic. If I "believe" that the sum of two plus two is equal to four, my belief is either true or false. If I "believe" that the world is a few thousand years old, my belief is either true or false. If I "believe" that Jesus rose from the dead, my belief is either true or false. If I "believe" that the Judeo-Christian God exists, my belief is either true or false. There is no sort of middle ground here. Since the results of empirical study are often extremely embarrassing to those who hold religious beliefs, they feel that the evidence should not be admitted–or even considered–because their religion is merely a "belief." If the results were beneficial to them, however, I guarantee that this evidence would be touted as justification for worshipping their god(s) of choice.

> *All humans look at things from what they know and write based upon this. You say that the Gospels differ in certain ways. This should be true based upon the human element "point-of-view." Even today if you have a car accident, every eyewitness account of the accident will vary.*

At the risk of sounding too blunt, this is a tired old argument that does not appreciate its own ramifications. The contradictions are not resolved–reasons are given for them. Something either *did* happen or *did not* happen. Details differ because different people recall them differently or create them differently. The details are either correct (consistent with reality) or incorrect (inconsistent with reality). This is a good demonstration of the lack of divine inspiration with the texts. What kind of all-powerful being, if it wanted anything to do with the Bible, would allow erroneous detail in his message to the world? Such a suggestion is absurd nonsense.

I would not go so far as to say that the gospel events didn't happen based solely on this observation, but the disagreement on key points (not simple points) is indicative of urban legend. As rumor spreads from person to person, each will typically add or subtract details from the last version. Furthermore, I completely agree with the reader's objection as it applies to everyday phenomena. The details of such stories, if they took place, will differ for various reasons. The insurmountable problem is trying to draw some sort of congruency between divine inspiration and human flaws when they supposedly appear in the same text. God had and still has unlimited opportunity to ensure the absence of contradiction, write the text himself, or tell us the story directly any time we request, but for some strange reason, God does not operate like this. He instead chooses to operate in the same manner as every other imaginary supernatural being from the ages of antiquity–in unverifiable secrecy. I suppose I will never understand why Christians will not accept the ramifications of this.

> *I could make two opposing websites and each one could be equally convincing. Not because the information is true or false, just because it's easy to rip apart people, their beliefs, and their ideas.*

I would disagree with this notion wholeheartedly. For instance, if one were to make a website defending a spherical earth and another defending a flat earth, each with the best evidence available, I hardly believe that each website would be equally convincing. There is good evidence for only one belief.

The writer's bad assertion here will help me make a critical point. Those who are unwilling to consider that the earth is flat will find justifications for believing it is spherical; those who are unwilling to consider that the earth is spherical will find justifications for believing it is flat; and those who hold no emotional investments in such beliefs will side with the party who has the best evidence (the spherical earth, of course). The same goes for religious affiliations. Those who are unwilling to consider that the Bible is divine will find justifications for believing it is fallible; those who are unwilling to consider that the Bible is fallible will find justifications for believing it is divine; and those who hold no emotional investments in such beliefs will side with the party who has the best evidence (the fallible Bible).

I would further disagree with the position that it is easy to rip apart beliefs and ideas. I believe it is easy to rip apart false beliefs and bad ideas, but not true beliefs and good ideas. If my belief is that one should do what is fair, just, and for the greater good, can a valid argument be raised that we should do just the opposite? If I state that molecules are composed of atoms, is it easy to rip apart such an idea? One can surely try to dismantle such strong positions, but will the objections withstand intense scrutiny? Good ideas and true beliefs are not easy to rip apart because empirical evidence or solid argumentation often supports them.

> *Truly wise students of the Bible leave room for the possibility of error in their own comprehension unless backed up by reliable sources and accurate knowledge.*

I would suggest that the truly wise would leave room for the possibility of error in their own comprehension indefinitely. It would be a huge mistake to assume that one's original unbiased conclusion would always stand the test of new evidence. Not that people join religion as a product of critical and impartial thought, but if they did, they should be willing to consider new ideas and interpretations that contradict even their most important beliefs. If reliable sources and accurate knowledge back the original position of the student, then his position is more likely to be the correct one. If he simply states that it is not possible he is wrong because he is backed by authority, which is what the writer's argument essentially states, the student makes an intellectual fool of himself. The psychological mistake that religious apologists make is that they begin with the premise of being correct, seek out the selective evidence that supports their premise, and remain within the confines of these beliefs indefinitely. It is most depressing to see otherwise intelligent people become victims of their preconceived notions.

> *You seem to have a problem with Christians worshipping God and reading the Bible.*

The inverse of the latter assessment is true because I wholeheartedly support Christians reading the Bible. As I mentioned earlier, I would almost suggest that Bible study should be a part of the public high school curriculum. I have always said that if more people read the Bible, less people would believe it. The existence of ignorant self-professed Christians attempting to impose certain biblical principles on society through misinformation is the problem I see. I have met more Christians who could not name the four gospels than ones who could, yet they are equally devout to the notion that the Bible is a product of divine inspiration. Furthermore, most Christians do not worship and know nothing about the Judeo-Christian God; and I have no problems with people worshipping benign ideas however they choose. I do however have a problem with those who teach their children about the validity of the Bible and the god therein. Most Christians do not know anything about God because extremely few of them read the Bible (more specifically the Old Testament) much less study it in any intense manner. They worship the god that they hear about in church–not the strangely gender-assigned one who spends his time giving instructions for trivial superstitious rituals rather than pertinent information for proving his existence, ceasing religious wars, or assisting his creations in their daily lives.

Furthermore, most of my writing does not deal with mainstream Christianity, and this much should be obvious to discerning readers. I've often argued that mainstream Christianity should essentially be renamed Salad Bar Christianity since almost all Christians pick and choose the parts of the Bible that they want to follow and ignore the parts that they don't like. After mainstream Christians make a dish of the religion that they prefer, they pass their conclusions down to their children who, in turn, pick and choose from those beliefs before passing them on. This practice is so rampant that the overwhelming majority of those who call themselves Christian know next to nothing about the Bible. I have no problem with those who follow only the better principles of the book, but the notion that something is moral or factual just because supporting passages can be found in the Bible directly contradicts the practice of Salad Bar Christianity (not to mention ethical behavior as a whole).

How do you know *that you're right about the Bible being wrong?*

I never claim to *know* that I am correct in my conclusions. I admit this much on a regular basis. I do not *know* that fairies do not exist either, but I can be *reasonably sure* based on the lack of evidence and known hoaxes throughout history that they do not. Smith handles this question about doubting human conclusions well:

> Doubt is not justified merely on the grounds that you can somehow "imagine" that you are mistaken. If in the face of such overwhelming evidence you wish to

> doubt the correctness of your judgment, then you must provide *reasons* for your doubt. If your skepticism [pertaining to human conclusions] is to be more than empty rambling, you must justify your doubt. This must consist of specifying why, in our particular circumstance, there is reason to suppose that our perceptual judgment is in error. Doubt cannot be applied indiscriminately; it arises *contextually* in specific circumstances when there is reason to suppose that we may be mistaken.[260]

Smith illustrates his position by drawing a contrast between doubts about the existence of a lake spotted in the desert (a situation in which there is good reason to be skeptical) and doubts about the existence of a lake in which one is currently swimming (a situation in which there is no good reason to be skeptical). In the same manner, scientific errors, historical mistakes, and other absurdities in the Bible led me to my conclusion about this particular version of a creator. Demanding that I defend what I believe is also a logically fallacious attempt to shift the burden of proof on the disbeliever. Even so, I am more than happy to explain what I believe and why I believe it.

If my conclusions appear wrong based on further evidence or alternate avenues of thought, my beliefs and thoughts change. My position is not religiously dogmatic. It is essential to note that those who make the positive claims are saddled with the burden of proof. I am most certainly wrong about a few things regarding the Bible. I have been wrong before, and I will probably be wrong again. This is the scientific method: forming tentative explanations, testing ideas, gathering data, and making rational conclusions based on those tasks. Due to the problems that I have noticed with the texts, I think the stories found in Greek mythology are just as likely to be true as those in the Bible. In sum, both have a seemingly insurmountable amount of explaining to do.

The level of evidence against the Bible is overwhelming, and that is astronomically unlikely to change. Will those on the other side admit to any chance at all, however minute, that they are wrong? Will they admit that God might not exist? The presumed responses to these two simple questions speak volumes about which party is the more rational and open-minded of the two. People simply find comfort in premature certainty when faced with the currently inexplicable.

> *I noticed a statement in your conclusion where you require counter arguments to be "probable" solutions. I'm left wondering how that should be defined. You seem to discount anything supernatural from "probability." To me, that's illogical. If God exists, then supernatural causes are probable. And by definition they will not be (fully) subject to human or even standard physical analysis. How are we to define "probable" in such a situation?*

Readers have criticized me more than once for demanding that apologetic responses be probable solutions to problems that I have presented. We should define "probable" in this sense as the most likely explanation for a question. If the Bible has an apparent conflict, is it more likely that it is the result of human error, or is the apologetic explanation of the apparent conflict more likely to be the author's intent?

Until we have evidence that anything in the supernatural exists, it is only appropriate to consider it improbable. Simply assuming that improbable things would be probable if God exists is no more logically coherent than beginning with the premise that God exists. If God is supernaturally altering a scientific experiment to provide different results, or if magical unicorns are altering a scientific experiment to provide different results, we have no way of knowing if there is a natural way to measure it. We can observe one as much as the other. If we beg the question of God's existence, or the existence of magical unicorns, then supernatural explanations become probable. Since we can plead for the existence of any supernatural entity we wish, we must first prove that one exists before attributing it to data gathered through observation.

Would the author of the preceding critique agree that it is not "probable" that Zeus, Allah, Vishnu, etc. carried out the steps necessary to make apologists of those respective religions give reasonable responses to problems presented? The Christian apologist shallowly and uncritically appeals to the "special" nature of his religion and commits the special pleading fallacy by only considering his god's existence while ignoring the balance of other deities. He wants us to consider that miracles are probable if God exists, but he fails to see that we can apply this line of reasoning to an infinite number of supernatural explanations. Just as the gods worshipped by the Romans, Greeks, Hindus, etc. are self-evidently ridiculous to the Jews and Christians, so is the Judeo-Christian God to anyone who has not fallen victim to the indoctrination of its existence. Mills elaborates with a nice example pertaining to the improbability of Jesus' resurrection:

> Suppose that I were standing near Kennedy's grave at Arlington National Cemetery, and the ground suddenly opened up revealing a coffin. I see the casket opening, and a man who looks exactly like John Kennedy sits up and walks away. Even under these bizarre circumstances, it is still more probable that: (a) I am misperceiving what is occurring, or (b) that something is playing an ingenious trick, or (c) that I am witnessing the filming of a movie, or (d) that I am dreaming, or (e) that the man I saw was not actually John Kennedy, or (f) that someone has slipped me a hallucinogenic drug, or (g) that I have fallen victim to psychosis or (h) that I am completely fabricating this story. Any of these explanations is infinitely more plausible than the assertion that John Kennedy genuinely rose from the dead. These explanations are more plausible even when I claim to be an eyewitness to the event. Whenever miraculous tales are secondhand or, like Scripture, are handed down from generation to generation, the veracity of the original stories is forever untestable and is thus unworthy of serious consideration. A naturalistic explanation–however far-fetched it seems–is invariably more likely to be accurate than a supernatural explanation.[261]

You have conflated appeals to legitimate authority, which carry much value, with appeals to illegitimate authority, which have no value.

I do not believe that I have ever done so. We can use appeals to authority that meet certain criteria as a supportive argument. It does not mean that something is necessarily true. If one wishes to argue a point, one needs to submit the argument that defends the point. If your only argument is that so-and-so person or number of people agree with your position, that is a weak argument. It does not even attempt to deal with the evidence. For instance, as I stated earlier, recent surveys indicate that over 99 percent of earth scientists believe that the planet is billions of years old. I make note of this statistic in my previous work, but I do not rest my argument on the earth's antiquity there. It is a legitimate appeal to authority, but I do not offer that the position is right on the sole basis of this statistic. Even with overwhelming support, I still took a lot of time to explain their arguments and explain why counterarguments are incorrect.

In any case, let me ask the readers a question so that I can really put this notion to the test. The vast majority of scientists report data that consistently yield an age of the earth in the billions of years. How would Young Earth Creationists feel if, instead of discussing the issue with them, I just kept asserting that they were wrong, that they knew nothing on the issue, and that they need to read articles written by legitimate authorities?[262] This is essentially what many have attempted to do when writing me–with the roles reversed–even though they are in the dwarfed minority.

Appealing to authority can be problematic enough, but people have an incredible innate tendency to submit to authority much more readily than they should. The Milgram study, an endeavor to determine exactly how much torture one individual is willing to inflict on another at the commands of an authority figure, is perhaps the best example of this phenomenon. The research team discovered that of the forty subjects involved, not one of them refused to deliver shocks to an innocent person after that person cried out in agony and demanded to be released from the experiment. Milgram explains by arguing that there is a sense of duty to authority within us deep enough to make the subjects willing to tremble, shake, perspire, agonize, dig their fingernails into their flesh, fall into fits of uncontrollable nervous laughter, and bite their lips until they bleed over their decisions to continue.[263] The ones receiving the shocks wanted to stop; the ones giving the shocks wanted to stop; the authorities simply gave the order to continue. If people are willing to submit physically to perceived authority to this degree, I find no trouble in believing that people will intellectually submit to perceived authority to a similar level of irrational degree, especially when that authority is providing information to their liking. Cialdini elaborates further and relates to a topic we discussed several chapters ago:

> Conforming to the dictates of authority figures has always had genuine practical advantages for us. Early on, these people (for example, parents, teachers) knew more than we did, and we found that taking their advice proved beneficial–partly because of their greater wisdom and partly because they controlled our rewards and punishments...It makes great sense to comply with the wishes of properly constituted authorities. It makes so much sense, in fact, that we often do so when it makes no sense at all...Once we realize that obedience to authority is mostly rewarding, it is easy to allow ourselves the convenience of automatic obedience. The simultaneous blessing and bane of such blind obedience is mechanical character. We don't have to think; therefore, we don't. Although such mindless obedience leads us to appropriate action in the great majority of cases, there will be conspicuous exceptions–because we are reacting rather than thinking.[264]

> *God shouldn't have to appear to every generation to maintain the life of our faith.*

I agree that it is unnecessary for God to appear in order to maintain the religion, but that is not the point I am trying to make when I note the convenient absence of God in the age of enlightenment and scientific scrutiny. The point is that some people will consider the matter critically and consequently expect evidence of such extraordinary claims. How do we know we are angering *God A* who exists, but not *God B* who does not exist? If we are to just take the matter on faith, why should we give credibility to one religion over another? Simply saying that we should believe in a certain god because he appeared to those before us is not an answer. Anyone can, and often did, make such a claim. If the Judeo-Christian God exists and wants us to believe in him, I only ask for definitive proof that he exists. If the Judeo-Christian God exists and wants us to believe in him based solely on faith, I only ask for a definitive argument as to why I should have faith in him instead of a different god.

It is this person's argument that God should not have to appear to everyone, and it is my duty to point out that God decided to appear at many points in the past for meaningless reasons. God appeared when he wanted to give directions for making curtains to go in his temple,[265] but he neglected to appear to Hitler and prevent the deaths of millions of his chosen people. God appeared when he wanted to have a wrestling match with Jacob,[266] but he neglected to appear when thousands of African children starved to death last week. God appeared when he wanted people put to death for working on the Sabbath,[267] but he neglected to appear during the Crusades when thousands of people were killing each other over who had the right religion. The reason to question comes not from God's decision to appear only at select times, but rather from the timing itself.

> *Following Jesus is not about "religion" but about a love relationship. I hope you've heard that idea stated many times in your life.*

Following Muhammad is not about "religion" but about a love relationship with Allah. This argument is equally valid because the speaker presumes the authority and veracity of his premise. As many Christians are aware that religion is inherently ridiculous and weak against scrutiny, they attempt to rid it of those shackles and make it something more reasonable. Some Young Earth Creationists even refer to Darwinian evolution by natural selection as a religion, typically under the name of Darwinism. The depressing part of this apologetic argument, however, is the number of times such universal arguments find their way to my inbox. Once again, any statement capable of being recycled by another religion never qualifies as evidence.

> *Any thinking person can make the same observations, but truly intelligent people don't completely dismiss the Bible.*

While I do not completely dismiss the entire biblical text, I doubt that this apologetic assertion can be widely defended. The meta-study analyses we reviewed earlier contain a number of studies that examined the relationship between levels of intelligence and levels of religiousness. What we observe is that the more intelligence a person exhibits, the more anti-religious a person tends to become. Whether increasing anti-religiousness leads to decreasing credibility given to the Bible is a question I cannot answer, but seeing as how increasing animosity against religion and increasing skepticism about the Bible seem to go hand in hand, I feel very comfortable speculating that my hypothesis is valid. I would assert that "truly intelligent people" realize that the Bible is a human document with serious flaws among some valid points, but they do not try to make poor justifications and absurd rationalizations for those flaws in order to make it fit with preconceived notions.

> *The basic content of your book heavily weighs in with me, but the difference between us is that I choose not to rush to judgment on such an important matter as God and the eternal truth of our existence.*

Rush to judgment? Is it truly a rush to judgment to conclude with great confidence that a position is likely incorrect when there is no evidence to support it and much counterevidence to dispute it? Do people with this position consider hundreds of other religious texts to be on the same level as the Bible and give them equal time before declaring that the Bible is the only valid work of divinity? Most people will not consider any text beyond the one that their society deems as special; an extremely select few will consider two or three more from other major religions; but virtually no one will consider all of them. That is what I call a rush to judgment.

We must remember that we do not need to have an answer for a problem before we start eliminating possibilities. For moderate and liberal Christian thinkers who have left fundamentalism behind, their erroneous consideration of a significant Bible drives their beliefs. Moreover, they never truly attempt to determine exactly to what extent the Bible is supposedly significant. As sure as I am that the earth revolves around the sun, I believe that objective people will look at the complete biblical picture and consider the book to be of no more value than any other ancient religious text, but rather much luckier in its survival.

> *It's preposterous for the created to imagine that we can observe and test every aspect of reality!*

It is most certainly not absurd because scientific study is the testing and observation of all natural phenomena. Without begging the question of supernatural existence, which this statement does since it deems us as "created," how can one argue that it is impossible to observe and test our reality? Are there things we cannot know yet? Absolutely. Are there things we may never know? Absolutely. Does this mean that we cannot reasonably eliminate logically absurd possibilities and suggestions like magical unicorns, talking donkeys, the Judeo-Christian God, and any other countless supernatural deities raised by countless individuals over the centuries? Why resort to supernatural explanations when they are not testable? Better yet, why use a supernatural explanation when a natural one will do?

An understanding of the physical universe in natural terms explains many of what would otherwise be life's mysteries. If anyone supporting this individual's suggestion provides one solid reason why we should consider the supernatural as an explanation for something in the natural world, this will change naturalistic philosophy as we know it. You just cannot beg the question of the supernatural and complain when naturalistic methods of questioning do not follow your prematurely supposed premise. As Mills explains, "Such 'logic' is identical to 'proving' Batman's existence by citing the eyewitness testimony of Robin, the Boy wonder."[268]

A handful of people have repeatedly demanded that I must be

able to solve all of the problems answered by Christianity if I expect them to abandon it, but my position is that such problems are often unanswerable at the present. My position is also irrelevant to whether or not the Bible is true and, therefore, irrelevant to the subject of my writings. Suggesting otherwise is creating a logically fallacious false dichotomy of Christian Theism versus my opinion, which also borders on a logically fallacious shift of the burden of proof. An opinion is not a required prerequisite for eliminating possibilities. I have never understood why humans are so uncomfortable with the answer "I don't know." Claims of ultimate knowledge are the property of cults; and Christianity fits many of the characterizations of a cult. In it, we see veneration, inerrancy, and omniscience of the leader Jesus Christ; coercive promises of the afterlife; absolute truth and morality; etc.[269] Scientific skepticism displays none of these.

One individual suggested that I was being nothing more than insulting when I called certain Christians ignorant or stubborn, but I'm not exactly sure where the insult lies. While the two designations seem to have politically unacceptable connotations, I use both descriptors in terms of their strictest definitions. If I believed that a herd of ten-pound elephants knitting cashmere sweaters on the surface of Jupiter created the earth, and if I refused to budge from my position regardless of the counterarguments offered, am I anything but stubborn and ignorant? Would the author defend me as readily if this were my position? Should I require that people disprove my belief or else give it proper respect? Should I declare that those who endeavor to prove these elephants should consider their existence and nonexistence equally since they cannot disprove them out of hand?

Besides, I often defend Christians throughout my writings while blaming the Bible and human psychology for their misguidance. I also think calling the majority of them stubborn and ignorant is a relatively mild offense compared with what some readers have hit me. For instance, one wanted to know why I am "so full of hate" and "trying to take it out on the only decent belief system the world has to give people hope." I wonder if this bigoted individual would consider me full of hate if I attempted to demonstrate the fraudulent nature of Islam or some other religion to which she did not belong. Another called my work "arrogant," insinuating that it takes an act of self-important pride to admit that you don't know which religion, if any, offers the correct view of the world. Preaching that you know the truth and were born into the truth, all the while claiming that there is no other truth, on the other hand, should not be regarded as arrogant. The hypocrisy found within some of my negative feedback is simply astounding.

But enough with the claims that my methods of argumentation are erroneous. I think it's only fair that we now investigate what some of my readers have attempted to pass off as "reasoning."

The Bible is true because God had a hand in writing it.

There are, of course, a variety of opinions as to exactly how much God participated in the creation of his holy word. These suggestions range anywhere from God ambiguously "inspiring" the authors while they were writing–to God dictating verbatim what he wanted in his manuscript, even straight through to the English King James Version in 1611.[270] Since just about anyone can find and interpret just about anything in the Bible to support a particular viewpoint, I am confident that people in every camp of thought could find textual justification for their respective positions on the subject of divine inspiration. After all, people are typically not the least bit interested in searching for evidence that disconfirms their beliefs. The majority of unbiased persons who hold the knowledge of a former religious follower turned freethinker, on the other hand, would not dare defend the unsighted belief that an omniscient and omnipotent being inspired the Bible, much less had a direct hand in writing it.

There is an extremely long list of objective reasons why we should not regard the Bible to be any more inspired than the hundreds of other ancient texts that came from the Ancient Near East. We should consider, above all, the superstitious age in which it was written, its failure to differentiate itself significantly from other contemporaneous mythological works, and the patently absurd claims of the Bible itself.

> *Of course if you look at the Bible presuming it is false and impossible (i.e. not even considering "what if it were true?") then nothing you read in it will be convincing.*

No matter how many times I explain this, it keeps popping up. "What if it were true?" is not the correct first question to ask. "Is it true?" would be a much more appropriate place to begin. I have addressed the remainder of the argument before. I did not begin my analysis by presuming it was false and impossible–in sharp contrast to defenders of the Bible who regularly begin by presuming that the book has validity. I began by searching for the truth and forming conclusions based on gathered information. Any person with no religious dogma to defend who begins an analysis on a work equally as ridiculous as the Bible, regardless of what religious message it offers, will come to the same conclusion. It is also incorrect to suggest that if one finds a work false, then there is nothing in it that we can consider convincing toward a specific viewpoint. But amazingly, look what the same person offered in the very next sentence of his complaint…

> *If we start off by assuming that the Bible is true, your entire body of work becomes evidence for the veracity of the Bible.*

"If we start off by assuming that the Bible is true," then we commit a strict violation of scientific principle. If we want to be this unscientific and start off by assuming that the Bible is true, my entire body of work can actually work either for *or against* the veracity of the Bible. If I offer evidence that does not agree with the assumption, the position that the Bible is true becomes weakened. If I offer evidence that does agree with the assumption, the position that the Bible is true becomes strengthened. Asserting that any evidence, regardless of the evidence, supports a proposition is epistemologically ridiculous. The writer should have just as well said, "If we start off by assuming that Hinduism is true, the Bible becomes evidence for the veracity of Hinduism." It would have been just as logically consistent if he had done so.

If one studies the Bible determined for it to be true, one will likely come away believing it is true. If one studies the Bible determined for it to be false, one will likely come away believing it is false. This goes for any book, any field, any belief, and any discipline. It is part of the human psychology that I spent so much time discussing. Since the utilization of such a disastrous discipline will only yield results that are consistent with preconceived notions, one should impartially study subjects to reach unbiased conclusions on them.

My views are not easily biased; I base them on what the authors wrote in the text. If someone presents a better translation or interpretation of that text, I am more than open to accepting it. I have no dogma to defend. Apologists will typically defend inerrancy and the like no matter how grim their situation. Conditions around me play no discernable part in the conclusions that I have made about the book. I have read the Bible, studied what it means, and arrived at conclusions that are unavoidable to anyone who is not trying to defend what they have been programmed with since childhood. If Christianity were just another weird religion practiced by a few thousand, no one would give it a second thought.

> *Just like if you start off by assuming that only psychological glitches and conditioning keep people believing in God, they will all be evidence for the power of conditioning and mental repression. Presuppositions make all the difference.*

This is a straw man because I offer no such idea. People believe in god(s) for a variety of reasons. The primary reason for a person's religion is the importance that the person's environment places on it. Bias, conditioning, and dissonance are strong factors in people not wanting to change their deepest beliefs, religious or otherwise. These extremely well documented phenomena are the cornerstones of persuasive psychology. The fact that they exist and play a strong role in decision-making is not in doubt. Most religious beliefs are inherently ridiculous, and the findings of persuasive psychology establish the reason for the beliefs. My conclusions, which are not presuppositions, follow my observations. The same cannot be said for the apologists.

> *You state that it is interesting no historians mention Jesus. Would not Jesus be a rather local phenomenon?*

It is true that Jesus did not travel widely, his emergence was of short duration, people were highly illiterate, and the word was spread mainly by the Apostles. However, historical stories of feeding five thousand people with a single plate of food, raising the dead, healing the blind, exorcising demons, walking on water, rising from the dead, and walking around with five hundred zombies with countless witnesses would hardly remain local for several decades. Think about what this man supposedly accomplished, and then consider how long it took the historians to record it. After that, look at mundane details that the historians of the era actually did record and consider how little time passed between the occurrence and documentation. It would be no different from the New York Times choosing to write about a kitten getting caught in a tree on the same day that someone assassinated the president. Such a decision would not make sense.

Why not consider the Apostles to be historians?

I would respond by asking what the Apostles wrote. No unbiased scholars and hardly any Christian scholars maintain that the Apostles wrote the gospels. The same goes for the decision to date these texts as anything earlier than the late first century.[271] And why not consider works like the Gospels of Peter, James, and Thomas if we're going to consider the Gospels of Matthew and John? If we take the leap and consider the gospel writers to be historians rather than worshippers who wrote merely to persuade, the further contradictions of non-canonical gospels destroy New Testament reliability. Even if we were to grant that the canonical gospels are historical documents, Matthew and Luke are clearly plagiarized from Mark and thus can hardly be considered novel works.[272] Matthew, in particular, relied heavily upon Mark except when it needed to correct the many patent mistakes with the earlier text.[273]

Given the fanciful details contained within the hundreds of ancient religions throughout the world, we can only surmise that urban legends were clearly alive and well two thousand years ago. As time passes, exaggerations blend with facts to create legends. Mark is the gospel considered least temporally removed from the events described, and it is consequently the least fanciful. In the first chapter of Mark, we see less substantial healings than the parallel versions found in the other synoptic gospels. In the sixth chapter, we find a Jesus who is unable to perform miracles because of the disbelief in the crowd. In the original ending of the sixteenth chapter, we do not hear from a resurrected Jesus, but rather testimony from a man at the tomb that they can find Jesus in Galilee.[274] Who is the man making this assertion? How does he know Jesus is in Galilee? Is he speaking of a physical resurrection? Do we have good reason to believe he is speaking symbolically or metaphorically? We don't know the answers to any of these questions because the story abruptly ends.

Later gospels embellish the story, turning the man into an angel and extending the story of the empty tomb into a divine encounter. Just as the urban legends of today's age grow to incredible proportions by word of mouth (or email) in a matter of days, it is the only logical conclusion that we are witnessing the same phenomenon in the gospels. A few decades in a highly superstitious era are more than adequate for the story to evolve to ridiculous status. People in this relatively enlightened age will believe just about anything in a week if they hear it enough.

Why would Jesus and the Apostles die for a lie?

People have died for lies, people have died for the truth, people have died for what they thought was the truth, people have been reported to die for a belief when they probably were not martyred at all, and people have been reported to exist when they may never have. The burden of proof is on the believer here to demonstrate that the Apostles were martyred for their beliefs. The reason that many Christians believe that the Apostles were martyred is the say-so of the New Testament, but if we are simply to accept New Testament reports that people were becoming martyrs for their Christian beliefs, why not simply accept the New Testament report that God resurrected Jesus from the dead? One step is just as logical as the next. For this reason, we must rely on extrabiblical reports to weigh the veracity of purported widespread apostolic martyrdom. Such reports are often unverifiable, inconsistent, and contradictory. The various traditions surrounding the death of Matthew are perhaps the greatest example.[275]

> *If you are right, and there is no Judeo-Christian God, or maybe no God at all, you may or may not know after death if you are right. But if you are wrong you will know forever. I have doubted, but decided the same thing you should. It is not worth risking Hell.*

In other words, we should believe in God, even if it is unlikely, because it is not worth the risk of being wrong. This is a very dated, yet still very popular, apologetic argument known as Pascal's Wager. It essentially argues that we should believe in the Judeo-Christian God because: 1) We gain nothing for saying that he does not exist and being right. 2) We lose everything for saying that he does not exist and being wrong. 3) We lose nothing for saying that he does exist and being wrong. 4) We gain everything for saying that he does exist and being right. In short, we only lose or break even for not believing, and we only win or break even for believing.

For several reasons, most forward thinking Christians abandoned Pascal's line of reasoning shortly after it was developed. Above all other reasons, Pascal's Wager is a false dichotomy, which is the erroneous belief that there are only two possible outcomes for a question. Pascal ignores a plethora of other possibilities. For instance, what if Islam is the right religion? In this scenario, God punishes Christians for blasphemy and the non-religious for denial. However, what if an unknown ancient European religion without an afterlife was the right one? In this instance, we will all go through our lives and eventually die, but some of us will have wasted absolutely everything on a delusion. As there are countless religious possibilities, it is not as simple as Pascal would like us to believe.

It is also incorrect to suggest that we gain nothing by abandoning false belief and superstition. Instead of wasting time in practices that are unnecessary, we can live increasingly productive lives that offer some sort of benefit to humanity. If you think about it, productivity costs from downtime in large corporations can reach into the millions; religion has been consistently occupying human thought for centuries. What if just 1 percent of the time spent on religion throughout history had instead been spent on scientific research? I think even many *Christians* would agree that we would be far better off than we are now.

Since one cannot help believing what one believes, it would be interesting to hear Pascal explain how we should utilize his practice. Moreover, why would an omnipotent creator consider our beliefs in him to be a more important attribute than our desires to improve the human race? Should our fellow man not require more attention than an all-powerful god? The Judeo-Christian God is petty in more ways than I could ever hope to count.

We should start reading the Bible knowing before we open even the first page that there are no mistakes.

The worst thing we can ever do to solve the question of the Bible's veracity is to follow an absurd suggestion drenched in misology. Replace "Bible" with "Qur'an" or any other holy document and you achieve equally disastrous results. This vicious abuse of reason is precisely how scores of religions have continued to survive for centuries. People across the globe consistently convince themselves that their holy books are infallible before they even open them. Smith said it best, "It makes no sense to accept the idea first and then search for evidence to support it. This is rationalization, not rationality."[276]

I certainly do not propose that the questions I raise have never been contemplated by Christians. The problem lies with their process of thinking through the potential problems. The vast majority will be consumed with confirmation bias and only look for answers confirming the validity and benevolence of the Bible. Most Christians will only look for an answer that satisfies the question the way that they want it to be satisfied. As I previously mentioned that creationists only look for answers to confirm Genesis, many doubting Christians will seek advice only from sources that will confirm the Bible. Once an individual gains the ability to look at the situation without a confirmation bias, it will become obvious that the book is one of hundreds that falls short of its claims.

Who needs textual analysis when you have God's divinely inspired Word as your evidence?

The ignorance is just nauseating. I thought that the statement immediately preceding this one was the worst example I was going to be able to include until this little jewel arrived shortly before I was going to release the book for publishing. I could elaborate forever on the absurdity of such a question, but if you have not received sufficient benefit from previous arguments in this section, chances are that a reasoned response to this question would not be of any considerable value to your psychological welfare.

On Christian Morality

The topic of morality is one that skeptical authors dwell on perhaps more than any other aspect of Christianity, and rightfully so. Surveys have shown that a majority of Americans believe faith in God is necessary for a person to be moral.[277] It makes good tactical sense to convince someone that a particular viewpoint is morally acceptable before attempting to convince them to come over to that viewpoint, but I have elected to do just the opposite in order to avoid accusations of emotional pandering.[278] Over the next few sections, I will attack the idea that God and morality are inseparable, not only by demonstrating facets of my own moral judgment, but also by attacking the inherent immorality that comes with believing in the sanctity of the Bible.

We need only look at the track record of the religious believers. Why is it that on every ethical issue that has been decided in the history of this country, the social progressives were right and the socially conservative Christian fundamentalists were dead wrong? Three hundred years ago, the social progressives had a crazy idea that it was wrong to hang and burn people for not belonging to the Christian faith. Once both sides settled this issue, the social conservatives realized that they were in the wrong but still fought the progressive idea that it was inhumane to slaughter the Native Americans and take their land under the idea that God wanted white people to occupy land between the two oceans.[279] Once both sides settled this issue, the social conservatives were again able to see that they were guilty of unethical behavior but still fought the progressive belief that it was wrong to kidnap innocent people from Africa in order to enslave them. One might think that the social conservatives would realize that biblical defenses for such a belief were immoral, but critical thinking has never been able to trump religious persuasion.

When the slavery issue was settled, the social conservatives once again saw the folly of their beliefs, but this of course did not stop them from fighting the absurd liberal proposition of allowing women to vote in elections. Time proved the social conservatives were once again wrong, of course, but they saw no harm in denying civil rights to those citizens that they grudgingly allowed an existence free from slavery. History once again demonstrated that the social conservatives were on the wrong side of morality, but it was now a matter of ensuring that couples with different skin tones couldn't get married. As you can see, the United States has always divided itself into those who fight to maintain situations that are comfortable for themselves (and their misguided morals) and those who fight for what is ethical. Just think what our lives might be like today if we were still following religious conservative ideology.

Since people change their fundamental beliefs only on extremely rare occasion, we simply have to wait for them to die out before society can progress. Social historians have called this phenomenon the *Planck Problem*. When I spoke of social conservatives admitting that they were wrong in the past, I do not speak of the exact same group of people, but rather a new generation who adopted the remaining socially conservative policies and continued to fight against further change. Social reform takes place when generations are replaced. I don't believe it's reasonable to assume that most of the social conservatives had actually changed their minds about slavery when Jim Crow laws were enacted. I believe it is much more reasonable to assume that a dwindling portion of them still wanted to reinstitute slavery, but they were outnumbered by a growing younger generation who had not been indoctrinated with the concept that slavery was a permissible practice. When growing discontentment emerged from the succeeding generation, the ones who were opposed to slavery but horrified at the idea of sharing a lunch counter were in turn replaced.

The contemporaneous batch of social conservatives for every age admitted they were wrong on every previous ethical issue that had been decided, but they continued to insist on being right about every contemporaneous issue that had not been widely accepted as wrong. It certainly won't be long before time deals them additional embarrassments in the form of gay marriage, stem cell research, and an individual's right to die. Even though we often view a person like George W. Bush as a staunch conservative, his position that people with different skin colors have the right to marry each other would place him as one of the most socially liberal presidents to ever live.

As of the time this book is being prepared for publishing, South Dakota has a near total ban on abortion. This strategic political movement, of course, arrives only a couple of months after the confirmation of the socially conservative Samuel Alito to the United States Supreme Court. Two points on the not-so-ironic if I may. First, if I were a contestant on a hypothetical game show on which I was given ten chances to guess which state would be the first to make it legally necessary for an eleven year old child raped and impregnated by her father to carry his baby for nine months, I'd begin celebrating as soon as the question was asked. My list of guesses would be as follows: Kansas for being the first to introduce Intelligent Design into public school, Tennessee for attempting to ban evolutionary biology and homosexuality, Arkansas for not allowing atheists to testify in court on the basis of their inherent immorality, Mississippi for not banning slavery at the state level until the 1990s, Georgia for placing evolution disclaimers in science textbooks and flying the flag of the Confederacy until 2002, South Carolina for erecting racist monuments on public property, Alabama for the push to display the Ten Commandments on government property, Texas for executing the mentally retarded, South Dakota for having nothing better to do, and Utah for being Utah.[280] If you're keeping count, all of those states have been strongly red for a while now. But should that come as any surprise? Should we be shocked that the socially progressive regions of the country are those with the most reputable universities?[281] Should we be shocked that they boast the greatest population of nonbelievers?[282]

The second point of irony is that if I were asked on the same game show whether a man was for or against a complete ban on abortion, based only on the information that he belonged to a white supremacy group at Princeton University, I would again celebrate as soon as I heard the question.[283] If getting both questions correct qualified me for the bonus round, in which I was asked whether the same man who was attempting to join the Supreme Court would actually admit remembering he was in a white male supremacist club twenty years ago, I would be driving home in a new car.

This is not to say that there is no way that he doesn't remember belonging to such an organization - because it's quite possible that he hit his head pretty hard in an automobile accident sometime between now and then. One must consider such a possibility when a man is so sorely lacking in morals and ethics. Our government is clearly broken as a result of conservative values, and religious thought has definitely had a hand in driving the impact. Harris elaborates:

> We live in a country in which a person cannot get elected president if he openly doubts the existence of heaven and hell. This is truly remarkable, given that there is no other body of "knowledge" that we require our political leaders to master. Even a hairstylist must pass a licensing exam before plying his trade in the United States, and yet those given the power to make war and national policy–those whose decisions will inevitably affect human life for generations–are not expected to know anything in particular before setting to work. They do not have to be political scientists, economists, or even lawyers; they need not have studied international relations, military history, resource management, civil engineering, or any other field of knowledge that might be brought to bear in the governance of a modern superpower; they need only be expert fund-raisers, comport themselves well on television, and be indulgent of certain *myths*. In our next presidential election, an actor who reads his Bible would almost certainly defeat a rocket scientist who does not. Could there be any clearer indication that we are allowing unreason and otherworldliness to govern our affairs?[284]

Recent polls of the American public support this position. When asked if they would be willing to vote for an otherwise well-qualified candidate, more than half would refuse to vote for an atheist, while a much smaller fraction felt comfortable discriminating against women, blacks, homosexuals, Mormons, Jews, and Catholics.

The Bible is an advanced and useful tool because we can extract bits of wisdom from it.

While we can certainly extract bits of ethical wisdom from the Bible, not all of the positions that we can extract are indeed ethical. The same can likely be said for just about every other religious work of antiquity. If one merely wishes to argue that the Bible is special due to insights that were offered way ahead of their time (which incidentally is a ridiculous assertion), we should consider how far behind God's chosen people were compared to other races of antiquity, particularly the Greeks.[285] Since a thorough analysis of the Greek cultural advancement over the Hebrews is far beyond the scope of this book, a brief summary will have to suffice.

While the Hebrews were content with being ruled by a so-called divinely appointed monarchy, the Greeks were advanced enough to have an aristocracy[286] (rule by the best) and a democracy (rule by the people). While the Hebrews were content with entertaining themselves by burning incense and dancing around campfires, the Greeks were busy writing stories for the theatre–having invented the genres of comedy, drama, and tragedy. While the Hebrews were content with their beliefs being guided by faith, superstition, and a violent god, Aristotle and other Greeks were discovering the principles of logic, reason, rational thought, and argumentation. While the Hebrews were content with believing that God was in control of all aspects of reality, Archimedes and other Greeks were laying the foundations of the scientific method. While the Hebrews were content with writing psalms that praise an egotistical god, the Greeks were busy developing musical theory. While the Hebrews were content with explaining their past by relying on myths, legends, and other oral traditions, Herodotus and other

Greeks were establishing the principles of unbiased, unemotional, nonjudgmental, and factual documentation of history.

While the Hebrews were content with breaking bird necks to cure leprosy, topically applying animal dung to cure various skin ailments, performing exorcisms to cure epilepsy, and praying to cure a number of untreatable afflictions, Hippocrates and other Greeks were developing rational anatomy-based medicine that relied on experience and observation. While the Hebrews were content with building temples for their god to dwell in, the Greeks were producing innovative architecture, sculptures, and paintings.[287] While the Hebrews were content with mundane stories and the writings of prophets, Homer, Sophocles, Aesop, Sappho, and other Greeks were writing some of the most powerful works of literature that the world has ever known. While the Hebrews were content with counting how many people belonged to each of their tribes, Euclid, Pythagoras, and other Greeks were inventing geometry and other advanced mathematics. While the Hebrews were content with believing whatever God or their other leaders told them about reality, Thales, Plato, Aristotle, and Socrates were busy not only inventing philosophy, but also writing some of the greatest philosophical treatises that the world will ever know. Yet after comparing the innumerable accomplishments of the Greeks to the unenlightened barbarity of the Hebrews, are we still to believe that the creator of the universe was working through the latter to carry his timeless message of paramount importance to future generations? Something is definitely wrong with such a position.

I could elaborate on the difference between the Greeks and Hebrews for the rest of the book without adequately drawing deserved contrast between the two groups, pointing out for example how Plato and Aristotle argued for their positions while Jesus merely gave assertions and threatened those who did not accept them, or how Democritus appreciated the vastness of the universe while any Hebrew thought he was the center of it, but I will instead put the issue to rest with one undeniably moving final observation.

Hippocrates, the aforementioned father of medicine who lived from approximately 460-370 BCE, once said, "Men think epilepsy divine, merely because they do not understand it." Yet four hundred years after the mortal Hippocrates realized that there had to be a natural, rational explanation for the mysterious medical condition, Jesus was allegedly curing epilepsy by casting out demons. Hippocrates realized that people attributed epilepsy to demonic possession only because they did not understand it. This leads us to perhaps the most important question I will pose in this book. How is it that the all-knowing, all-powerful creator of the universe sent a messenger, the savior of all humanity, who knew less than an ordinary man who had been dead for centuries? How could Hippocrates have a better understanding of the world than Jesus? Why should we hold Jesus as a superior teacher? It does not make sense.

There are considerable problems with the philosophies of Jesus that so many have deemed insightful and groundbreaking. What if Franklin Roosevelt had decided to love Adolf Hitler as he loved himself–or had followed the philosophy that we should turn the other cheek once the Japanese bombed Pearl Harbor? Should we love our neighbors as we love ourselves and turn the other cheek if they are determined to cause us harm? Smith takes issue with these biblical disciplines and asks:

> Why? For what possible reason should one offer oneself as a sacrificial animal in this way? Such questions, however, do not apply to Jesus, because he is interested only in obedience, not in presenting rational arguments. In fact, when viewed in this context, these commands begin to make sense. We are not to judge others, Jesus says, which is merely another facet of suspending one's critical faculties. We are to tolerate injustice, we are to refrain from passing value judgments of other people–such precepts require the obliteration of one's capacity to distinguish the good from the evil; they require the kind of intellectual and moral passiveness that generates a mentality of obedience. The man who is incapable of passing independent value judgments will be the least critical when given orders. And he will be unlikely to evaluate the moral worth of the man, or the supposed god, from whence these orders come.[288]

For every passage that someone could offer as substantiating for a given position like the one Jesus provides, we could certainly find another in the Bible that offers a contrasting position. Since we have to use reason and ethical judgment to decide when principles like "do unto others" are the proper course of action, why not just replace such an inferior philosophy with "do what is for the greater good." If an omnipotent being truly inspired ethical guidelines provided in the Bible, is it too much to ask for those guidelines to be superior to what the human mind can develop?

Since the biblical guidelines are inferior to what we can develop, we can only reasonably conclude that they were products of inferior minds. The Bible offers advice that its readers can apply only in certain areas, except that it foolishly fails to elaborate to any important extent and subsequently passes them off as absolute boundaries of morality. If God had a hand in the creation of the Bible, why did he lack such providential foresight? Why could the Greeks (and even I) develop superior codes of morality?

One doctrine of the New Testament that should definitely not sit well with progressive thinkers is the promise of hell for disbelievers. Granted that there is very little textual support for the mainstream idea of eternal punishment, I will still treat the issue as canonical since it is a major force in conservative sects of the religion. This idea of an infinite deity eternally torturing sentient beings simply because they see no reason (or flat-out refuse) to worship it is the cruelest absurdity one could ever dream. The punishment can serve no other purpose but to satisfy God's egotistical desire for revenge. It is not a means to separate the saved from the unsaved because that process can be resolved in a number of ways that do not involve punishment. It is not a means to dissuade sinful behavior because many do not believe and many who do still sin. It is not a means to rehabilitate because the punishment is eternal; and if it is not eternal as a growing number of Christian scholars believe, there are a number of ways to mend the individual that are far more effective and ethical.

Even worse, the process is unethically enforced under duress. God demands, "Do what I say or be tortured for eternity." Simply offering someone a dichotomy of everlasting torture or everlasting happiness with the prerequisite that one must follow certain actions is not ethical behavior. What choice would there be in such a situation? It is absurd, if not for any other reason, because it conflicts with the inherent freedom to believe as one chooses. We did not see or hear what the Bible claims, and God has not addressed us directly concerning these claims. We have only a book of hearsay testimony–a composition reading and sounding nothing different from superstition, written many centuries ago in a superstitious age to provide superstitious people with a refuge from reality. We have a right–and when absurd, an intellectual duty–not to believe such things. People should have the option not to exist for eternity and thus be exempt from the reward/punishment system if they want no part of such ambiguity. I for one would certainly never want to reside in the domain of a being who arbitrarily kills people at his own discretion. Smith elaborates:

> The threat of punishment for disbelief is the crowning touch of Christian misology. Believe in Jesus–regardless of evidence of justification–or be subjected to agonizing torture. With this theme reverberating throughout the New Testament, we have intellectual intimidation, transcendental blackmail, in its purest form. Threats replace argumentation, and irrationality gains the edge over reason through an appeal to brute force. Man's ability to think and question becomes his most dangerous liability, and the intellectually frightened, docile, unquestioning believer is presented as the exemplification of moral perfection.[289]

Furthermore, I am confident that the ideas of heaven and hell create less moral attitudes for the people who believe in them. Petty and Cacioppo report a tendency for people to be less vulnerable to actual belief changes when they are able to attribute their reasoning and actions to external rewards and punishments.[290] Cialdini provides a great example of this phenomenon in the form of a research project involving citizens of Iowa. After receiving tips for energy conversation from a researcher, it was noted that the utility records from the sampled group showed no real energy savings. With a similar group who were, in addition to receiving the energy conservation tips, promised to receive a reward via having their names printed in the newspaper, utility records showed a dramatic decrease in energy consumption. However, once the promise of reward was later pulled out from this group, energy consumption decreased even further! Cialdini explains:

> Strangely enough, when the publicity factor was no longer a possibility, these families did not merely maintain their fuel-saving effort, they heightened it... In a way, the opportunity to receive newspaper publicity had prevented the homeowners from fully owning their commitment to conservation. Of all the reasons supporting the decision to try to save fuel, it was the only one that had come from the outside; it was the only one preventing the homeowners from thinking that they were conserving gas because they believed in it. So when the letter arrived canceling the publicity agreement, it removed the only impediment to these residents' images of themselves as fully concerned, energy-conscious citizens. This unqualified, new self-image then pushed them to even greater heights of conservation.[291]

This phenomenon provokes an interesting question. If people are initially motivated by reward, but that motivation is better maintained by the satisfaction of the moral behavior itself, could the promise of eternal life in paradise based on our faith and works ultimately hinder us from bettering ourselves? Even Jesus encouraged moral behavior primarily to achieve the heavenly reward. Smith elaborates:

> The precepts of Jesus, almost without exception, are accompanied by the promise of a divine reward. Be humble, counsels Jesus, "and your Father who sees in secret will reward you." Be kind to the poor and

> disabled, and you "will be repaid at the resurrection of the just." Even the much heralded Sermon on the Mount (regardless of which of the conflicting versions one accepts) is saturated with divine sanctions: "Blessed are the poor in spirit, for theirs is the kingdom of heaven." "Blessed are the pure in heart, for they shall see God." On the reverse side of supernatural sanctions, of course, was the threat of punishment for those who will not listen and obey...There can be no doubt but that those precepts are strictly otherworldly in emphasis. Jesus does not prescribe standards of behavior on the basis that they will contribute to man's happiness and well-being on earth. He issues commands, or rules, backed by the brute sanctions of heaven and hell, with the specific choice of sanction determined by how well one obeys.[292]

It is unfortunate that Jesus, the earthly incarnation of the universe's all-knowing, all-powerful creator, did not have the results from Cialdini at his disposal. If he had, Jesus would have realized that people likely behave more ethically without the continued promise of a reward for doing so.

> *What kind of a country would we live in if we lost respect of the Ten Commandments? Certainly not one I would want to live in.*

The only argument I have heard more absurd than the one about the Ten Commandments being good moral guidelines is that they are the basis of our national laws; and this statement essentially argues both. I will start with the more ridiculous suggestion of the two, that the founders of the country based our laws on the Ten Commandments. We can dispatch this idea for a number of reasons without ever reviewing the rules themselves.

Congress *unanimously* approved of the Treaty of Tripoli, drafted in 1796 under George Washington and signed in 1797 by John Adams, which stated, "the Government of the United States of America is not, in any sense, founded on the Christian religion." That it was not founded on Judaism, Islam, or any other religion that includes these Commandments should already be evident. James Madison, considered the Father of the Constitution, wrote of a "total separation of the church from the state" when describing the terminology of the First Amendment, which itself states, "Congress shall make no law respecting an establishment of religion." Neither the Constitution nor the Declaration of Independence makes a single reference to Christianity because the founders of the United States were primarily Deists. These facts alone render the idea of the United States being a Christian nation nonsense, but we can investigate further still by reviewing each Commandment.

1) Do not have other gods. 2) Do not make idols. 3) Do not misuse God's name. 4) Observe the Sabbath. After considering these first four, I would like to hear from someone who can explain to me how our laws require us to observe a specific religion. If I am right, and I think I am, the four Commandments listed here requiring religious observance do not exist as laws. Quite the opposite, I believe that the government is not granted the legal right to force you to observe the Christian religion.

5) Honor your father and mother. That's another law I'm obviously not familiar with. 6) Do not murder.[293] This one is actually in the books. 7) Do not commit adultery. While there are some very old laws in certain jurisdictions that prohibit adultery, they are no longer enforced. 8) Do not steal. This one is actually a law. 9) Do not lie. Lying is against the law in courts and to government officials but not to the public as a whole. We will count number nine as one-half and say that we have two and a half Commandments thus far that are part of national law.

10) Do not covet. In other words, do not be greedy and desire what your neighbors have. I think there is actually a name for an economic mode of society that thrives on groups of people trying to outdo and outperform other groups of people, all in an effort to look

better while putting the other groups of people out of business. The name of this practice escapes me at the moment. If only I could… oh yes, I remember now. It's called *capitalism.* Our country's philosophical foundation for commerce is based on a direct contradiction of the final Commandment, which is somehow a basis for the laws of our land. Sure. Well, there you have it. US law agrees with the Ten Commandments 25 percent of the time.[294]

Now we can move on to the idea that the Commandments are a proper moral code. If we begin with the premise that the foolish egomaniac deity in the Old Testament actually exists, even though we have no good reason to believe so yet many great reasons to believe the opposite, then we should perhaps obey the first four Commandments to appease this creature. Remember what's in store for us if we refuse. Still, is it ethical for a being to create us and demand that we worship him in a certain way to appease his desires while the alternative of apathy might be an eternity of unimaginable torment? Is this what an ethical god would do? I would argue that the first four Commandments are indeed a form of duress, and therefore unethical.

Should we honor our parents if they have done us wrong, perhaps through physical, mental, and sexual abuse? Is it unethical for someone to murder another person when it is absolutely necessary to serve the greater good? Is it unethical for agreeing married couples to have outside relationships that increase satisfaction and bring no harm to anyone? Is it unethical for someone to steal when it's the only way to feed his starving family? Is it okay to lie to someone when the lie is for the greater good?

What is the harm in coveting what someone else has… oh wait, there is more to that one: Do not covet "your neighbor's house, wife, slaves,[295] animals, or anything else that belongs to him."[296] Most of us are remotely aware that women were treated as possessions in the Old Testament, but what is this business about the Bible saying we are not supposed to be greedy of our neighbors' *slaves*? No wonder the makers of those huge stone monuments like to abbreviate that last one. Speaking of those stone monuments, why do they not engrave the penalties for breaking those Commandments? They are, after all, punishable by death in almost every instance.[297] Do those who proclaim the Bible to be a book of moral character have the slightest idea what it says? It takes religion to make good people think bad things.

The Judeo-Christian God gives us absolutes in the Ten Commandments, yet any omniscient being worthy of a second look would know that there are no absolutes when it comes to morality. Now I'll admit that I'm a pretty smart guy, but I'm nothing compared to an entity with an infinite IQ that, quite simply, knows everything. Even so, I am going to attempt to create a more ethical system based around ten rules, and to add to the degree of difficulty, I am going to use similar principles as the biblical foundation. I will keep the first four rules the same since God apparently knows how he wants ego to be satisfied.

5) Honor your parents unless an enlightened society would agree that they have greatly wronged you. 6) Do not kill a human being unless it is necessary to protect the welfare of the innocent. 7) Do not commit adultery against a partner with whom you have an ongoing promise to stay faithful. 8) Do not steal unless it is an absolute, last resort necessity for the greater good. Make amends as soon as possible. 9) Do not lie unless the lie serves a higher, more ethical purpose than the truth. 10) Do not treat other people as objects or own innocent unwilling people as property.

There you have it. I have a greatly inferior mind compared to the perfect Judeo-Christian God, yet I can develop a much more superior ethical code than the one he provided. To save my life, I cannot figure out how to make Christians accept the necessary ramifications of this. To the one who asked what type of world we would live in if we lost respect of the Ten Commandments, my answer is an enlightened one. Still, many of my readers have taken great offense to my position that social taboos like adultery are not always immoral, but this only goes to demonstrate how some individuals cannot step outside of what society has conditioned them to think. Couples who mutually agree to have extramarital affairs are by definition committing adultery, but they are not cheating or causing each other injury. If there is no harm to those involved, or if the benefit for each outweighs the harm in a particular instance, I see no reason to think that such actions serve anything other than the greater good.

Unable to grasp this concept, more than one individual has used the atrociously inappropriate analogy of a student cheating on a test in school. They simply see a commonality in the word "cheating" and think that they are making a valid argument. Students and teachers must abide by a set of regulations set by a governing body who acts in the best interest of those involved. The body does not leave it up to the pupils and teachers to decide if they should arbitrarily cheat. Still, I will not even say that cheating on a test is an absolute wrong because, again, there are no absolutes in morality. It is certainly wrong for a student to cheat in the vast majority of conceivable cases (as it would be in the vast majority of conceivable adultery cases), hence there is a need to enforce a sweeping rule against it, provided that there is an opportunity for the student to appeal to a governing body in order to see if the act can be justified.

If cheating on one test in high school enables a student to pass a class so that he can get into college and later go on to cure cancer, then cheating was certainly for the greater good. When one cannot know such outcomes, however, one is best to serve what appears to be for the immediate good by not cheating. One should consider other factors involved, such as the unfairness to other students who might be competing against a cheating student for a position in college, but there is no correlative to this in the example of a couple who mutually agree to have external sexual relations. It is no one's business except the members of the family. I have said it before, I will say it again, and I will continue to say it: there are no absolutes in morality. Shermer addresses the issue well:

> Morals do not exist in nature and thus cannot be discovered. In nature there are only actions–physical actions, biological actions, human actions. Humans act to increase their happiness, however they personally define it. Their actions become moral or immoral only when someone else judges them as such. Thus, morality is strictly a human creation, subject to all sorts of cultural influences and social constructions, just as other human creations are. Since virtually every person and every group claims they know what constitutes right versus wrong human action, and since virtually all of these moralities differ from all others to a greater

> or lesser extent, reason alone tells us they cannot all be correct. Just as there is no absolute right type of human music, there is no absolute right type of human action. The broad range of human action is a rich continuum that precludes pigeonholing into the unambiguous rights and wrongs that political laws and moral codes tend to require.[298]

We simply cannot tell children that it is always wrong to steal, lie, cheat, fornicate, or even kill. We can show our children as many examples as possible when such actions are likely right and when they are likely wrong. We can tell a child that it is not okay to steal video games from Wal-Mart in almost every conceivable situation by explaining how such an action would affect all parties involved. Wal-Mart is a company owned by the public that offers goods in exchange for currency. Video games are a source of entertainment and not essential for life. Assuming that Wal-Mart has not harmed our children in any direct fashion, stealing from the store is stealing from individuals who have invested their savings in the livelihood of the company. In this instance, I feel comfortable concluding that it is not okay, for the greater good, or ethically permissible to steal video games from Wal-Mart.

On the other hand, we might be able to tell a child that it is okay to steal $100 from a man who once assaulted someone and left them with a $500 hospital bill, provided that the money goes to benefit the victim of the crime. In this hypothetical instance, let us say that a judge found there was no evidence that the attacker committed the crime, yet we know it was the same person because we were eyewitnesses and knew the attacker personally. Since the victim is not going to receive justice through legal avenues, this will probably be the only opportunity for the victim to receive compensation. In this instance, I feel comfortable concluding that it is okay, for the greater good, and ethically permissible to steal the money.

Let's just be silly for a moment though. What if someone was going to murder your family if you did not steal a loaf of bread from Wal-Mart? It is okay to steal in that instance, right? If so, is it correct to suggest that stealing is an absolute wrong? Saying that it is *almost* always wrong to steal is probably a good thing to tell your children. I would do the same. My point is that an absolute rule is not a good idea. As our society advances, we need to learn to think in terms of overall happiness and suffering instead of following rules that we have been told are perfect determinates of right and wrong.

With many similar examples in a child's memory, he can apply fair reasoning in other hypothetical and real-life scenarios. A rational child can now decide, to the best of his ability, when it is right and wrong to steal. The child is much better equipped to make the proper decision more often than a child who is told that it is an absolute wrong to steal. This potential for adaptation is why absolutes do not provide what is right and wrong. We cannot say stealing is wrong because it is a divine law or because it is a human law. No objective philosopher that I know of in the past several centuries would ever support the notion of absolutes in morality. However, if we find ourselves unable to determine if stealing is right or wrong in a particular instance, we can say that when in doubt, follow the guideline of not stealing. The Bible does not display this advanced level of thinking; it simply provides an absolute rule not to be broken. Christians cannot demand the use of common sense to satisfy these shortcomings because it begs the question that the authors had any to begin with. Considering that the book contains a plethora of absurdities, such a notion would already be in serious question.

> *The evils perpetrated by consistent atheists, even through just the last century, make the evils of inconsistent Christians pale in comparison.*

This statement is grossly misleading, but I will get around to addressing that issue in a minute. Atheism is a religious *stance*, not a religious *belief*. There is no philosophy or morality inherently linked to it or divorced from it. I will assume that the writer is primarily referring to the dictators of Russia, in which case Lenin and Stalin literally worked millions of people to death under a brutal regime. The problem with claiming that atheism has caused the injustice is that their religious beliefs did not drive them to be the men that they were. How many people were killed strictly because the killers had no belief in a god? A lengthy treatise on the subject of Russian history over the past two hundred years will have to wait for another day, but while we can say that a great travesty took place under regimes led by atheists, we cannot say that atheism was the cause of the injustice. If Lenin and Stalin are guilty of mass murder, their lack of a proper ethical code is the reason. According to Smith:

> This irrational and grossly unfair practice of linking atheism with communism is losing popularity and is rarely encountered any longer except among political conservatives. But the same basic technique is sometimes used by the religious philosopher in his attempt to discredit atheism. Instead of communism, the sophisticated theologian will associate atheism with existentialism–which projects a pessimistic view of existence–and he will then reach the conclusion that atheism leads to a pessimistic view of the universe. It seems that the next best thing to convincing people not to be atheists is to scare them away from it.[299]

The writer makes the common Christian mistake of confusing correlation with causation on this particular issue. Also, notice how the writer also refers to the atheists as "consistent." In other words, he wants us to believe that it is, by definition, consistent for atheists to perpetuate evil because atheism is consistent with evil. This is nothing but hateful bigotry coming from an ignorant Christian, and I think very little of people who think this way. The Christians, on the other hand, who perpetuate the very same evils are "inconsistent" with *true* Christianity. Whether you call them "inconsistent" types or "untrue" types, the same *No True Scotsman* fallacy is being committed. Here is one example from a different reader...

> *It's interesting that the historical evils you attribute to Christians are almost all the result of those people violating*

the principles of Christianity. Therefore, much of the evil you attribute to Christianity (including the Crusades) is the result of UN-Christianity.

For whatever action the writer deems to be a black mark on Christianity, he claims that it is "un-Christian." There is no such defining line (or "principles of Christianity") as to whether or not a person is or is not acting like a Christian. This individual's definition would have to be arbitrary, because by strict definition, a Christian is someone who is like Christ, which *also* happens to be an arbitrary description. Anyone offering this logical fallacy simply wants us to think that the evils in society perpetuated by those who claim to be Christians are not really acting like Christians and we should therefore not consider them as such.

The objective classification of subjective qualities is where the fallacy is committed. A person who considers himself a Christian by following what he believes to be proper Christianity is considered a Christian by the standards of society. His actions are driven by his beliefs, which are in turn driven by his Bible and his church. Thus, the only issue of importance with these actions is whether they were carried out in the name of Christianity. In other words, were the horrible actions throughout history in part the result of Christians following their beliefs? The answer is affirmative to all the examples in America's history I provided in *Biblical Nonsense*: Native American genocide, religious persecution, African slavery, and female subordination. There is more than enough biblical text to support these past movements, and these specific events would have been eliminated or greatly reduced without Christian beliefs fueling them. But getting back to the original line of argument…

Where atheism reigns, there has always been mass murder and an increase in human enslavement and suffering. Atheistic regimes are responsible for the deaths of hundreds of millions of people and the repression and enslavement of hundreds of millions more.

Since the writer does nothing but assert his position, I will do the same and say that monotheistic religions have proven to be more violent throughout history than polytheistic and non-theistic religions.[300] The notion that mass murder, enslavement, and suffering exist under atheistic regimes is no doubt true. We can say the same about Christian regimes and other Christian governments throughout history. The type of regime is irrelevant, however, because the issues at hand, once again, are the evils carried out strictly in the name of Christianity. Those who offer this reader's assertion can knock down their straw men all they want, but discerning readers are going to know that they are not dealing with the real issue. Furthermore, I would like those with views similar to this individual to support (with hard evidence) the assertion that atheistic regimes are responsible for the deaths of hundreds of millions of people and the repression and enslavement of hundreds of millions more. I would also like them to explain how areas with polytheistic religions are more peaceful and have less suffering than monotheistic societies. Do more gods equal more happiness?

The apologetic argument disintegrates into the assertion that a Christian dictator would not have committed such atrocities, but this position is likewise without merit. In order for a leader to operate a moral regime, he needs one thing that Christianity, stripped of its components, does not provide: a moral code. One can be a Christian and claim Christian beliefs without adopting every aspect of the faith. Thus, we must add a sense of morality as a virtue for an ethical foundation to be free of the atrocities we witnessed in the former Soviet Union. However, since we have added morality, we no longer need religion. The only principle we needed from the beginning was a sense of morality; and since no one can deny that the witch burners and crusaders had just as much religious faith as the Christians of today, it only makes sense that faith is at best irrelevant and at worse an impediment to moral behavior.

We have now further reduced the argument to a suggestion that Christians often have an attached code of morality, which is not something I would dispute. But so do most atheists. The question then becomes which group has the highest probability of producing an individual with ethical behavior. I do not know the definitive answer on this subject, but suggestions made elsewhere in this text provide a hint that it may be leading toward the nonreligious.

Where Christianity has been consistently practiced, people enjoy the highest levels of literacy, prosperity, and peace.

Such as South America and Africa? South America is almost entirely Christian while Africa is half-Christian and half-Muslim. How are the literacy, prosperity, and peace in these regions? They are the two most illiterate, impoverished, and war torn continents in the world. Seeing as how this observation does not support the individual's case, this is obviously not the point he intended to convey. What he intended to express, I assume, is the success of places like the United States. Yes, America is better off than most countries on peace, literacy, and prosperity, but even the US is now quickly sliding out of the top twenty in fields like literacy and education,[301] all the while constantly involving itself in foreign wars and other unmerciful affairs.

No one can deny that the US is historically the most prosperous country in the world, but was the success not due to a harsh Capitalist government that forced children as young as six to work unsanitary jobs for eighty hours a week during the Industrial Revolution just to feed themselves? Was the success also not due to kidnapping and enslaving people from other countries in order to gain free labor and get ahead of the competition? Was the country itself not obtained through violent warfare and attempted genocide of a peaceful race that welcomed us with open arms? It seems that these very "UN-Christian" principles are part of what led to the country's prosperity. Perhaps the one who made this suggestion wanted us to think of the prosperity of Western Europe and Japan as well, but I would suggest checking out the religious demographics of those areas. The vast majority of those populations consider religion irrelevant, and they have regarded it as so for quite a while.[302]

Christian believers are responsible for most of the world's advancements.

Harris handles this assertion well enough to allow me to pass on giving my own two cents:

> It is a truism to say that people of faith have created almost everything of value in our world, because

> nearly every person who has ever swung a hammer or trimmed a sail has been a devout member of one or another religious culture. There has been simply no one else to do the job. We can also say that every human achievement prior to the twentieth century was accomplished by men and women who were perfectly ignorant of the molecular basis of life. Does this suggest that a nineteenth-century view of biology would have been worth maintaining?[303]

I was into pornography and sexual relationships before I became Christian and it only brought me pain and confusion. Now that I'm learning God's way, everything from my past only makes more sense.

I am always sorry to hear that people have had misery in their past, regardless of the sources. While I find nothing at all ethically wrong with pornography and sexual relationships, considering the tendency for some people's preoccupation with these practices (or any other potentially addictive practices) along with the overwhelming disapproval from society on such practices, discontentment does often seem to follow. Since some individuals can handle this lifestyle without pain and confusion while others cannot, we should not consider the avoidance of pornography and sexual relationships a moral absolute. Furthermore, this testimony is a personal experience. I do not doubt that such positive transformations take place when individuals join Christianity, but they are not evidence of a belief's veracity. Countless people can purport countless transformations from countless religions and philosophies.

Adam and Eve are the cause of our sin and suffering.

Other than the fact that they are fictional characters, there is a fundamental flaw with blaming Adam and Eve for causing the downfall of humankind. When God created Adam and Eve, they did not know good from evil because they had not yet eaten of the fruit. If one cannot tell what is good from what is evil, then one has no way of knowing what is right and what is wrong. While one can understand the association that good is right and evil is wrong, one cannot apply what is right and wrong without first knowing what is good and evil. Since good and evil were concepts unknown to them, Adam and Eve could not have known that obeying God was good and that disobeying God was evil. They could have appreciated that they were told not to eat the fruit, but they would have had no way to evaluate the morality of not doing so. The story, being a very primitive and spontaneous piece of mythology, presupposes that they had this knowledge and were appropriately punished for not acting properly.

More importantly, God, being omniscient, had the foreknowledge that this was going to happen to the beings the he created entirely the way he wanted them to be. Thus, Adam and Eve had no chance of escaping their fate because God knew they were going to do it and God created them wanting to do it. The world is exactly how God created it, envisioned it, and knew it would become. If he is displeased with how things turned out, he needs to look no further than himself. Many Christians have even suggested that God does not punish children who cannot understand the ramifications of their actions, yet here he punishes two adults who have the minds of ignorant children. Consistency is clearly too much to ask.

> *As a free society, we have a right to hold whatever religious beliefs we choose and a right to instill our beliefs into our children.*

I wonder if this right would extend to those who believe that their deity of choice wants them to molest children and to teach their own children to do the same. I asked the mother of three who made the assertion how she would feel if a man was taught in childhood that God wanted him to molest her children. Would she rather him abide by his religious upbringing, or instead rely on reason and observation to evaluate the consequences of his actions? Does she still think people have a right to indoctrinate their children with religious beliefs if the ideals of such an institution bring about more harm than good? I cannot say for sure because she would not respond directly to that rebuttal.

The point I am attempting to make here is that if Christianity brings more harm than good to society, we have an ethical duty not to spread such beliefs. Furthermore, if a belief system teaches people to worship and appreciate an evil god, do we not have an ethical duty to speak out against it? Dawkins reports the cruelest of all study results: children overwhelmingly approving of genocide as moral behavior in situations where those with the same religion are the aggressors–but overwhelmingly disapproving otherwise.[304] If this does not tell us that it is time to step in, what will? Children have the right to be free from the potential moral damage and cruel nonsense inflicted by childhood indoctrination.

To an unbiased outside observer, the Christian idea of morality is often strange to say the least. Those of us who take the time to observe and understand the religious movement realize that most people probably would not think the same way under different circumstances. Most Christians will admit to not understanding many of God's rules and simply appeal to his higher ethical understanding as to why we should follow heinous biblical guidelines for our moral codes. Others will naturally become bigoted against anyone who thinks he can know more about ethics than the creator of the universe. The problem here is that religious followers simply beg the question of God's involvement in the rules. Instead of declaring God perfectly ethical and concluding that his rules must also be ethical, the proper analysis would be to determine if the rules are ethical before deciding whether they originate from a perfect god.

Dawkins summarizes my personal position on biblical morality quite well:

> The God of the Old Testament is arguably the most unpleasant character in all fiction: jealous and proud of it; a petty, unjust, unforgiving control-freak; a vindictive, bloodthirsty ethnic cleanser; a misogynistic,

> homophobic, racist, infanticidal, genocidal, filicidal, pestilential, megalomaniacal, sadomasochistic, capriciously malevolent bully.[305]

The Old Testament portrays God as a being that experiences pleasure from distributing strange and ridiculous punishments for breaking his equally strange and ridiculous laws. This deity is also guilty of torturing innocent people for the sins committed by others, murdering millions of our fellow human beings, and forcing his own creations into slavery. Furthermore, he unambiguously supports the very institution of slavery and the practice of severely oppressing women into a state of subordination. Had the invented Judeo-Christian God held the moral fortitude to believe otherwise, he would have surely exercised his unlimited power to ban these customs. Instead, he makes promises to deliver a multitude of cruel punishments, including perhaps an eternal torture of unimaginable proportions, for those who refuse to bow down and worship him.[306]

If you ask Christians to describe their quasi-chosen god of worship, you will often hear such descriptors as *wonderful* and *loving*. This choice of selective designation seems commonplace within the Christian community. In fact, most churches ignore the Old Testament all together so that the members feel comfortable propagating this view. Christians take it for granted that the Bible is benevolent and true. They are rarely given reason to question it; and when this happens, such suggestions are quickly dismissed. Very few realize that God once ordered people put to death for incest, homosexuality, bestiality, adultery, perjury, kidnapping, blasphemy, rebellion, worshipping other gods, working on the Sabbath, disobeying a judge, disobeying a priest, approaching a sanctuary, prophesying incorrectly, attacking your parents, cursing your parents, practicing witchcraft, having premarital sex, and not controlling your livestock.[307] Yes, the same god who allowed the rape of women war captives and the beating of slaves for no reason once ordered people to death for these relatively benign offenses.[308]

Even fewer Christians realize that the prophets claim God will kill men, have their children smashed, and have their wives raped; punish children for the iniquities of their fathers and distant ancestors; lay waste to entire cities and make the lands desolate; set people, animals, and even plants on fire because of his anger; send so much evil that people would rather be dead than suffer; give away the property of men, including their wives, to other men; kill young men and allow their children to die from a famine; cause everyone to become drunk so father and son will kill one another; not hear the cries of the people or acknowledge their sacrifices; make people hungry enough to eat their own children and friends; burn entire cities with the inhabitants still inside; break people's bones and knock their teeth out with stones; force fathers and sons to eat each other and scatter their remembrance; be comforted by killing everyone with pestilence, plagues, and swords; lay dead bodies around idols and spread their bones around the alters; kill righteous men and forget their good deeds if they ever turn to sin; turn daughters into whores and wives into adulterers; kill children when they come out of their mothers' wombs; tear people apart and devour them like a lion; kill children and unborn fetuses because their parents worship other gods; sell the children of Israel into slavery in a far away land; kill inhabitants of entire cities if they have a corrupt government; consume every living thing from the face of the earth; send people to steal Jerusalem, rape the women, and enslave the rest; and send plagues on people and animals to rot away tongues and eyes.[309]

A lengthy treatise of all of God's deplorable actions was another questionable undertaking that I performed in my first work. I am not sure it was the most reasonable course of action since one tends to become numb to the violence after reading monotonous details for a while. It can be difficult to remain cognizant that the stories are not about numbers; they are about human beings. An estimate on the number of victims in the Old Testament who paid the ultimate price as a result of God's questionable judgment is nearly impossible to determine, but it's somewhere in the millions.[310] The Judeo-Christian God is a mass murderer, plain and simple. Moreover, these estimates *still* do not include all of the deaths resulting from petty religious bickering that continues to this day.

To keep the matter of God's most deplorable actions to a respectable level, I will succinctly point out the following: he killed the firstborn sons of all Egyptian families because their Pharaoh decided to not let the Israelites out of slavery (after he intentionally hardened the Pharaoh's heart to make him feel this way); he ordered Joshua and others to kill every breathing thing in dozens of cities so that the Israelites could occupy the land; he frequently punished children for the sins of their parents; and he even had two bears maul forty-two children for making fun of a bald man's head.[311] Once again, however, a long list of every deplorable thing God did in the Bible is beyond the scope of this book. Instead, I wish to focus on the singular act of drowning the entire world.

Even if we suppose that the *adults* in Noah's era deserved to die slow and torturous deaths, what association could we conceivably make between their decisions and those made by the adolescent victims of the flood? Couldn't God have just placed the innocent children and animals aside for a while so that they wouldn't drown? If not, how about a humane death at the very least? Drowning is a horrible way for people to die. As a result of hopelessly treading water for hours, their muscles burned due to large amounts of lactic acid production. Once they finally gave up, went under, and held their breaths, acidic carbon dioxide eroded their lungs until the unbearable pain forced them to inhale where there was no air for them to breathe. The water brought into their lungs robbed their bodies of oxygen, causing them to go numb. As water violently rushed in and out of their chests, the currents eventually laid their heavily breathing, slowly dying bodies at the bottom of the ocean. The inhaled water caused their lungs to tear and bleed profusely. As their blood supply dwindled, their hearts slowly came to a halt. Even so, their brains continued to process information for another couple of minutes. They were patently aware that death was imminent, yet they could do nothing to speed it or prevent it. I imagine that their final reflections would have been on what they did to deserve such treatment. Drowning is *not* a quick and painless death.

God did this to nearly every living thing in the world because he saw man was evil. The Bible tells us so.[312] Infants and children can hardly be considered corrupted by the influence of evil. God, being omnipotent, had a choice of rescuing them from evil or murdering them. He chose murder. No matter how one twists or adds to the text, that fact remains. We do not need to look for alternative reasons to fit predetermined beliefs when the reasons are already given. This is what God did to every man, woman, child, baby, and animal on earth because *he* made the mistake of creating us this way! To make matters disgustingly worse, the flood accomplished *nothing*! The omniscient God realizes *after* the flood that a man's imagination is evil from youth.[313] He seemingly allows us to be evil to this day, just like those he purportedly drowned in the flood. Any human being under any system of jurisprudence on earth would be heavily punished for such actions, but because it's God, we let it go. He is presupposed to be ethical, therefore his actions must have some ultimately honorable purpose. Even if this was the sole befuddled and immoral act carried out by God, I am positive that I could not bring myself to worship him. However, as I mentioned earlier, this was only the beginning of his mass-murdering spree.

> *Why not also suggest that God create a whole squadron of nannies after the flood to take care of all of those innocent children? Indeed, why not ask God to change the channel for us so we don't have to get up or even pick up a remote? If* [Jason] *Long wants God to erect Wham-o Force Fields during the Flood, how can he refuse the person who says God ought to help him fix his leaky roof? If he wants God to feed people directly, how can he refuse the person who wants God to change the channel? He cannot, for there is no place that one can warrant a stop. God is omnipotent! And since that means nothing is beyond God, nothing is too much to ask.*

This abusive apologist narrowly treats this situation like a false dichotomy. I am a limited being, but I could come up with a few dozen alternative methods through which God could have spared innocent children from drowning to death. One would assume that an omnipotent being, such as the Judeo-Christian God, could come up with more ideas in one second than I could produce in a dozen lifetimes. For instance, assuming for a moment that the parents deserved what they received, God could have personally taken care of all of the young children until they developed sufficiently to take care of themselves. This way, he could have taught them to live the moral lives he wished for their parents. Is this too much to ask from an omnipotent being? The apologist apparently believes so, but I do not.

The apologist–very disturbingly–also suggests that it would make just as much sense for us to expect that God should change the channels on our televisions as it would for us to expect him not to murder innocent people. He later went on to claim that I contradict myself when I say that God *should not* have any business in what same sex couples do in their bedroom but that God *should* take an active role in explaining to us which religion is correct since we invariably continue to send millions to their deaths over this very argument.

I wholeheartedly agree that an omnipotent being would have no more trouble feeding starving people than he would changing a television channel, but God's omnipotence has nothing to do with what are reasonable levels of direct involvement from him. The issue is not what is too much for God to do; the issue is what is too much for *us to expect* God to do. Changing channels on a television is an easy, relatively pointless task that we are more than capable of handling. Developing a self-sustaining society in Africa that sees thousands of God's Christian followers die yearly from disease and starvation has proven to be much more difficult for humanity to tackle. Spending the time to describe in detail how he wants the curtains in his temples to look, but avoiding situations like the one in Africa make God hypothetically guilty of unreasonable cruelty. I hope you will take careful notice of how my position often contrasts with those who defend the Judeo-Christian God.

> *The God Jason Long wanted came with a key on its back and did what it was told; and when he didn't get it, he threw a temper tantrum.*

The dictator that Ronald Goldstein wanted came with a key on its back and did what is was told; and when he didn't get it, he threw a temper tantrum. Can you imagine a Nazi apologist from the 1940s offering such a statement in defense of a Jewish complaint against the actions of Adolf Hitler? While just about anyone can see that the apologetic Nazi statement would be heavily insulting and do nothing to solve the complaint raised, most people unnecessarily feel a need to find a discrepancy between the two scenarios. There is none. One complaint deserves just as much review as the other.

It is not my intent in bringing up Hitler to simply appeal to emotion. I am trying to make a definite point. Both Hitler and God are absolute leaders who commit seemingly reprehensible acts under the premise that they are benevolently working for the greater good. If we simply assert that God is good without reviewing his actions first, why do we not do so for Hitler? If we simply assert that the difference is God's omniscience, how can we be certain that he is a benevolent creature in the first place? Because the Bible says so? Because we have always been told so? Because we are ridiculed by misguided apologists if we do not believe so?

I do not suggest that we should be able to control God with a key in his back, but I do suggest that we should not respect him if he is able to kill innocent children and hide when we are most in need of a simple explanation. Of course, since knowledgeable Christians worship this god in spite of his misdeeds, one would reasonably assume that they would stick up for him under any circumstances. I do not fault this apologist or any other Christian for making moronic excuses for God because this is what they have learned to do. They begin with the premise that God is good and rationalize contrasting evidence as being for the overall good since it is the will of God. This form of confirmation bias is completely backwards from rational decision-making. It makes much more sense to observe the qualities, outcomes, and effects of certain actions before making a determination on whether they are ethical. This is a common mistake of switching the premise and conclusion.

We see this a lot in Battered Wife Syndrome, a state of mind in which the female victims begin with the premise that their husbands love them and arrive at the conclusion that their husbands only abuse them out of love. The rational conclusion, on the other hand, can be made by observing the actions; observing the qualities, outcomes, and effects of the actions; and drawing the conclusion that husbands are not committing the actions due to their love for their wives. Just as the battered wives erroneously begin with the premise that their husbands beat them out of love, apologists erroneously begin with the premise that all of God's actions are resultant from his love for us. The correct way to determine whether one is behaving ethically is to evaluate the actions and render a decision based on collected observations. The incorrect way to make such a determination is to start with the conclusion and find justification for the observations. We should not simply presuppose that God is all-knowing and all-loving, especially when such divine horrors are involved. Objections to God's unethical behavior are valid points to consider and should not be answered by simply asserting omniscience and omnibenevolence. Answering such objections by insulting those who offer them is a fruitless, juvenile practice.

> *God lifted the souls of the children before the demise of the flood.*

This is a classic case of adding something to the Bible that is not there in order to eliminate cognitive dissonance. The reader offering this solution realizes that the act of drowning children is unequivocally cruel (unlike the previous apologist), begins with the premise that God is not cruel, and invents a necessary scenario that will eliminate the uneasy feeling created from reading my argument. Does the Bible actually say something about lifting the souls of the children before the flood? No, but if it makes Christians feel better about what God did, they are likely to swallow it. Some have rid themselves of doubt and cognitive issues using similar avenues…

> *The killing of these children was actually merciful, for they have skipped over all the hardships and problems you and I must face every day.*

If I brutally murdered people in order to save them from this earth and send them straight to heaven, is it merciful? If not, why do we apply this reasoning to an entity just because it is of superior quality? Omniscience is irrelevant in the scenario because the question is strictly concerning the sending of people into heaven who the speaker has already presupposed to be headed there. Again, the Christian realizes that the act was cruel, presupposes that God is not cruel, and invents an immoral scenario that eliminates the uneasy feeling created by my argument.

God is omniscient. He knows who is wicked and who isn't.

God's supposed omniscience does not solve the ethical problem of his actions. Assuming God is omniscient, he knows that people of other religions cannot help believing what they believe. They believe in their respective deities just as much as God's followers believe in God because that is what their parents have taught them to believe. Being the creator of something does not give him an *ethical* right to kill innocent people, nor does it automatically grant him the quality of having perfect moral character. Two parents create a child, yet they cannot do as they please with it because they might do things that are immoral and harmful to the child.

Furthermore, the writer's line of argument is irrelevant since God kills people for explicitly stated purposes that indicate their innocence. We could not even *attempt* to explain away the moral dilemmas by saying that God knows their supposed wickedness when the Bible clearly states that certain victims are not wicked. Regardless, why does God even feel the need to inflict mass torture and death on his insignificant created beings who do not want to worship him? If apologists would only stop making excuses around their preconceived notions and start appreciating the absurdity of the matter, we could move beyond such useless exchanges.

What logic is there in the fact that the being who promises us eternal life out of his love for all humankind is the same entity who often murdered millions of people for morally bankrupt reasons? The biblical god is not *wonderful* and *loving* as Christians claim because these unenlightened followers base such crude assessments on the more positive New Testament. The God of the Old Testament, on the other hand, is pure evil and full of perpetual anger; he even admits as much. No one who creates and needlessly kills millions of people can honestly be called *wonderful* and *loving*, deity or not. Most people certainly would not think it was fair if they saw their fellow man being tortured just because his parents raised him with a different version of the creator, yet we give God immunity because we presuppose that it is for an ethical reason. I cannot emphasize enough how this way of thinking is the complete reverse of rational decision-making.

God barbarically killed millions of people in the Old Testament because they were not "fortunate" enough to belong to the Israelite tribe. Had these alleged victims belonged to the lineage of Jacob, they obviously would not have suffered the full wrath of God. Nevertheless, what chances did they realistically have of converting to worship the Hebrew deity when their own parents conditioned them to think according to their local customs? Even today, God's evil demands require us to murder billions of non-Christians because their parents unknowingly continue to practice this same form of powerful conditioning.[314] The consequences of obeying God's directions should give us the presence of mind to refrain from following such orders without first analyzing the morality of the demands in question. Widely distributed directions from a fair god should be self-evidently moral or have a satisfactory explanation as to why they are necessary. Otherwise, we may be repeating the same evil accomplishments of our ancestors. Lucky for us, however, God conveniently ceased his murdering and slave driving when modern philosophers, enlightened thinking, and accurate historical records began to appear.

The Bible does not treat women as inferior.

After thousands of years of recorded history, we are just now arriving at a point where women are starting to receive fair and equal treatment in many progressive societies. It is an irrefutable historical fact that some of the major sources of this unsolicited oppression were drawn from references of women's treatment in both the Old and New Testaments. The Bible takes a clear and undeniable stance in its avocation for the unequal treatment of women because the Old Testament authors clearly intended for women to play the role of a man's servant from birth until death. Women were bought and sold as sex slaves, stoned to death if physically unable to prove their virginity, and undeniably treated as the complete property of their husbands. The subsequent works of Paul and his peers show only how gullible they were in so readily accepting the Hebrew Scriptures as divine ordination. Since a lengthy treatise on the treatment of women in the Bible is beyond the scope of this book, I will discuss only the issue of rape and simply refer readers to other works if they want the complete picture.[315]

The punishments for rape are perhaps the most disturbing regulations in the Bible. While God ensures that the authors list it as a crime under most circumstances,[316] we must realize that there are two contrasting conditions to consider in the event that a Hebrew woman is sexually violated: whether the victim is married (or engaged) or a virgin. The fine for committing one of the most heinous acts imaginable against a virgin woman without God's permission is a pound of *silver* paid to her *father* and a forced *marriage* to the *victim*.[317] Yes, God's idea of justice for the raped woman is to be horrendously punished again by forcing her to marry the man who savagely attacked her. This disgusting rule is nowhere near what most people would consider an ethical resolution, and it's certainly not a decision rendered by any court I would like to be facing. On the other hand, a man who rapes an engaged virgin or a married woman will be stoned to death, not because he committed a brutal atrocity against the woman, but because he "violated another man's wife."[318]

Note the shamefully sharp contrast in disciplinary action between raping a woman with a husband and raping a woman without a husband: *death* versus a pound of *silver*. Since being raped is certainly all the same to the woman, it now becomes clear that God feels the *husband* is the one who is the victim of the attack. Raping a woman of your choice who does not have a husband allows you to marry the woman of your choice, but raping a woman who already belongs to another man warrants the death sentence. I could talk for days without overstating the evil absurdity of these rules. I simply cannot have any respect for any Christian who reads these regulations, acknowledges them, and makes excuses for them because they are part of the *Old* Testament. At *no* time should this philosophy have been law.

As I alluded to earlier, there is also a third category of rape guidelines in the Old Testament that applies to women of foreign nations. After Moses follows God's instructions to defeat the Midianites in battle, his army takes thousands of war prisoners. Moses then orders his army to kill the remaining men, boys, and women who have already slept with a man, "but all the women children, that have not known a man by lying with him, keep alive for yourselves."[319] If taking a human war trophy based solely on the prisoner's gender and sexual status is not implied permission to commit rape, I honestly do not know what is. However, we actually do not require implications because the Bible tells us exactly what to do when a female virgin is taken prisoner in warfare...

> *It has been groundlessly asserted, that Moses here authorised the Israelites to make concubines of the whole number of female children; and an insidious objection against his writings has been grounded upon this monstrous supposition. But the whole tenor of the law, and especially a statute recorded in Deuteronomy 21:10-14, proves most decisively to the contrary. They were merely permitted to possess them as female slaves, educating them in their families, and employing them as domestics; for the laws concerning fornication, concubinage, and marriage, were in full force, and prohibited an Israelite even from marrying a captive, without delays and previous formalities; and if he afterwards divorced her, he was to set here at liberty, "because he had humbled her."*[320]

I disagree with very little of what this individual argues, but I rather strongly disagree with how he tries to make the issue benign. Note that, according to the apologist, the Israelite is prohibited from marrying his prisoner without "delays and previous formalities." Naturally, we would like to know what these delays and formalities are that the person references.

> When thou goest forth to war against thine enemies, and the LORD thy God hath delivered them into thine hands, and thou hast taken them captive, And seest among the captives a beautiful woman, and hast a desire unto her, that thou wouldest have her to thy wife; Then thou shalt bring her home to thine house; and she shall shave her head, and pare her nails; And she shall put the raiment of her captivity from off her,

> and shall remain in thine house, and bewail her father and her mother a full month: and after that thou shalt go in unto her, and be her husband, and she shall be thy wife. And it shall be, if thou have no delight in her, then thou shalt let her go whither she will; but thou shalt not sell her at all for money, thou shalt not make merchandise of her, because thou hast humbled her.[321]

In other words, if you want to make the prisoner your wife, you must shave her head, cut her nails, remove her prisoner clothing, and allow her to mourn the fact that you murdered her parents along with everyone else in her city for one month before you can marry her and "go in unto" her. How exactly does the apologist propose that these regulations make it ethically permissible to marry and have sex with someone who obviously would not have the same desires? How exactly does letting the woman go if you are not sexually pleased with her make everything morally acceptable? Are we expected to believe that the female prisoner had a right to refuse this process? The Bible does not even indicate that the local *Hebrew* women are given this luxury. It is clear that the kidnapped woman was forced to marry and have sexual relations with her barbaric captor whether she wanted to or not. This is rape, and no apologist wants to deal critically and honestly with the matter. It is all about defending the Bible at any sickening cost.

I once had a very lengthy debate with a Jewish apologist (pursuing a dual Ph.D. in psychology and Jewish studies) regarding the translation of the Midianite story. Here is the relevant portion of the passage: "[31:17] Now therefore kill every male among the little ones, and kill every woman that hath known man by lying with him. [31:18] But all the women children, that have not known a man by lying with him, keep alive for yourselves." [322] Before we proceed, consider that Moses' army had previously killed all of the grown men in battle.

The intent of the passage seems straight forward, but that has never stopped apologists from twisting the text in order to make the Bible fit with their predetermined beliefs. According to the Jewish apologist, the word *women* (*ishshah* in Hebrew) in the eighteenth verse should have been translated as *every*. In other words, God says to keep *all* children alive that have not slept with a man. Since the apologist's alternative translation is indeed supported by a small minority of other cases in the Old Testament, we might have to accept the apologist's suggestion if the passage appeared in a vacuum. However, the passage must be viewed in context for us to understand it properly. After doing so, we must ask why the order would be to 1) kill all of the boys, 2) kill all of the non-virgin girls, 3) save all of the virgin boys and girls.

Command number one does not say to kill all of the non-virgin boys; it says to kill all of the boys. You cannot kill all of the boys, then save the virgin ones. When pressed to explain why the sexual status exception was listed for the girls and not the boys in verse *seventeen*, the apologist immediately chided me for not knowing that we were supposed to be discussing verse *eighteen*. However, it should be clear to discerning readers that verse seventeen is relevant to the context of verse eighteen. It was obvious that he could not reasonably ignore the given translation because there is a contrast between the boys and girls with regard to whether they had previously had sexual relations. We could then only reasonably render verse eighteen as speaking of *female* children, not *all* children. The apologist's attempt to save all of the virgin children, regardless of gender, failed.

When the apologist realized that I was not going to let him ignore the context of the passage, he changed his tune. After further review, he determined that the English word *not* was incorrectly added to the translation of the seventeenth verse. Again, considering the translational possibilities, this explanation would have been valid in a vacuum, but I pressed him to explain why the text would say 1) kill all of the boys, 2) kill all of the non-virgin girls, 3) save all of the non-virgin girls. His explanation was that verse eighteen was stating an exception to the two commands in verse seventeen. In his own words, "Do A and B, but not B."

The amount of conditioning this young man was under simply astounded me. This laughable method of argumentation was the only way he could eliminate the uneasy feeling from the cognitive dissonance that I had placed on him. He honestly thought that the order should be translated as, "Kill all of the young boys and all of the young girls, but don't kill all of the young girls." He was going to do anything in order to make that text not say something he did not want it to say, even if it meant claiming that it would make sense for someone to say, "I like apples and oranges, but I don't like oranges." The apologist's attempt to save all of the girls, regardless of sexual experience, failed.

As far as I know, he still believes his ridiculous suggestion to this day. The stupidity of such an argument from an otherwise intelligent person made me want to cry. Raping a woman who follows another religion warrants you God's indifference, and no textual manipulation can change that. Most apologists would never attempt a defense like the one given. Instead, they attempt to make the issue as benign as possible by ignoring the underlying ramifications. Here is one example:

> *Forcing the man to marry a raped woman is actually beneficial because no other man would ever want to marry her.*[323]

With a million pages at my disposal, I could not elaborate sufficiently on how backwards this idea is. For most readers, a single sentence is probably not needed due to its self-evident nature. It is disturbingly shameful that someone would actually have the audacity to offer such a sorry excuse for his god. Did this person ever stop to consider that the woman would perhaps prefer that the man be punished and she be allowed to go about her difficult existence as a single woman? Did this person ever stop to consider that God could have provided a moral code for a man not to eliminate a woman from consideration for marriage if someone had previously raped her? At the very least, did this person ever stop to consider that God could have eliminated such actions from occurring so that we would never need such a backwards policy? It is amazing how God chose to create beings with such punishable immorality.

I of course know what most of the progressive Christians are screaming in their heads: "All of this stuff about rape is in the *Old* Testament. Times were different then. God doesn't want us to follow those rules anymore. That's why he sent Jesus to burden our sins." But I ask you, why did God *ever* allow this? Those were real people living back then. God ordered his followers to rape someone's sister because she had not been raised to follow the religion of Abraham. God forced someone's daughter to marry the man who raped her in order to punish the rapist and provide security for the victim.

God was in complete control of establishing codes of morality, yet he offered this cruel nonsense as his moral standard. It is simply much easier and employs infinitely more common sense to disregard such hatred as the product of barbaric men rather than defend it as the holy word of a perfect god. How could an omnipotent creature ever allow such a pitiful mess to represent him? Throwing your hands up and declaring that there *must* be a reason because of God's infinite benevolence is no better intellectually than declaring Hitler a good man and molding explanations for his actions around that premise.

Ephesians 5:21 involves mutual submission between a man and a woman.

Although the idea that women are to be submissive to men is nearly consistent throughout the Bible, apologists like to reference this singular passage in Ephesians that supposedly corrects the problem. The suggestion of mutual male/female submission does not succeed, as I will show, but even if it did, how does one explain the remainder of passages that support female subordination? Ephesians 5:21, which states, "submit to one another out of reverence for Christ" is the most common defense submitted against the argument that women are assigned to inferiority, as if God suddenly changed his mind after allowing all sorts of cruelties and injustices against them for centuries in the Old Testament.

There are several problems with using this verse as an equal rights argument. First, Paul addresses a general audience in his letters. When he wants to address specific roles, such as the role of a husband or wife, he will say so. He does this three times in the next few verses. After addressing the general population and telling them to submit to each other, as a message of general kindness, he addresses wives, husbands, and children specifically, beginning in verse twenty-two. Wives are told to submit to husbands in everything, as husbands must submit to Christ. Husbands, on the other hand, are told to *love* their wives as they love themselves.

Paul had the perfect opportunity to say that husbands should also submit to their wives, if this was what he intended in verse twenty-one, but he did not do so. If he truly meant for husbands and wives to submit to each other, why was he redundant with just the instruction for wives? There is obviously no mutual submission here. Paul is consistent with his oblivious bigotry of women in his other works, and there is no reason to believe that he promoted equality between the sexes. And even if the apologetic suggestion was God's will, why could he not get his ideas across properly the first time? Why the need for a clarification centuries later?

I am perfectly aware, however, that there is a radical departure from tradition in Ephesians. Paul tells men to set aside their own desires and to give their complete love to their wives. Before, in the Old Testament, husbands treated their wives like simple objects. Paul is one of the first biblical characters to humanize women, but he still orders them to be submissive to their male leaders. Husbands who love their wives completely can still order them to do what they think is best, and the wives must obey. This is bigotry. It is ridiculous beyond comprehension to assume that a god would inspire something so unenlightened, much more so with what we see him allegedly inspiring in the Old Testament.

Of all the worthwhile things Paul could have written, Ephesians 5:21 is the nonsense with which we are left. I am not divinely inspired, yet I can do better than Paul: "Submit to each other: wives to your husbands, and husbands to your wives. One shall not have dominion over the other. Work together to achieve solutions to your problems. Listen to each other. Love each other as you love yourselves. Give yourselves completely to each other, so long as you do no harm to yourselves. Consider yourselves equals since you *are* equal." No divine inspiration, yet I am more enlightened than the father of Christianity who was inspired by an omnipotent, omniscient being. For the life of me, I cannot understand why apologists will not accept the ramifications here.

> *It's important to know whether God is* describing *or* deciding *the punishment of women. Adam and Eve's actions automatically resulted in certain consequences. It is quite reasonable to read it as God's description of those consequences, rather than as his prescription.*

No, it is irrelevant. God is in complete control of the creation. He can decide to punish women into inferiority, assign them into inferiority, declare that they were inferior to begin with, or describe them as being inferior creations. It makes no difference because God had the opportunity to create whatever scenario he saw fit. Otherwise, why call him a god?

If God wanted men and women to have equal places in society, one must assume that God would have said so. If God wanted women to be superior to men, one must assume that he would have said so. If God wanted men to be superior to women, one must assume that he would have said so. If God did not care, one must assume nothing would have been said. It is clear, however, what God says in the Old Testament. One can easily take the Adam and Eve passage out of context and say that it is equally likely to be a description or prescription, as if it truly mattered. However, to make matters worse for this suggestion, God sure picks a curious time for a *description* - right after Adam and Eve have refused his orders. You just do not see many superiors going up to their inferiors to give them *descriptions* of their nature after they have disobeyed them.

What this suggestion seems to be is just another wild impractical scenario that does not invalidate the preconceived notion that God is a loving figure who would not force one sex to be ruled by another. Those who desperately don't want it to be a punishment will not see it that way even when context clearly demonstrates that it is. I am certainly open to the idea that it is a description and not a prescription, but one must demonstrate that this is a reasonable position to take and how exactly the distinction can exist. The apologist did not do this because he likely could not.

> *Look at the context of Genesis 3:16, look at the words chosen, and look at what other similar words* could *have been chosen but were not.*

There is obviously a rank double standard within the apologetic community. When I criticize Old Testament authors for describing the earth as a *chug* (circle) instead of a *kadur* (sphere), I hear that the chosen word is sufficient because the intent is clear (even in the age of flat-earth beliefs, mind you). The true context of Genesis 3:16 is obvious to anyone who is not emotionally concerned with the outcome. I do not care one way or another whether the passage talks about female subordination; and even if I did, there are plenty of other verses that show how women were treated as inferior. If my interpretations of all of those are wrong, then there is plenty more wrong with the Bible in science, history, and other aspects of morality. If all of those conclusions are wrong, then I am wrong. I don't mind. I've been wrong before. I am willing to accept any possibility, but when a certain text is blatantly wrong on a number of key issues, I decrease that possibility dramatically. Apologists are just not willing to back down one inch from their position because it damages the entire notion of perfection or divine inspiration.

I wish the person who offered this suggestion would have written back and elaborated on alternatives to the author's word choice. I never heard from him again. Since I do not know the Hebrew translation of every word in the Bible, I wish someone would enlighten me on what I supposedly do not understand. From what I *do* understand, however, *mashal* is consistently used to convey exercising authority or dominion: the sun ruling the day, Abraham ruling his property, Joseph ruling Egypt, several kings ruling their lands, etc. Not once, out of eighty-one instances, is *mashal* used to describe something benign like the writer is suggesting.[324]

I am sure there are harsher Hebrew words, just as there are no doubt lighter ones, but this does not take away from the fact that God is declaring one sex will have dominion over another. The husband has final authority over the wife, just as kings have authority over their lands, just as Joseph had authority over Egypt, just as Abraham had authority over his property, just as the sun has authority over the day. God told Adam his punishment for eating the forbidden fruit was a future in which he would have to suffer during his work, but God passed over another perfect opportunity to describe how husbands should rule together with their wives–if such an idea was truly God's intention, as the apologist hopelessly asserted.

> *There's a difference between stating a natural result and changing the rules. The universe was already created. God*

> *had no need to change the rules. He simply was stating already-existent truth.*

Men ruling over women was a "natural result?" That's weak and deplorable. What would God say to those who questioned the order of things? "Look, women, it's just natural that you're going to be ruled by men. I could say that this is unjust and see that it isn't carried out by using my omnipotence, or I could have made things a different way to begin with, but I'm not going to change the rules. Sorry about the millennia of injustice, that's just the way things are." This trivializes the Judeo-Christian God in ways that I can only begin to imagine. It's more damaging to the Bible's credibility than a bigoted god. He is now a lazy, indifferent one. God creates an unethical situation knowing full well that women are going to suffer as inferiors for millennia but isn't going to change the rules because it's what he decided was a "natural result." I could elaborate further on the pathetic nature of this attitude, but I think I have sufficiently made my point. I will conclude by urging all Christian men to use their intrinsic common decency, not the Bible, when deciding how to treat a woman.

> *The Bible does not allow slavery in the sense that you're thinking.*

The common apologetic response to the question of how God feels about slavery is that he *definitely* opposed the historical tradition. The long-time practice of holding innocent individuals against their will could very well be the worst crime humankind has ever committed. The Judeo-Christian God, who is purported to love his people to a degree that we could never comprehend, would certainly have to declare some explicit opposition to violent forms of slavery, wouldn't he? As you might have already guessed, the Bible contains not one mention of God's desire to end slavery. Out of all the "thou shalt nots" and multitude of rules that he provides for us; out of all the chapters that God spends giving us intricate directions for making candles, tents, and temples; and out of all the chapters that God inspires the authors to spend on telling us who begat whom; not once does he *ever* take the time to abolish, admonish, or reject violent forms of slavery.

Since God is supposedly omniscient, he knew that a time would arrive when the results of his silence would include the capture, torture, castration, dehumanization, and/or murder of tens of millions of African abductees around the world. Even with his unlimited knowledge, God still neglects to spend two seconds of his infinite time to ensure that we have his documented denouncement of slavery. Using elementary deduction and common sense on this scrap of information, we are already able to conclude that it was not displeasing in the eyes of the Judeo-Christian God for a more powerful individual to own a lesser one.

Does the presumably apathetic preference of God toward slavery mean that we are left with a distant ruler demonstrably indifferent toward the institution? In such a case, perhaps he wants us to use our judgment on whether or not it is morally acceptable to own other people. Regrettably, an in depth analysis of the Bible tells us that this cannot be the case either. As hard as it may be to accept, even for those doubtful of the Bible's authenticity, God and the multitude of his appointed biblical authors are strongly vocal in advocating cruel forms of slavery.

God explicitly allows slaveowners to beat their living property and declares that the slaveowner "shall not be punished: for [the slave] is his money."[325] God clearly believes that a non-Hebrew slave is nothing more than a financial investment of the owner. The only way that the law can distribute a punishment for the physical onslaught is if it results in the slave's death, yet God does not provide us with the exact punishment.[326] One of the heralded Proverbs even educates its readers that a slave "cannot be corrected by mere words."[327] Furthermore, the New Testament includes a number of writers who encourage slaves to be submissive to cruel masters, as well as a number of other writers who discourage slave rebellion.[328]

The question now becomes why God would have such statements in his holy word if he did not approve of slave ownership and a regular slave beating. Sure, we can attempt to justify the early practice of slavery as offering protection for the weak, but the guidelines go well beyond what is ethical. I think there is little doubt that God, who necessarily had the foresight of the later forms of its practice, was not displeased with the practice getting out of hand. Any decent person knows that this lifestyle is humiliating and demoralizing, not to mention just plain wrong, because freedom is essential to a healthy and happy existence.

How can you believe that God is a *wonderful* and *loving* creator when he inspired the men who wrote the Old Testament to claim that they were divinely encouraged to promote slavery of foreigners who worshiped different gods? How can you believe that God is a *wonderful* and *loving* creator when he allowed women to live as slaves because the men believed that females were the inferior gender? The Old Testament writers even say that God sold slaves and gave rules to Moses permitting his people to beat the male slaves and rape the female slaves.[329] These are not *wonderful* and *loving* decisions.

Ask yourself a tough question: Did God actually say and do all these horrible things, or were the authors probably trying to advance ulterior motives by tricking a gullible audience into believing that these ghastly commands were truly of divine origin? Please take time to consider the ramifications of a god who would not take two seconds to warn people about how slavery would get out of hand by including clear condemnations among his textual encouragements for beating slaves. And if you decide that the Bible contains something God did not say, why would God allow it to turn out that way? If the Bible is wrong on slavery, might it not also be wrong on female subordination? And if wrong on female subordination, then wrong on morality in general? And if wrong on morality, then wrong on history? And if wrong on history, then wrong on reality? And if wrong on reality, then wrong on the existence of the vile Judeo-Christian God itself?

Addendum: Letter From A Preacher

I was prepared to send this book off for publishing with the material you've read up to this point, but I could not resist delaying the process after I received the following letter from an individual who identifies himself as a preacher. Since the issues raised do not necessarily impede on the other topics previously covered, I left the letter pretty much as it found me.

> *An atheist assigns himself to life without ultimate purpose. Yes, atheists enjoy many smaller meanings of life–like friendship and love, pleasure and sorrow, Mozart and Plato. But to be consistent with his atheism, he cannot allow for ultimate meaning. Yet, if the atheist is honest, he will admit to feeling that there is something more to existence–something bigger.*

Ignoring the fact that I don't exactly consider myself an atheist and have never really identified myself as one,[330] perhaps the preacher would like to offer an argument (instead of an assertion) as to why there is no ultimate purpose or meaning outside of a creator and why the atheist must feel something bigger. Assertions filled with rhetoric do not make arguments. I am also quite disturbed that friendship, love, Mozart, and Plato are "smaller meanings of life." What atrocities is one capable of committing if he relegates such ideas to smaller meanings of life?

If an atheist feels that enjoying these subjects is his ultimate purpose, the preacher has already invalidated his earlier assertion. Perhaps the preacher meant to assert that the atheist assigns himself to life without a purpose *with which the preacher agrees* should be an ultimate purpose. In which case, it is the duty of the preacher to demonstrate that the ultimate purpose he perceives is the only possible ultimate purpose. As you can see, ridiculous assertions often create tangled webs.

> *Someone said, "The blazing evidence for immortality is our dissatisfaction with any other solution."*

Does the preacher not spot the blazing irony in this statement? The suggestion states that the best reason we have to believe we are immortal is due to the comfort in *believing just that.* Mark Twain similarly once said, "One of the proofs of the immortality of the soul is that myriads have believed in it. They have also believed the world was flat."[331] The idea of heaven has thrived for centuries for three major reasons: 1) it is comforting, 2) it is indoctrinated heavily during childhood, and 3) it is non-falsifiable. There will most likely never be hard evidence for the absence of an afterlife. As Smith put it, "The dead cannot return to demand a refund."[332] The apologetic suggestion is yet another example of a Christian coming unbelievably close to truly understanding his position, yet falling short because of interference from his confirmation bias. He sees in that statement what he wants to see, I suppose, but I could not possibly find what he likely intended to share.

> *To maintain his position, the atheist must suppress the feeling that there is more to life than temporal pleasures.*

The "temporal" portion I do not disagree with, but the "pleasures" aspect is a clear assertive attempt to portray atheists as creatures purely seeking pleasure. If the preacher chose to research *hedonism* in more depth, he probably would not have made this mistake. Otherwise, the rules of logic now force the preacher to explain how hedonism and atheism can be used interchangeably. I really shouldn't feel the need to point out that many atheists have their own codes of conduct that are more than acceptable under common decency laws (and are often very superior to traditional Christian codes), but if this line of thinking is popular in the clergy, apparently someone needs to do so.

> *His controlling bias against God will not allow him to accept that we are designed.*

The preacher extends this idea because he had just offered the previously discussed Design Argument as proof that God exists, but I decided not to tackle the argument again since I have dealt with it previously in the text. As far as addressing his suggestion that I have a bias against God, I will accept most any assertion with a reasonable argument to back it up. On the other hand, I have often found that apologists will readily admit that they will not accept any argument that is contrary to their beliefs. I will again ask readers to determine which party holds controlling bias that will not allow them to consider the other party's arguments objectively.

There is no shortage of Christians who will admit that nothing will change their belief in God's existence. To date, no one has offered a plausible reason for such blind faith. I once drew the analogy of two separate tribes that resided in an area with a large blanket covering the ground. While no member of either tribe has seen the grass under the blanket, one group has been convinced for thousands of years that it is blue–and the other, red. While every member of each tribe has been indoctrinated to accept the correctness of his or her beliefs, no one can actually lay claim to absolute certainty of the color. An apologist for the blue grass has an enormous amount of arguments at his disposal, as does the apologist for the red grass. Each thinks his case is a slam-dunk since each has strong emotional and pseudo-intellectual attachments to his belief. What good is either apologist who will not admit to the slightest chance of being wrong? This matter seems patently silly to us only because our societies did not raise us to believe in blue or red grass, but rather in Christianity or Islam.

A controlling bias that there is likely no grass, if such a phenomenon exists within the grass skeptics, could not possibly be more damaging than a controlling bias within the believers for a certain color of grass. When you are already convinced of a position, counterarguments are not going to be convincing. It is clear that once you accept supernatural concepts like God and Satan, which you have never encountered yet you believe to have powers beyond human comprehension, just about any suggestion is considered wholly plausible. Consider this historical example offered by Sagan:

> In the witch trials, mitigating evidence or defense witnesses were inadmissible. In any case, it was nearly impossible to provide compelling alibis for accused witches: The rules of evidence had a special character. For example, in more than one case a husband attested that his wife was asleep in his arms at the very moment she was accused of frolicking with the devil at a witch's Sabbath; but the archbishop patiently explained that a demon had taken the place of the wife. The husbands were not to imagine that their powers of perception could exceed Satan's powers of deception. The beautiful young women were perforce consigned to the flames.[333]

> *Yet, ironically, the atheist has to believe in miracles without believing in God. Why? Well, one law that nature seems to obey is this: whatever begins to exist is caused to exist. The atheist knows that the universe began to exist and since the universe is, according to the atheist, all there is, the very existence of the universe seems to be a colossal violation of the laws of nature (i.e. a miracle).*

Since I am also not going to repeat the earlier refutation of the Kalam version of the Ontological Argument, I will simply refer readers to the section where I previously discussed it. As for this "miracle," perhaps a "colossal violation of the laws of nature" might be considered a miracle, but a colossal violation of the *known* or *perceived* laws of nature would hardly be held in the same regard. When Einstein proposed that Newton's law of universal gravitation could not apply to large objects, did people shout "Miracle!" or did we simply have a better understanding of what nature's laws were? Deeming an act a miracle simply because it violates our contemporaneous understanding of the universe is patently foolish and requires omniscience from the one making such a suggestion in order to rule out all possible natural causes. Smith has something nice to say about this:

> The problem is that one is never justified in claiming that a given occurrence falls outside the realm of natural law. Such an assertion, even if it made sense, would require omniscience. All that one may say is that an event cannot be explained with reference to *presently* known laws, but this does not mean that the event cannot be explained with reference to principles as yet unknown. No man can lay claim to omniscience, and no man can claim to possess a noncontextual and unalterable knowledge of all physical laws. While one may assert that something is presently unexplained, one may never conclude that something is inherently unexplainable.[334]

> *An atheist must also suppress all notions of morality. He is not able to declare any quality to be morally superior to another. Such admissions require an absolute standard of goodness and duty. Without this, there is no basis for an atheist to declare peace better than war or love better than hate.*

How does one need an absolute standard of goodness or duty to declare that war is worse than peace–or rape is worse than homosexuality? No absolute standards of morality are necessary to observe the consequences of each state because, first of all, they are *relative* comparisons. In the Bible, God declares that rape is punishable with a monetary fine in many cases, but homosexuality is punishable by death. Is a monetary fine worse than death? Is this the absolute standard of goodness that the preacher is looking for?

Without the Bible, even the overwhelming majority of Christians can appreciate the fact that rape is worse than homosexuality. No religious absolute standard of goodness tells us that this is so, yet any rational person can perceive that homosexuality is not morally inferior to rape. Why is this? God never spelled it out, so is there an inborn ability to determine certain levels of ethical behavior? If God simply programmed morality into us, how do we differ between this programming and our developed ethical notions? The preacher cannot answer these questions because his answers are contradictory to his previous assertions.

> *For there to be evil, there must also be some real, objective standard of right and wrong. But if the physical universe is all there is, there can be no such standard. How could arrangements of matter and energy make judgments about good and evil true?*

I would hardly argue that evil would be determined *objectively* rather than *subjectively*, and I have already supported my position to my satisfaction in the morality section. Since the preacher asserted that morality must be objective, let him also back his claim. However, it is clear that the preacher is making assertions that he has no desire to support with arguments or reasoning. In addition, these "arrangements of matter and energy" are clearly responsible for creating consciousness, which is undeniably eliminated once the matter and energy are removed. This is demonstrable through empirical testing and observation. The rules of logic now force the preacher to argue that God magically removes a person's thought processes once the matter or energy is removed, but this is a strict violation of choosing the simplest explanation for a phenomenon. There is evidence for one argument, while the other relies on assertive dogma. I cannot believe that anyone would actually make this argument, but then again, I can.

> *The atheist must also live with the arrogance of his position. Although he realizes that he does not possess total knowledge, his assertion that there is no God requires that he pretend such knowledge.*

How ironic. Just as the preacher commits the blunder of chastising atheists for not accepting omniscience-requiring miracles, he accuses atheists of utilizing omniscience for disbelieving in God. Very much to the contrary of the preacher's suggestion, atheists most often argue that they have no reason to believe in God and/or that they have good reasons to disbelieve in God. Asserting that there is no god is pretty much the academic equivalent of asserting that there is a god. It would serve the preacher well in the future to understand his opponents' positions–and perhaps his own. Furthermore, the act of claiming that one knows the origin of the universe without doubt and without evidence, even in the face of contrasting religious stories and scientific counterevidence, should be covered under any reasonable definition of arrogance.

> *The atheist must also deny the validity of historical proof. If he accepted the standard rules for testing the truth claims of historical documents, he would be forced to accept the resurrection of Jesus Christ from the dead. The extensive manuscript evidence of eyewitnesses to the resurrection is presented in an unbiased, authentic manner. The account of Jesus' resurrection is strongly validated by standard rules for judging historical accuracy.*

Perhaps you have heard of a certain man that I think it's now time to discuss. According to his followers, his story takes place in a land under control of the Roman Empire when an angelic messenger announced his upcoming birth to his mother in the year 4BCE. While his mother was human, his father was a divine being. Not much is known about his childhood, other than the time he spent discussing philosophy and religion with his elders. As he became of age, he roamed about the Near East with his disciples teaching moral codes to live by, driving demons out of possessed individuals, and working all sorts of other miracles. Most notably, he healed the lame, blind, and dead simply by laying his hands upon them. Crowds loved him and followed him, but the Roman authorities, believing such acts to be unlawful, sought to kill him. Following his death, he miraculously reappeared to his disciples. One of whom doubted that he had truly returned to life, to which this man offered his hand as proof. Soon thereafter, he left the earth and entered into heaven.

This, as you probably do not know, is the story of Apollonius of Tyana. I would give you more information on him had the Christians not burned all of the books he wrote. While no freethinking individual would ever believe that this man actually did all of these things, they are nevertheless written in his earliest known biography. Although Apollonius pre-dates Jesus of Nazareth, we have no solid evidence that Jesus was based on Apollonius since the gospels pre-date the earliest extant version of this story. However, the point of relaying the tale is to demonstrate that so-called saviors were a dime a dozen in the times before scientific scrutiny. So much for "standard rules for judging historical accuracy."[335]

The paramount aspect of Christian faith is the unwavering belief that there was indeed a man named Jesus from Nazareth, the supernatural son of God, who performed such feats. This character performed a variety of incredible miracles and attributed their possibility to the faith that his followers held in his heavenly father. Such an extraordinary being would eventually be crucified for his teachings, as the story goes, only to follow through on his promises of resurrecting from death and returning to his disciples shortly thereafter. Before his ultimate reunion with God, he pledges to descend one day in order to take all of those with him who believe in following his examples. Suffice to say, this is the mother of all extraordinary cultish claims requiring extraordinary evidence.

At the present, it is honestly impossible to verify or dismiss Jesus as a historical person because we lack evidence and crucial eyewitness testimony. Thus, the Christian belief of Jesus being a true historical figure is entirely predicated upon blind faith in the legitimacy of the New Testament writers. Even if we assume a successful completion of an endeavor to legitimize some sort of historical Jesus who lectured on various subjects of life, which is indeed most likely the case, the burden of proof would still be on the shoulder of the apologist to prove the typical claims of outlandish miracles. These allegations of mystic performances are what are relevant to our analysis.

If Jesus Christ was merely an ordinary man with extraordinary teaching abilities, or if he was a legend born from the obvious necessities of turbulent times, the entire foundation of the New Testament quickly implodes. While we are still unable to offer the undeniable proof that contradicts all gospel claims, once we sit down and actually read the outlandish suggestions found within the New Testament, we *can* easily deduce the incredibly overwhelming unlikelihood of Jesus ever having lived a life anything like the one depicted in the gospels.

Paul began writing about Christ twenty years after his supposed death, but he does not talk about any earthly miracles and rarely touches on any aspects of an earthly existence. When he does do so, a few scholars maintain that they are suspect interpolations of the work. We must also wonder why Paul was not able to locate someone else who could personally testify to the physical existence of Jesus Christ and the historical events surrounding his residency. He mentions meeting Peter and James, two of Jesus' Apostles, but he relates nothing regarding their verbal exchanges.[336] Paul should have also had the ability to meet with thousands who had witnessed Jesus' miracles. Furthermore, he missed many perfect opportunities to talk about some of the events surrounding Jesus and even consistently told the Romans (those who actually sought out and killed Jesus) that many of his writings needed to be taken on faith.

First century historians and other writers fail to mention any of the incredible events purported in the gospels, which were themselves written at least forty years after the alleged resurrection. There are no known records mentioning Jesus made prior to 49 CE, and the earliest date ascribed to the gospels by secular scholars is about 75 CE. This often-overlooked exclusion might be understandable, perhaps even anticipated, if there were no reputable historians, authors, or philosophers around to document the unique phenomena purported by the New Testament. However, this supposed explanation cannot be the case. The quintessential reason is Jewish author and philosopher Philo of Alexandria (15 BCE - 50 CE), a devotedly religious man with a volume of work sizable enough to fill a modern publication of nearly one thousand pages with small print.

Even though Philo was adamant about the legitimacy of the Hebrew scripture, not once does he indicate that he knew the first thing about a historical Jesus. However, Philo *did* choose to refer to the son of God in the form of *Logos*, which is to say a spiritual medium between God and man. As it stands in the biblical world, the supernatural son of the universe's almighty creator was supposedly performing unprecedented miracles and fulfilling prophecies that this philosopher spent his life analyzing, yet Philo, living well before Jesus' birth and well after the crucifixion, *never* mentions such occurrences! This fact alone should assuredly convince you that the gospel authors based a great deal of their work on rumors, urban legends, and mere fiction.

Other historians and philosophers, while not strictly religious writers, never mentioned Jesus' influence on society. The most notable of which include Jewish author and historian Justus of Tiberias from Galilee (35-100 CE[337]), Roman author and philosopher Pliny the Elder (23-79 CE), Jewish Roman author and historian Josephus Flavius (37-100 CE),[338] Greek philosopher and writer Apollonius of Tyana (4 BCE–100 CE), Latin rhetorician of Roman History Valerius Maximus (20 BCE–50 CE), and Roman author and philosopher Seneca the Younger (4 BCE–65 CE), not to mention the twenty or so other known writers from the first century,[339] the five hundred resurrected in Matthew,[340] and the thousands who allegedly witnessed these miracles but weren't moved enough to have them documented.

All sorts of second century historians write about Jesus when the gospels start emerging on the scene, but no first century historians give him the briefest mention. So what exactly are the preacher's standards for strong historical validation for a common event, let alone a phenomenon unique to human history? For example, if we accept Josephus' dubious 93 CE mention of Jesus as evidence for his miraculous works, must we not also accept Josephus' claim that the Pamphylian Sea parted for Alexander the Great?[341] If we accept historian Suetonius' 112 CE mention of "Chrestus" as evidence for the historicity of Jesus, do we also accept his testimony that Roman Emperor Vespasian healed the blind and lame simply by touching them?[342] Smith elaborates on this problem:

> "The Christian encounters a problem of selectivity. On what basis can he believe in the miracles of Christianity and yet deny the reported miracles of other religions? How does one distinguish historical miracles that are worthy of belief from those that are not? Or, to push the point further, after one has conceded the validity of

> recorded miracles, how does one distinguish historical fact from mythological fancy?...Without rational standards with which to sift nonsense from possible fact, without a means to separate the possible from the impossible, there could be no study of history for man. And since a miracle by definition, does not conform to rational standards, it is absurd to speak of a "historical miracle"; it is a contradiction in terms. If one admits the veracity of historical miracles, one has abandoned rational guidelines; if one abandons these guidelines, however, one cannot speak of *anything* as being historical–including miracles–since one has destroyed one's tool of discrimination."[343]

I have never honestly understood the apologetic position that the skeptic must accept the story of a dead man coming back to life based on the (alleged) say-so of a few witnesses and historians. If I can gather one hundred people to write reports that claim I was killed and came back to life a week later, would the "standard rules for testing the truth claims" of these documents force people to accept that the story is true? Hardly. Common sense tells us that there are many explanations more likely than the one reported. Which suggestion should we find more likely: the rules of the universe fell apart two thousand years ago, or superstitious people were mistaken two thousand years ago? It is intellectually unacceptable to believe in the absurd resurrection claim based upon the works of anonymous authors who recorded (perhaps second-hand) the testimonies of individuals whom we know little about (particularly in the case of Mark and Luke).

A possible explanation as to why there was apparently a growing belief in the early second century for a physical resurrection has been found in psychological study of eyewitness behavior. According to Sagan, the results of one such study imply that witnesses of events become convinced of suggested incidents that did not happen. Subjects in a controlled experiment were made to watch a film of a traffic accident, and the researchers mentioned the presence of a stop sign that was not in the film. When the researchers revealed the deception, some subjects vehemently protested the assertion and stressed how vividly they remembered a stop sign being in the film. Moreover, as more time passed between the viewing and revealing, people were increasingly convinced of their original belief in a stop sign.[344]

Perhaps as the rumor of a resurrection grew at the turn of the century, members of an older generation could have "remembered" details of the event. One could have "remembered" a guard at the tomb; one could have "remembered" someone who saw Jesus after the resurrection; one could have "remembered" seeing him go into the sky. We do not fully know why the belief in a resurrection exploded in the second century, but we can certainly eliminate implausible suggestions.

Jesus was not even a significant figure in the philosophy of morality, and I could hardly imagine how any teacher with the supposed backing of an omnipotent being could possibly be any more inept. Absolutely nothing he says is worth more than a passing mention in the history of philosophy. Why does he scoff at the ancient laws of hand washing, stoning, fasting, taking an eye for an eye, and working on the Sabbath, yet at the same time say that he came to uphold, not change, the laws of Moses?[345] Why does he offer reward as the primary motivation for moral behavior?[346] Why can we find all of his teachings in the Old Testament and other works of those who lived before him?[347] Why is his celebrated golden rule, "Do unto others as you would have them do unto you," predated centuries before by Confucius, among others? [348] Why are his philosophies greatly inferior to those predated centuries before by the intellectual giants Plato and Aristotle, among others?[349] Why does he tell his followers to give away whatever is asked of them and to not resist anyone doing them harm?[350] Why does he tell others that they must hate their own families before following him?[351]

"Do unto others as you would have them do unto you" might be a good rule of thumb, but the selection of this singular quote is very uncharacteristic of the majority of biblical material. For every apparent benevolent guideline offered in the Bible, I could find an equally unjust one. How about "Kill everyone who worships a different God"?[352] It seems to me that one must not simply heed advice given in the Bible, but instead decide on what is the more appropriate course of action through inductive reasoning. Just because a philosophy can be located in the Bible does not self-demonstrate that it should be replicated, held in esteem, or regarded in any way as ethical.

Instead of just laying down an ethical framework for humanity to follow, why does Jesus speak in parables that he himself admits are difficult or impossible for some to understand?[353] Instead of telling these parables using slaves and masters, why not say that slavery is unjust?[354] Instead of telling these parables using virgins and husbands, why not say that women are equal to men?[355] Why did he not condemn the vast majority of the cruelty found in the Pentateuch? Is any of this what we should expect from the offspring of an infinitely wise being? If he gave lectures morally superior to those found in the canonical gospels, why does God allow this contradictory mess to represent him? Instead of leaving the task to a dozen or so gospel writers who frequently disagree with each other on critical issues, why did he not take the time to ensure the world's salvation by writing down his own infallible version of the events? It all sounds so suspiciously flawed, human, unoriginal, and divinely uninspired. Smith explains nicely:

> If we ignore what Jesus said about himself and consider only what he said about morality, he emerges as predominately status quo. This poses a problem for Christian liberals. Strip Jesus of his divinity–as many liberals wish to do–and, at best, he becomes a mediocre preacher who held mistaken beliefs about practically everything, including himself; and, at worst, he becomes a pretentious fraud.[356]

The problem with the public accepting the conclusion that Jesus was an insignificant philosopher is also explained well by Smith:

> Many Christians feel that Jesus, regardless of what he said, must have been the greatest moralist because he was, they believe, the "Son of God" (however this phrase may be interpreted). Few Christians reserve judgment, read the Gospels and, on the bases of an objective evaluation, conclude that Jesus was outstanding. Instead, believing as they do that Jesus was a divine figure, they assume beforehand that whatever he said must be vitally important, because to believe otherwise

> would be to cast doubt on his divinity. And this is tantamount to blasphemy.[357]

Jesus was even among those guilty of making false prophecies. The most condemning of such prophetic statements were his predictions of a return to earth during the long-passed era that he designated. Even though you have no doubt been told repeatedly that the Bible does not indicate when Jesus is going to make his return, such statements are demonstrably false. The truth is that Jesus failed to follow through on the promises unambiguously included in the text as his own words.[358] I imagine such a bold declaration of Jesus' failure may be difficult to swallow at first for two primary reasons: you've received an overwhelming wealth of information to the contrary, and it seems that Christianity would crumble at Jesus' failure to reappear. Probably for these very same reasons, early Christians found a way to circumvent the problem and convince their associates not to renounce his imminent return.[359]

> *It is the atheist's anti-supernatural bias that keeps him from allowing history to prove anything.*

No, it is the freethinker's uniform standard of proof that causes him to reject absurd claims. Extraordinary claims require extraordinary evidence, yet the arguments for the resurrection do not even amount to ordinary evidence and are actually plagued by tremendous amounts of counterevidence.

> *Finally, the atheist must admit that human beings are not importantly different from other animals. According to the atheist, we are simply the result of blind chance operating on the primordial ooze, and differing from animals by only a few genes. Yet, the wonders of human achievement and the moral dignity we ascribe to human beings just do not fit with the claim that we are no different than the animals.*

Did you notice how humans go from being "not importantly different from other animals" to "differing from animals by only a few genes" to "no different than the animals"? Perhaps the preacher's position would be more worthy of consideration if he made a consistent argument. Either we are different, or we are not. What does "importantly different" mean anyway? The notion that we are "the result of blind chance operating on the primordial ooze" is an obvious appeal to emotion that isn't even grounded in fact. Anyone who holds the least bit of evolutionary understanding realizes that it is not a function of chance. I could again fill a page debunking this notion, but I will instead point out that the foundation for evolution (i.e. natural selection) is the complete opposite of chance. Anyone who believes otherwise simply needs to study evolution more in depth.

Since we determine our differentiating characteristics by the relative difference in our DNA, I would agree with the assessment that (on some level) we actually do differ from animals by a *few* genes (in the case of the chimpanzee, 1 percent[360]). It is an empirical, testable, observable, falsifiable fact; and I realize that facts sometimes get in the way of predetermined beliefs. However, we must acknowledge one or the other as true, and it is much easier to change our position than it is to change the facts. "Achievement" and "moral dignity" are the products of our intelligence, which is clearly linked to our genetic code. If you change our DNA even slightly (e.g. one mutation out of thousands of correct replications is believed to result in Autism[361]), you can eliminate the individual's capacity for advanced thought. Change our DNA a little more, and you would have a Neanderthal. Change it a little more still, and you would have a chimpanzee. DNA is certainly the strongest predictor of an organism's ability to reason and achieve.

> *The realities of human creativity, love, reason, and moral value seem to indicate that humans are creatures uniquely made in the image of God.*

Either that - or the realities of those qualities seem to indicate that humans have a genetic code for advanced intelligence and emotion. This position has empirical evidence; the preacher's position has none. At the risk of sounding glib, the preacher does not have the intellectual curiosity to understand his opponent's position and is comfortable in the belief that "God did it" can solve anything. In actuality, the realties of human creativity, love, reason, and moral value seem to indicate that they are beneficial to the continuation of our species. Those who posses such characteristics are more likely to survive, find a mate, and pass such qualities on through procreation. Those who never possessed them likely found it much more difficult to survive. The selection is therefore natural, not supernatural.

> *Always remember that the atheist's problem with belief in God is not the absence of evidence but the suppression of it.*

This would be true only if such evidence existed and if atheists had a driving conscious desire to disbelieve in a supreme being. I have seen no argument that met either case. The Christian theist's problem of believing in the Judeo-Christian God is not the absence of evidence pointing toward biblical fallibility, but rather his indoctrination, conditioning, and biases that have taught him to hold his religious principles as unquestionable.

> *You have to believe in something.*

Many readers have noticed that while I am enormously concerned with the illegitimacy of the Bible, I never take the time to talk about my own religious perspectives. I originally chose not to do so because they were not relevant to the veracity of the Bible. To put the matter to rest, I will declare that I do not follow any particular religion. Since I do not subscribe to a specific religious belief, I pretty much find myself following the basics of secular humanism as a moral guideline. In other words, I base my decisions and actions upon reason and observation rather than religious convictions and ancient superstitions. I ask myself what is right and what is for the greater good–not what a man said that God said he wanted us to do, which anyone can of course ascertain from one of the many books written during the height of human gullibility. I do what is right because it is right–not because an omnipresent voyeurist is going to reward me for doing so.

Even though I meet the classical definition of an atheist,[362] I also frequently refer to myself as agnostic because I know of no way to be certain about supernatural existence–I can only eliminate possibilities. Now that is not to say that I am uncertain whether the Judeo-Christian God exists. I am in no more doubt on that issue than the existence of any of the hundreds of other gods invented in the era. I simply will not rule out the (unlikely?) possibility of a higher power that is beyond the scope of human understanding–the Thomas Jeffersonian God, if you will.

More than one reader has suggested that calling oneself a secular humanist is a thinly veiled attempt to avoid the term atheist, but it is not a matter of what term one prefers because the two schools of thought are independent and sometimes even contradictory. Atheism is a religious stance that there is insufficient evidence to declare the existence of a god; humanism is a philosophy that one should do what is for the greater good without the expectation of a supernatural reward. Since there are a number of Christian individuals who belong to humanist groups,[363] it would not make much to sense to call them Christian atheists. Many Christians (and perhaps a few atheists) use the term interchangeably because they simply do not know the difference. I hope that this practice will soon cease.

Afterword

For the Christian Fundamentalist:

I do not know how many more talking donkeys, talking snakes, global floods, heavenly towers, six day creations, ten-foot Goliaths, forty day periods without food and water, anthropomorphic gods enjoying the smell of burnt animal flesh, ridiculous rules and regulations, declarations of prayer over medicine, wacky visions and hallucinations, transformations of water into blood or wine, exorcisms, dead bodies returning back to life, and bets between deities you would need before you are comfortable calling the Bible an absurd piece of mythological literature. You, however, do not see it as mythology because you begin with the premise that it is not. It is clear that you would believe in it, no matter what claims it made, because you likely were taught to believe in it before you were taught how to tie your shoes. While the best advice I can offer you is to drop your preconceived notions and instead see if you can arrive at your original conclusions by impartially analyzing the evidence and engaging in common sense, I know that you will not heed such advice. Belief is comfortable; skepticism is difficult. You are almost certainly lost forever, and I mourn for you.

For the Progressive Christian:

You are far wiser and more fortunate than your fundamentalist brothers and sisters in Christ, but there is still more to gain. Please consider how you were destined from birth to have the beliefs of society instilled within you. Conditioning from society and your biases toward wanting there to be a god and afterlife are preventing you from rational decision-making. The worst thing you could do is read this book, agree that I have made some good points, and shrug the matters off as explainable in some fashion. If you were interested enough on the subject of the Bible's veracity to read this book, you owe it to yourself to discover the truth no matter where it leads.

For the Rationalist:

I very often hear rationalists only going after the logical misinformation presented by Christians before giving up in disgust and wondering why they can't appeal to people's intellect. I have even caught myself doing it on more than one occasion because we are often provoked with misinformation from Young Earth Creationists and other disreputable apologists. We must remember, however, that it can be nearly impossible to alter a person's stance on an important topic by invoking the use of logic and rational thought when emotional irrationalism protects so much of that person's stance.

Be thankful that you have not wasted your life in the quasi-comforts of false beliefs. Billions of people have died believing in religious myths, but you are not among them. Never will you obsess over pleasing some fictional judge, jury, and executioner. Since not everyone is as fortunate as you have turned out to be, you may want to consider helping others who have fallen victim to superstitions enacted by the societal powers of psychological persuasion.

Notes

1 Actually, most people who accomplish such feats tend *not* to believe in the veracity of the Bible, but we'll get to this issue later.

2 From first to last: the two greatest books of my generation on skepticism, the two greatest primers ever written on disbelief in God, and the two current best-sellers on religious criticism. From this point forward, each work will be referred to simply by author.

3 A lesser-known tale in the Bible, found in the twenty-second chapter of Numbers. It's a new favorite of mine after having watched the movie *Shrek*. In the tale, a donkey argues with its master after receiving a number of beatings for lying down on the job. I often wonder how many people would leave the faith out of embarrassment if they only knew this story was in the Bible.

4 Typically, single-family American Christian households located in Christian neighborhoods during the mid-to-late twentieth century. That's just about everyone, right?

5 Angels: May 10-13, 2007 Gallup Poll accessed from http://www.galluppoll.com/content/?ci=27877&pg=1. Noah and Jesus: ABC News Primetime Poll February 6-10, 2004 accessed from http://www.pollingreport.com/religion2.htm. Psychics: Living TV Paranormal Report 2002 accessed from http://www.50connect.co.uk/50c/faithnews.asp?article=5375 (a survey of the UK – I've picked on the US enough for one footnote).

6 A survey indicating that one-half of all Americans can't name *any* of the four gospels (or the first book of the Bible) has recently been published by Stephen Prothero, head of Boston University's religion

department, in his book *Religious Literacy: What Every American Needs to Know – and Doesn't*, published by HarperOne.

7 This is an allusion to Jesus' statement found in Matthew 7:5. Matthew is one of the four canonical gospels for those of you in the previously mentioned majority.

8 Harris, Sam. *The End of Faith: Religion, Terror, and the Future of Reason*. New York: W. W. Norton & Company, 2004. 72.

9 *American Religious Identification Survey 2001*. Kosmin, Barry A., et.al., eds. The Graduate Center of the City University of New York. 19 December 2001. <http://www.gc.cuny.edu/faculty/research_studies/aris.pdf>.

10 Although the current retention rate of Christianity is "only" 84 percent, it is quite reasonable to believe that the figure was much higher throughout the vast majority of the religion's reign.

11 Barrett, D. et.al., eds. *World Christian Encyclopedia (2nd Ed.)*. New York: Oxford University Press, 2001.

12 Petty, Richard E. and John T. Cacioppo. *Attitudes and Persuasion: Classic and Contemporary Approaches*. Iowa: William C. Brown Company, 1981. 184.

13 Smith, George H. *Atheism: The Case Against God*. New York: Prometheus Books, 1989. 15.

14 Shermer, Michael. *Why People Believe Weird Things: Pseudoscience, Superstition, and Other Confusions of Our Time*. New York: Henry Holt and Company, 2002. 258.

15 Shermer 292.

16 Promises of eternal agony should certainly apply.

17 Petty and Cacioppo 72-73.

18 Bible: Matthew 13:47-50, Mark 9:42-29, and Revelation 14:9-12.

19 Bible: Matthew 13:41-50, Matthew 25:31-46, and Revelation 20:11-15.

20 Bible: John 3:16.

21 Petty and Cacioppo 80.

22 Dawkins, Richard. *The God Delusion*. Boston: Houghton Mifflin Company, 2006. 174.

23 This task isn't as difficult as it may sound, considering how wide of an influence this single religion has over America.

24 This reminds me of a joke about an Eskimo and a missionary. The missionary shares the typical story of salvation through Jesus Christ and the punishment without, to which the Eskimo inquires whether those who have not heard of Jesus would be punished for not accepting him. When the missionary admits he can't say for certain, the Eskimo asks, "Then why did you even tell me?"

25 Slevin, Peter. "Battle on Teaching Evolution Sharpens." *Washington Post.* 14 March 2005, online edition: <http://www.washingtonpost.com/wp-dyn/articles/A32444-2005Mar13.html?nav=rss_topnews>

26 Bible: Matthew 18:3, NIV.

27 Smith 322.

28 Dawkins 3.

29 Yes, that's the Bible.

30 Years later, I am *still* trying to figure that one out.

31 It's interesting to note that a much higher percentage think they should be displayed in public schools and government courtrooms. Grossman, Cathy Lynn. "Americans get an 'F' in religion." *USA Today.* 7 March 2007, online edition: <http://www.usatoday.com/news/religion/2007-03-07-teaching-religion-cover_N.htm>. November 29-30, 2005 Fox News / Opinion Dynamics Poll accessed from http://www.foxnews.com/story/0,2933,177355,00.html.

32 Harris 19.

33 Cialdini, Robert B. *Influence: The Psychology of Persuasion.* New York: William Morrow and Company, 1993. 57.

34 Or to reflect Cialdini's example, decades after those beliefs have been backed with emotional bets.

35 Shermer 296.

36 Ibid.

37 Shermer 283-284.

38 Shermer 59.

39 Shermer 277.

40 Cialdini 110-111.

41 Shermer 299-300.

42 Petty and Cacioppo 107-108.

43 One of the most widely touted Creationist websites, answersingenesis.org, offers this is in their statement of faith: "No apparent, perceived or claimed evidence in any field, including history

and chronology, can be valid if it contradicts the Scriptural record." <http://www.answersingenesis.org/home/area/about/faith.asp>

44 Bible: Genesis 30.

45 Qur'an: Sura 54 (Al-Qamar).

46 A few years ago, I spoke with an apologist who, in order to harmonize the layers of the Grand Canyon with the six-thousand-year-old age of the earth, claimed that the Colorado River once flowed uphill.

47 Shermer 46.

48 Sagan, Carl. *The Demon-Haunted World: Science as a Candle in the Dark*. New York: Ballantine Books. 232-233.

49 It is also worth noting that the number of people who leave specific denominations for non-denominational worship greatly outweighs the number moving in the opposite direction. *American Religious Identification Survey 2001*. Kosmin, Barry A., et.al., eds. The Graduate Center of the City University of New York. 19 December 2001. <http://www.gc.cuny.edu/faculty/research_studies/aris.pdf>.

50 And again, this goes back to the earlier point of extended religious environment running deeper than you might think. The widespread perceived appropriateness of believing that a man rose from the dead gives artificial credence to such an absurd claim.

51 I believe that there is an indisputable contradiction committed between two authors on the subject, which is a position I will defend later in the section.

52 A list of studies and surveys used to compile these figures can be found online at http://www.adherents.com/Religions_By_Adherents.html.

53 UFO apologists actually have it a bit easier than biblical inerrancy apologists. The former can admit hoaxes and mistakes because they need only a single substantiation; the latter must defend the entire package.

54 From The TalkOrigins Archive, accessed online at http://www.talkorigins.org/indexcc/CD/CD011_3.html.

55 It is widely known that Ronald Reagan, the leader of the free world during much of the Cold War, used his wife's astrologers to assist in his scheduling, security, and perhaps, his foreign policy. Scary thought, no?

56 The printing press, for example, is much more widely used in Christian regions.

57 A diploma mill is an institution that hands out degrees like candy. Accrediting bodies do not recognize them. They're usable, but meaningless. The US Department of Education has a searchable database of accredited institutions online at http://www.ope.ed.gov/accreditation/Search.asp.

58 Petty and Cacioppo 62.

59 Cialdini 222-223.

60 Petty and Cacioppo 63.

61 "The Monkey Suit." *The Simpsons*. FOX. WTTE, Columbus. 2006 May 14.

62 Petty and Cacioppo 74-75.

63 Leon Festinger, in Petty and Cacioppo 137, 140.

64 Petty and Cacioppo 141-142.

65 Petty and Cacioppo 137.

66 We will assume that the detective is equally competent on each matter.

67 An exact figure is difficult to estimate, but this percentage is consistent with the opinions of psychologists who specialize in the field of marital infidelity. Gerhardt, Pam. "The Emotional Cost of Infidelity." *The Washington Post*. 30 March 1999: Z10.

68 Sixty-seven percent is actually the most conservative estimate since it assumes that the largest religion on the planet, Christianity, is correct. This value is much higher if we consider specific dominations. Catholics and Protestants, for example, have different biblical canons, which would further increase the likelihood of being born into the wrong religion. If Judaism were true, the value would soar to over 99%.

69 More on this later.

70 I have quoted the condensed version from Petty and Cacioppo 125.

71 Hardyck, J.A., and Braden, M. "Prophecy fails again: A report of a failure to replicate." *Journal of Abnormal and Social Psychology*, 1962, *65*, 136-141. I have quoted the condensed version from Petty and Cacioppo 139.

72 Any reasonable person would dismiss such a claim almost immediately, but this is not the point I wish to discuss.

73 A group known as the Preterists.

74 Westen, D., Kilts, C., Blagov, P., Harenski, K., and Hamann, S. "The neural basis of motivated reasoning: An fMRI study of emotional constraints on political judgment during the U.S. Presidential election of 2004." *Journal of Cognitive Neuroscience* (2006).

75 Petty and Cacioppo 152.

76 Petty and Cacioppo 155.

77 The historian Tacitus makes this allegation in his *Annals*, but the veracity of the full account has long been in dispute.

78 Diocletian ordered such measures in an "Edict against the Christians," published in the year 303.

79 Petty and Cacioppo 159-160.

80 Cialdini 249-252.

81 Cialdini 257.

82 I've often considered that the very nature of the book's vagueness and interpretability serves as ample evidence for its lack of divine inspiration. Never mind that contradictions are apparent; the very possibility of people *thinking* it is contradictory may well demonstrate that it's not inspired by a perfect being.

83 Bible: Matthew 2:1.

84 The primary source being *Jewish Antiquities* (Book 17 Chapter 8 Section 1) by Josephus Flavius (from page 570 of *The New Complete Works of Josephus*, translated by William Whiston and published by Kregel Academic and Professional, 5th edition (1999).

85 The year designated centuries later as Jesus' birth (1 CE, since there is no year zero) was misplaced, but there's nothing wrong biblically about that.

86 Bible: Luke 2:1-5.

87 Compiled from Richard Carrier's excellent essay, "*The Date of the Nativity in Luke (5th edition, 2006)*," published online at http://www.infidels.org/library/modern/richard_carrier/quirinius.html.

88 Ibid.

89 Or as the apologist might think to himself, "This explanation may be far-fetched, but nothing is more far-fetched than God making a mistake in his Bible."

90 Bible: 1 Timothy 2:8, KJV.

91 Bible: Matthew 6:5-6, KJV.

92 A lesser-known online apologist, that is, who incidentally supports the doctrine that the inerrant Bible "is the supreme and final authority in all matters on which it speaks." How's that for objectivity?

93 Incidentally, this particular apologist refuses to provide links to his opponents' comments, presumably so he can misrepresent what they say. His reasoning? "It gives small minded people something to complain about." In this particular instance, I think it is obvious that he hopes to distract his audience with a straw man rather than attack my true position. I certainly don't mean to apply that most apologists are like this. Most are kind and well intentioned; this individual is the exception.

94 Of the twelve major translations, nine are consistent with my interpretation. <http://www.blueletterbible.org/cgi-bin/versions.pl?book=1Ti&chapter=2&verse=8&version=KJV#8>

95 One exchange is documented online at http://www.allexperts.com/user.cgi?m=6&catID=2004&qID=4605848; the other two were through personal emails. One holds a Ph.D. in classic languages; the other two are natives of Greece who study the ancient form of the language.

96 Bible: 26:34, 22:34, and 13:38, respectively.

97 Bible: 26:69-75, 22:56-61, and 18:17-27, respectively.

98 Bible: Mark 14:30

99 Bible: Mark 14:66-72.

100 He would probably like to appeal to the other oldest (currently) discovered manuscript, Codex Sinaiticus, since it omits all three duplicate crowings in Mark 14, thereby making the matter much easier to deal with, but he likely knows that the manuscript is greatly corrupted. Furthermore, we begin to see the stupidity in arguing for biblical inerrancy when the closest documents we have to the originals are heavily edited copies made centuries after the events that they report. We will also discover an enormous problem for Christians, much later in this book, if they wish to appeal to the reliability of the Codex Vaticanus manuscript.

101 The reality is that we have absolutely no idea what the original texts said, but the consensus from secular historians is that the alterations began when copyists noted contradictions among the gospels.

102 A point on which scholars disagree.

103 And since it was considered the first crowing of the day, as the argument goes, Jesus was correct to say that the cock would not crow that day until three denials were made.

104 If you're confused by now, you should be.

105 Mark 14:72, however, does not say that the cock crowed twice, but rather that it crowed a second time (without mentioning the first crowing, which the apologists removed from 14:68). This explanation is plainly incoherent.

106 I have no idea how that's supposed to eliminate the contradiction.

107 The same way that we would say "before two shakes of a lamb's tail."

108 After all, there are several additional contradictions within the stories of Peter's denials.

109 The only crowing, in fact, that has a chance of fitting his conjecture (out of many that do not). Or alternatively, that the second crowing was a pointless redundancy and/or a time-significant crowing, which would also eliminate the need to accept argument number three.

110 For example, the author of Mark misattributes (in 1:2-3) Malachi 3:1 as being the words of Isaiah. In defense of this blunder, we are told that since it was common for writers to combine works of the prophets into a single unit of work, it is not erroneous to suggest that a person said something he actually did not.

111 So unlikely, in fact, that it took me quite a while to grasp what exactly the apologist was attempting to argue. The likelihood of the apologetic solution is further damaged when the other contradictions of the story, the timing of the denials and to whom Peter was doing the denying, are considered.

112 I compiled such a list, focusing on the strongest cases, in *Biblical Nonsense*, published by iUniverse.

113 Smith 111-112.

114 *An Introduction to Logic* by Irving M. Copi and Carl Cohen is an excellent reference for detecting fallacious logic.

115 Smith 96.

116 Petty and Cacioppo 84.

117 Bible: Matthew 10:37.

118 Smith 308.

119 Beckwith, Burnham. "The Effect of Intelligence on Religious Faith." *Free Inquiry*. Spring 1986.

120 Bell, Paul. "Would you believe it?" *Mensa Magazine*. February 2002. 12-13.

121 Harris Interactive Poll #59 from October 15, 2003, accessed from http://www.harrisinteractive.com/harris_poll/index.asp?PID=408.

122 For those of you getting in a huff, men comprise more than 50% of the extremely intelligent and extremely unintelligent ends of the spectrum. In other words, while the average man and woman are of equal intelligence, men are more likely to be extremely intelligent/unintelligent and less likely to have normal intelligence. Because I suppose that only those near the highly intelligent extreme of the spectrum have an increased chance of escaping the religion, this may explain why the data are skewed toward men.

123 A social club comprised of those who have IQs in the top 2 percent of the United States.

124 Unitarianism is a liberal, non-dogmatic, pro-reason branch of theology that does not believe in the divinity of Jesus and wants to keep government secular.

125 Data taken from the MENSA FAQ, accessed from http://www.faqs.org/faqs/mensa/faq/.

126 Even as far back as 1914, 70 percent of greater scientists expressed doubt or disbelief in a personal god. Larson Edward J. and Larry Witham. "Leading scientists still reject God." *Nature*, Volume 394, Number 6691. 313.

127 Dawkins 100.

128 Dawkins 101.

129 Dawkins 100.

130 Petty and Cacioppo 80-82.

131 Shermer 297.

132 Smith 325.

133 Petty and Cacioppo 39.

134 Research has also shown that there is likely an advantageous genetic predisposition, acquired through natural selection, to certain

potentially dangerous situations.

135 Two such practices are cognitive behavioral therapy and systematic desensitization therapy.

136 Given the widespread belief of the supernatural, one could make the assertion that it is instinctive to believe in a god or gods. However, one cannot make the argument that it is instinctive to believe in a *particular* god, which is the issue we wish to investigate.

137 Or perhaps by some lower level justification, such as "The Bible says it, I believe it, that settles it."

138 Cialdini 70-71.

139 Petty and Cacioppo 200.

140 Petty and Cacioppo 72.

141 Petty and Cacioppo 228-229.

142 For example, "The fool says in his heart, 'There is no God.'" Psalms 53:1, NIV.

143 Petty and Cacioppo 234-235.

144 Petty and Cacioppo 257.

145 *Atheists Are Distrusted.* American Sociological Association website, accessed from http://www.asanet.org/page.ww?section=Press &name=Atheists+Are+Distrusted.

146 Petty and Cacioppo 259-260.

147 The percentage of people who believe in ESP (50%) is larger than those accept evolution (49%) – with out without God. Both polls are from Gallup: June 8, 2001, and March 5, 2001, respectively.

148 Shermer 26.

149 Cialdini 188-190.

150 Cialdini 1, 4, 7, 29, 40, 172.

151 Dawkins 35.

152 STEP from *American Heart Journal* April 2006, MANTRA from *Lancet* volume 366, and the 2001 Mayo Clinic coronary care unit trial are perhaps the three most definitive investigations on the topic.

153 Dawkins 63.

154 Deuteronomy 6:16 comes to mind, which just so happens to contradict 1 Thessalonians 5:21, which orders us to "test everything and hold on to the good."

155 Mark 6:5-6, perhaps.

156 This example is taken from *Biblical Nonsense.*

157 Petty and Cacioppo 85.

158 Cavett Robert, renowned speaker.

159 Cialdini 119.

160 Cialidini 152.

161 Petty and Cacioppo 85.

162 Recall the fundamental difficulty in accepting contradictory apologetic interpretations.

163 Petty and Cacioppo 140.

164 Petty 223.

165 Cialdini 117.

166 Cialdini 145-151.

167 Petty 223.

168 Cialdini 61-64.

169 Stars: Matthew 24:29; Mark 13:25; and Revelation 1:16, 6:13, 8:10, 12:4. Possessions: Matthew 9:32, 12:22-28, 17:15; Mark 9:17; and Luke 9:39, 11:14-20, 13:11.

170 The irony is that they seem to appreciate that the very nature of religion is absurd. Could this be a form of projection?

171 Sagan 21.

172 Dawkins 340.

173 For a more elaborate explanation, please see *Biblical Nonsense.*

174 Geologist Nicolas Steno established the principle of superposition in 1669, which states that sedimentary layers are deposited in a time sequence. Geologist William Smith established the principle of faunal succession in 1799, which states that the location of fossils in those rock layers consistently appear in a reliable order. While there were ideas for evolution prior to Charles Darwin's work, the theory was not widely accepted until 1859.

175 Radiometric dating did not come along until the early 1900s.

176 There is a terrific debate in the scientific community over what constitutes "life." Viruses were once excluded out of hand because they require very specific conditions to reproduce, but they can often metabolize with assistance and even adapt to their environment. Most remarkably, viruses are capable of self-assembly, a characteristic that provides a viable hypothesis for abiogenesis. Prions are merely clusters of protein that can cause other cells to take on prion-like characteristics. Is this reproduction? If not, why not? Any definition of life is arbitrary

by nature.

177 The study of how life began.

178 Nothing to Atoms: There are working theories by Stephen Hawking, among others, that predict the creation of matter from fluctuations in a quantum vacuum. More on this later. Atoms to Molecules: This is a well-established rule in chemistry. Molecules to Amino Acids: The 1953 Miller-Urey experiment established that an electrical charge passing through molecular compounds of water, methane, hydrogen, and ammonia could produce amino acids. Amino Acids to Proteins: This is a well-established rule in biology. Proteins to Prions: More accurately, prions *are* proteins. Viruses are merely proteins mixed with nucleic acids.

179 http://www.msnbc.msn.com/id/20249628/

180 Dawkins 283.

181 Cialdini 116.

182 This is not to say that all homeopathic medications fail to work since some really aren't following the principles when they aren't diluted very much, and the side effects of such substances just happen to mimic the disease itself. Dawkins (167) also points out a possibility that I had not considered too heavily before. "Homeopaths may be achieving relative success because they, unlike orthodox practitioners, are still allowed to administer placebos – under another name. They also have more time to devote to talking and simply being kind to the patient."

183 The standard level of confidence for running a statistical analysis is 95%. This means that the researchers want to be 95% sure that their result did not occur by chance, which leaves a false positive in 5% of cases. If you run twenty tests, you're likely to get a false positive that you can use to support your product.

184 Also relevant is Stephen Jay Gould's observation of the Arkansas State Supreme Court case McLean v. Arkansas. He realized early on that his side would win because court hearings require proof – not speeches.

185 That is to say, the age of the universe in Big Bang cosmology.

186 We will get to the problems of this story shortly.

187 An excellent website dedicated to debunking or confirming urban legends of all varieties.

188 http://www.snopes.com/religion/lostday.asp

189 http://www.films.com/id/12620/The_100_Greatest_Discoveries_Top_Ten.htm

190 I compiled a more elaborate list of reasons and defenses in *Biblical Nonsense*. Wikipedia actually has some nice material on the subject as well, under the topic *Documentary Hypothesis*.

191 Sagan 91.

192 The reign of Gilgamesh is believed to have taken place around 2700 BCE, much earlier than the Noachian Flood, purported in the Bible to have taken place around 2350 BCE. The Sumerian Epic is believed to have been recorded around 2000 BCE; Moses, the author traditionally assigned to the Noachian Flood, wasn't even born until around 1550 BCE. Scholarly dating for the recording of the Noachian Flood would be placed at least an additional five hundred years after Moses' alleged time of death.

193 These are way too numerous to deal with here, but I addressed over one hundred of them in *Biblical Nonsense*.

194 Mills, David. *Atheist Universe: The Thinking Person's Answer to Christian Fundamentalism*. California: Ulysses Press, 2006. 139.

195 Bible: Genesis 7:19-20.

196 Ryan, William and Walter Pitman. *Noah's Flood: The New Scientific Discoveries About The Event That Changed History*. New York: Touchstone (2000).

197 In the latest poll I could find, "only" 60 percent of Americans still interpret the story as a literal truth. ABC News Primetime Poll February 6-10, 2004 accessed from http://www.pollingreport.com/religion2.htm.

198 Harris 20-21.

199 A process by which one attempts to explain an apparent problem by analyzing all possible interpretations and explanations in extraordinary detail.

200 Till, Farrell. "A Reply to Skeptic X on Circumcision Requirements." *The Skeptical Review*, accessed from http://www.theskepticalreview.com/JFTBobbyCutOff.html.

201 Dawkins 242.

202 William Mumler used double exposures in the 1860s to make ghostly images appear in otherwise normal photos. The trick can be

easily replicated.

203 Margaret Fox admitted the hoax in 1888, forty years after she initiated the phenomenon.

204 The American public's familiarity with Bigfoot is attributable to the grainy Patterson-Gimlin film produced in 1967. The family of Ray Wallace, the man who started the North American Bigfoot craze in 1958 by faking footprints, confessed that he was involved in the making of the film. Philip Morris, a North Carolina costume maker, admitted in 2002 to having made and sold the costume to Roger Patterson for a "prank." Bob Heironimus, the man who wore the costume in the film, eventually came forward as well.

205 Doug Bower and Dave Chorley confessed in 1991 that they had been performing the prank since 1976, long before the fad entered into the mainstream. The practice of producing increasingly complex crop circles is now a common hobby in England.

206 The popular grey aliens were unknown until NBC broadcasted the abduction story of Betty and Barney Hill. Now they account for 75 percent of US abductions, compared to 20 percent or less elsewhere. Before the emergence of the greys, aliens were alleged to be anything from blobs of hair to metallic asparaguses, commonly hailing from within our own solar system.

207 Sagan 277.

208 Typically, 30-60 percent, depending on how the question is asked.

209 See http://www.answersingenesis.org/articles/am/v1/n2/who-begat-whom for a rebuttal.

210 Mills 147-148.

211 Harris 296.

212 Isaiah's use of *almah* in Isaiah 7:14 and Jesus' use of *miseo* in Luke 14:26 come to mind.

213 Paine, Thomas. *Age of Reason.* New York: Willey Book Company, 1942. 99.

214 Joshua 10:12-14.

215 http://www.blueletterbible.org/cgi-bin/versions.pl?book=Jos &chapter=10&verse=13&version=KJV#13

216 Sagan 29.

217 First Thessalonians 5:21 comes to mind: "Prove all things;

hold fast that which is good."

218 Smith 141.

219 Sagan 34-35.

220 Shermer 94.

221 Sagan 297.

222 Sagan 210.

223 May 10-13, 2007 Gallup Poll accessed from http://www.galluppoll.com/content/?ci=27877&pg=1

224 Okay, I didn't try to resist and was actually very glad when I rediscovered it in my saved emails because I instantly knew how I was going to utilize it. Imagine what other frank honesty people might miss by not checking the endnotes consistently!

225 Petty and Cacioppo 68.

226 Mills 71-72.

227 A string is a theoretical one-dimensional object whose existence unifies several theories of physics. String theories are in turn unified by M-theory. Interesting stuff, but off-topic.

228 Mills 73-74.

229 The universe with its strictest definition of all existence, not the universe as we now perceive it. Our observable universe obviously began about fourteen billion years ago with the Big Bang.

230 Recent evidence of an accelerating universe works against the idea of an oscillating universe. If the matter within the universe is accelerating away from its point of origin, gravitational forces among the matter might not be sufficient to pull everything back together.

231 This argument comes from William Lane Craig's *Reasonable Faith*. Craig is widely considered by believers and skeptics to be the best on his side of the debate.

232 Richard Dawkins' *The Blind Watchmaker* is the perfect place to begin.

233 Smith 267.

234 Shermer 153.

235 Smith 268.

236 Smith 260-261.

237 Mills 102.

238 Some theologians and philosophers do not make this distinction.

239 Of course, this is the same person who made the following asinine statements (taken from Mills 249-251): 1) "In order for the universe to sustain even one life-support planet, each one of these ten billion trillion stars is a necessity. If the number of stars in the observable universe were any greater, or any fewer, life would be impossible." 2) "If the Earth were one half of one percent closer to the sun, water on Earth would boil off. If the earth were one half of one percent farther from the sun, all the water would freeze." 3) "Only two percent of stars have planets around them." 4) "The position and the mass and the orbit of every solar system planet plays a critical role in life on planet earth." 5) "Only spiral galaxies can contain planets in stable orbits around their stars." An astronomer making such claims would be equivalent to an architect making these: 1) "A building constructed with trillions of bolts would fall over if you removed one of them." 2) "A building constructed a mile from a swamp would sink if it were moved ten feet closer." 3) "Only two percent of buildings use a particular brand of bolts, although there are trillions of buildings, and only a handful have been inspected." 4) "If we took off the awning over the front door of a building, the building couldn't sustain itself." 5) "A perfectly squared building is the only kind capable of existing, although I have not seen anyone else attempt to build something different." We must remember that Hugh Ross is one of the most widely respected apologists in the world.

240 Dawkins 143-144.

241 Mills 113.

242 Mills 222.

243 Shermer 80.

244 Whinnery, James E. "Psychophysiologic Correlates of Unconsciousness and Near-Death Experiences." *Journal of Near-Death Studies*. Volume 15, Number 4, Summer 1997.

245 LSD, mescaline, etc.

246 Sagan 268-269.

247 McDowell, Josh. *Evidence that Demands a Verdict*. California: Here's Life Publishers, 1979. 16-17.

248 A full discussion of this point is beyond the scope of this text. I am merely stating my opinion on the matter and not asking you to accept it uncritically. My intent with the first question is to focus

solely on the reasons why biblical harmony would exist if in fact it does. Recommended reading: Farrell Till's "The Uniqueness of the Bible," accessible at http://www.infidels.org/library/modern/farrell_till/unique.html.

249 Again, a thorough investigation is beyond the scope of this text. Larry A. Taylor summarizes the canonization process well in his "The Canon of the Bible," accessible at http://www.infidels.org/library/modern/larry_taylor/canon.html.

250 Carrier, Richard. "The Formation of the New Testament Canon." Secular Web. <http://www.infidels.org/library/modern/richard_carrier/NTcanon.html>

251 Ibid.

252 Romer, John. "Testament: The Bible and History." Connecticut: Konecky & Konecky (2004).

253 Infancy Gospel of Thomas, especially Chapters 3-5, 14. Andrew Bernhard's translation available online at http://www.gospels.net/translations/infancythomastranslation.html.

254 Ironically, even the Greek word *parthenos* used in Matthew does not necessarily mean *virgin*, as repeatedly demonstrated in Homer's *Iliad*: <http://www.perseus.tufts.edu/cgi-bin/ptext?lookup=Hom.+Il.+1.1. Compare the Greek and English versions, especially at 22.111.>

255 Mills 21.

256 "With God all things are possible." KJV.

257 The idea that free will is an illusion is complete nonsense, which of course, leaves us with only one alternative.

258 Sagan 171.

259 Smith 53.

260 Smith 157.

261 Mills 164.

262 I realize that I have done this to some degree in this book, but I have given such nonsense more than enough attention in the past.

263 Cialdini 208-214.

264 Cialdini 218.

265 Bible: Exodus 26.

266 Bible: Genesis 32:24-30.

267 Bible: Numbers 15:32-36

268 Mills 187.

269 Shermer 119.

270 For some reason, the inspiration almost always seems to travel no further. I consistently found humor in the fact that people in my church thought that they were closer to God because they spoke in seventeenth-century King's English. What a remarkable exhibition of ignorant Western prejudice!

271 Mark would be the earliest, probably written around 70 CE. Scholarly consensus places the rest from 75-105 CE.

272 Burton Mack elaborates on this point well in chapter nine of his book, *The Lost Gospel: The Book of Q & Christian Origins*, published by HarperSanFrancisco.

273 I included a list of these alterations in *Biblical Nonsense.*

274 The Vaticanus (along with the Sinaiticus), which an apologist apparently used earlier to defend the crowing contradiction, does not contain Mark 16:9-20. If one wishes to submit this manuscript as the sole reason to remove the contradiction, consistency also forces one to remove the resurrection from the earliest gospel. This fun little game of textual criticism is the consequence of a thoughtless god who ceases his divine inspiration before ensuring proper translation. No one has ever been able to explain to me the value of divine inspiration for texts that no longer exist.

275 Till, Farrell. "How Did the Apostles Die?" *The Skeptical Review.* July 1997. Accessed from http://www.infidels.org/library/magazines/tsr/1997/4/4front97.html.

276 Smith 225.

277 Mills 20.

278 That's why this section is near the end of the book rather than the beginning.

279 An idea called Manifest Destiny, established perhaps by John L. O'Sullivan. He argued that God had given the United States a mission, a moral ideal that superseded other considerations, to spread Republican Democracy across North America. The idea was widely swallowed hook, line, and sinker. This just goes to show how any action can be easily justified to an unenlightened populace by invoking the will of God.

280 Those last two are a joke, kind of.

281 Morgan, Kathleen and Scott Morgan. *Education State Rankings*

2006-2007. Kansas: Morgan Quinto Corporation, 2006.

282 Glenmary Research Center's "Religious Congregations and Membership in the United States, 2000." Data available in graphical from at http://www.valpo.edu/geomet/pics/geo200/religion/adherents.gif.

283 Sethi, Chanakya. "Alito '72 joined conservative alumni group." *The Daily Princetonian*. 18 November, 2005, online edition: <http://www.dailyprincetonian.com/archives/2005/11/18/news/13876.shtml>

284 Harris 39.

285 The Egyptians incidentally were not too far behind.

286 In my opinion, the best form of government. Not a traditional aristocracy of the wealthy, but one of the enlightened – the philosophers, as Socrates called them.

287 None of the paintings still exists, but we have anecdotal reports of their appearance often being indistinguishable from reality.

288 Smith 325.

289 Smith 169.

290 Petty and Cacioppo 173.

291 Cialdini 100-103.

292 Smith 316-317.

293 The popular rendition of *kill* is a poor translation of the Hebrew *ratsach*.

294 If you're wondering, our laws are based on English Common Law.

295 The Hebrews often use the same words for slave and servant, but I feel that this is the proper translation of *ebed* and *amah* in the context of desiring possessions. Distinctions are made in the Hebrew language for all male and female servants, just as they are in the English language for *voluntary* male and female servants (i.e. butler and maid), hence the Western translating bias.

296 Bible: Exodus 20:17, NIV with correction.

297 1-2) Deuteronomy 17:2-5. 3) Leviticus 24:14-16. 4) Exodus 35:2. 5) Leviticus 20:9. 6) Leviticus 24:17. 7) Deuteronomy 22:22. 8) Stealing is not a capital offense, but the thief is sold into slavery if necessary to compensate the owner (Exodus 22:1-3). Some biblical scholars believe the intent was to not "steal people." In which case,

kidnapping is also a capital offense (Exodus 21:16). 9) Deuteronomy 19:18-19 (in cases of perjury). 10) God apparently has no desire to (or capability of) punishing thought crimes.

298 Shermer 123.

299 Smith 22.

300 Actually, the point should be self-evident. Consider the histories of Christianity and Islam against the histories of Hinduism and Buddhism. Sagan (296-297) points out the observations of anthropologists: "The ones with a supreme god who lives in the sky tend to be the most ferocious – torturing their enemies for example. But this is a statistical correlation only; the causal link has not been established, although speculations naturally present themselves."

301 United Nations rankings for 2002, as reported by CBS News on 26 November, 2002, located at http://www.cbsnews.com/stories/2002/11/26/world/main530872.shtml. Just about any study would suffice.

302 "Among Wealthy Nations, U.S. stands alone in its embrace of religion." 19 December, 2002. The Pew Research Center for the People and the Press. <http://people-press.org/reports/display.php3?ReportID=167>

303 Harris 108-109.

304 Dawkins 257.

305 Dawkins 31.

306 For an elaboration of these points, see *Biblical Nonsense*.

307 Bible: Exodus 21, 25; Leviticus 20, 24; Numbers 17; Deuteronomy 17-22.

308 These issues will be covered later.

309 Isaiah 13:15-16, 14:21; Jeremiah 4:7, 7:20, 8:3, 8:10, 11:22, 13:14, 14:12, 19:9, 50:32; Lamentations 3:1-16; Ezekiel 5:10, 5:12-13, 6:5, 18:24; Hosea 4:13, 10:14, 13:8, 13:16; Joel 3:8; Micah 3:9-12; Zephaniah 1:2-3, 14:2, 14:12-15

310 A little over two million by one count, not including the unknown number in Noah's flood, Sodom, Gomorrah, and the cities that God ordered destroyed. http://dwindlinginunbelief.blogspot.com/2006/08/how-many-has-god-killed.html

311 One apologetic defense for God sending the bears to kill the children argued the following: 1) The children could have been as old

as fourteen or fifteen and should have known better; 2) Baldness was probably rare and embarrassing, or possibly a sign of mourning; 3) The group was the likely equivalent of a modern street gang. I will let the defense speak for itself. Exodus 7-12, Joshua 6-11, 2 Samuel 24:10-17, 2 Kings 2:23-24.

312 Bible: Genesis 6:5-7.

313 Bible: Genesis 8:21.

314 Deuteronomy 13:12-16, 17:2-5; 2 Chronicles 15:10-15; among others.

315 I include a chapter in *Biblical Nonsense*. Another good essay, "The Status of Women in the Hebrew Scriptures," has been written by the Ontario Consultants on Religious Tolerance: <http://www.religioustolerance.org/ofe_bibl.htm>. An exhaustive (and sometimes overreaching) list can be found online in the Skeptic's Annotated Bible at http://www.skepticsannotatedbible.com/women/long.html.

316 Yes, only under *most* circumstances. We will get to that shortly.

317 Bible: Deuteronomy 22:28-29.

318 Bible: Deuteronomy 22:24. If the woman does not cry loud enough to draw attention, however, the community should consider the attack consensual if it took place within the city. Thus, the whore must also be stoned to death per God's instructions. It obviously does not matter if the woman is too scared to scream because God's law provides no such exception.

319 Bible: Numbers 31:17-18.

320 Scott, Thomas. "Numbers 31:17," The Treasury of Scripture Knowledge. Blue Letter Bible. 1836. 9 Jul 2004.

321 Bible: Deuteronomy 21:10-14, KJV.

322 Bible: Numbers 31:17-18, KJV.

323 No, I did not make this up.

324 Strong, James. *Strong's Exhaustive Concordance of the Bible.* New York: Abingdon Press (1967). 854, C74. Also see the Blue Letter Bible online reference at: http://cf.blueletterbible.org/lang/lexicon/lexicon.cfm?Strongs=H04910&Version=kjv.

325 Bible: Exodus 21:21, KJV.

326 Bible: Exodus 21:20-27. If a slave is merely disabled permanently by the beating, he is to go free. However, I would hardly

consider inherent freedom to be a fair compensation for permanent blindness.

327 Bible: Proverbs 29:19, NIV.

328 Bible: Ephesians 6, Colossians 3, 1 Peter 2, 1 Timothy 2.

329 Bible: Judges 2-16, Exodus 21:20-27, Numbers 31.

330 In the strictest terms of atheism, lacking a specific belief in a god, I suppose I would fit.

331 In his 1900 Notebook. For more priceless Twain quotes, I recommend *The Bible According to Mark Twain*, edited by Howard G. Baetzhold and published by Touchstone (1996).

332 Smith 310.

333 Sagan 121.

334 Smith 213.

335 A recently discovered stone tablet from the first century BCE also indicates that a messianic death and three-day resurrection was likely part of Jewish culture before Jesus was ever born: *New York Times*. 6 July, 2008, online edition: <http://www.nytimes.com/2008/07/06/world/middleeast/06stone.html?_r=2&pagewanted=1&hp&oref=slogin>

336 Bible: Galatians 1.

337 Some of the dates for these ancient writers are approximate.

338 Two small paragraphs, approximately 0.01% of his work, mention Jesus, but the passages are widely regarded as tampered. Reasons for this position include the use of Christian language from a Jewish author, the brevity given to such an important figure, the interruptive nature of the passage, the ignorance of early Christian writers and missionaries about this passage, its discovery by an admitted fraud, its rejection by a growing number of Christian scholars, and Origen's explicit statement that Josephus does not mention Jesus. The only portion still considered authentic is the phrase, "James, brother of Jesus," which is widely interpretable. An entire book could be written over the dispute of this passage, but this will hopefully summarize the matter in a decently sized paragraph.

339 None of whom wrote about material relevant to Jesus – but wouldn't these stories, if true, have at least motivated some sort of incorporation?

340 Bible: Matthew 27:52-53.

341 *Jewish Antiquities* (Book 2 Chapter 16 Section 5) by Josephus Flavius (from page 109 of *The New Complete Works of Josephus*, translated by William Whiston and published by Kregel Academic and Professional, 5th edition (1999).

342 Suetonius. *The Lives of the Twelve Caesars, Volume 10: Vespasian.* Chapter 7. Online book catalog from Project Gutenberg, etext 6395.

343 Smith 216-217.

344 Sagan 139.

345 Bible: Mark 7:1-13, John 8:1-11, Luke 5:33-38, Matthew 5:38-42, Matthew 12:1-8, Matthew 5:17-18, Luke 16:17.

346 Recall the promise of reward in Matthew 6:5-6 for praying in secret.

347 Smith 317-319 lays out a nice case.

348 Ibid.

349 This is an opinion, of course, but one shared almost unanimously among secular philosophers.

350 Bible: Matthew 5:38-42.

351 Bible: Luke 14:26.

352 Bible: Deuteronomy 13:12-16, 17:2-5; 2 Chronicles 15:10-15; among others.

353 Bible: Matthew 13:10-17.

354 Bible: Matthew 22:1-14.

355 Bible: Matthew 25:1-13.

356 Smith 319.

357 Smith 312.

358 Such a realization has even prompted a movement of individuals called Preterists who believe that Jesus has already returned and fulfilled those promises. Bible: Matthew 16:27-28, 23, 24:29-34, 26:62-64; Mark 9:1, 14:24-30, 14:60-62; Luke 9:27.

359 Bible: 2 Peter 3:1-8.

360 The exact value depends on how the measurement is taken. The total difference in the entire DNA is 4 percent; the difference in the functional part of the genome is 1 percent. Weiss, Rick. "Scientists Complete Genetic Map of the Chimpanzee." *Washington Post.* 1 September, 2005, online edition: <http://www.washingtonpost.com/wp-dyn/content/article/2005/08/31/AR2005083102278.html>

361 "Gene Mutation Linked to Risk of Autism." Canadian

Broadcasting Corporation. 16 October, 2006, accessed from http://www.cbc.ca/cp/HealthScout/061016/6101606U.html.

362 One who lacks belief in a god, as opposed to the contemporary connotation of absolute knowledge that one does not exist. A Gallup Poll taken from May 10-13, 2007, accessed from http://www.galluppoll.com/content/?ci=27877&pg=1, indicates that as many as 14 percent of Americans qualify as atheists under the classical definition.

363 Do a quick search on Google, and you'll come up with several forums and books on Christian Humanists.

Made in the USA